The family, women and death

International Library of Anthropology

Editor: Adam Kuper, University of Leiden

Arbor Scientiae
Arbor Vitae

A catalogue of other Social Science books published by Routledge &
Kegan Paul will be found at the end of this volume.

The family, women and death
Comparative studies

S.C. Humphreys
Department of Anthropology
University College London

Routledge & Kegan Paul
London, Boston, Melbourne and Henley

First published in 1983
by Routledge & Kegan Paul Ltd
39 Store Street, London WC1E 7DD,
9 Park Street, Boston, Mass. 02108, USA,
296 Beaconsfield Parade, Middle Park,
Melbourne, 3206, Australia and
Broadway House, Newtown Road,
Henley-on-Thames, Oxon RG9 1EN
Set in IBM Press Roman by
Donald Typesetting, Bristol
Printed and bound in Great Britain by
T.J. Press Ltd., Padstow, Cornwall

Library of Congress Cataloging in Publication Data

Humphreys, S. C. (Sarah C.)

The family, women and death.
(International library of anthropology)
Bibliography: p.
Includes index.
1. Greece – Social life and customs – Addresses,
essays, lectures. 2. Greece – Social conditions
– Addresses, essays, lectures. 3. Family – Greece
– Addresses, essays, lectures. 4. Women –
Greece – Addresses, essays, lectures. Death –
Addresses, essays, lectures. 6. Funeral rites
and ceremonies – Greece – Addresses, essays,
lectures.
I. Title. II. Series.
DF93. H85   1982   306'.09495   82-23093

ISBN 0-7100-9322-5

Contents

Acknowledgments

An early version of chapter 1, *'Oikos* and *polis'*, was delivered in 1972 as a seminar paper at the Centre des recherches comparées sur les sociétés anciennes in Paris, and began an exchange of ideas about the relation between public and private domains in Greece from which I have derived a great deal of profit and encouragement. An Italian translation of substantially the present text was published in *Rivista storica italiana*, 91, 1979, pp. 545–63.

Chapter 2, 'Public and private interests in classical Athens', was written for a conference held at Princeton University in April 1977 and published in the *Classical Journal*, 73, 1977/78, pp. 97–104. I should like here to express my gratitude to Princeton University for its hospitality and to Bob Connor for organising the conference, as well as thanking the *Classical Journal* for permission to reprint the paper.

Chapter 3, 'Women in antiquity', was written as introduction to a collection of essays edited by Mario Vegetti and myself, to be published by Boringhieri, Milan. Apart from the papers by Marylin Arthur, Dominique Gérin, Geoffrey Lloyd and Giampiera Arrigoni, the papers discussed in my introduction have already been published elsewhere, in English or French, and references are given in the bibliography of this volume to the original publications.

'Greeks and "others" ' is a revised version of a short communication contributed to a colloquium at Cérisy-la-Salle in June 1975 on 'Problèmes de terminologie: discrimination, races et racisme', organised by Professor Léon Poliakov and published in Poliakov, ed., *Ni Juif ni Grec*, Mouton, Paris/Hague, 1978, pp. 75–9. Besides the works already referred to in the text, mention should be made of the two seminal contributions to the study of Greek ethnography by Pembroke (1967) and Benardete (1969), and of the more recent article by Rossellini and Said (1978).

'Greek sexuality' was published in the *Classical Review*, 30, 1980, pp. 61–4; I am grateful for the permission to reprint it here.

An early version of chapter 4, 'The family in classical Athens', was delivered in April 1981 as a lecture at the University of Illinois, Chicago Circle, Wellesley College, and Mount Holyoke College. I should like to thank all who discussed the paper with me on those occasions, and especially Betsy Gebhard, Mary Lefkowitz, Bill McFeely and Carole Straw.

Chapter 5, 'Family tombs and tomb cult in ancient Athens', is reprinted by kind permission of the Society for the Promotion of Hellenic Studies from *Journal of Hellenic Studies*, 100, 1980, pp. 96-126. I should like to thank C. Clairmont and D.M. Lewis for pointing out errors in the original text, and D.M. Lewis also for supplying references to *IG* i^3.

Chapter 6, the foreword to Fustel de Colanges's *The Ancient City*, is reprinted by kind permission of the Johns Hopkins University Press (original publication Baltimore, 1980). It represents a long-standing collaboration with Arnaldo Momigliano on problems connected with Fustel's *Cité Antique*, and, as with a previous joint paper (Humphreys, 1978, pp. 177-208, 'The social structure of the ancient city'), Professor Momigliano has generously allowed his own part of it to be reprinted in a 'contributino' rather than in one of his own *Contributi.*

Chapters 7 and 8, 'Death and time' and 'Comparative perspectives on death', are reprinted by kind permission of Academic Press from *Mortality and Immortality: the Anthropology and Archaeology of Death* (1982), proceedings of a research seminar in archaeology and anthropology organised by me in London in June, 1980, edited by myself and Helen King.

Chapter 5, Fig. 1 is reproduced by courtesy of W. de Gruyter, Berlin, from *Kerameikos* VI.1 (Kübler, 1959), Abb. 4-20.

Plate Ia-b and Plate IIa are reproduced by courtesy of the Antikenmuseum StMPK, Berlin; Plate Ic, by courtesy of the National Museum, Athens; Plate IIb by courtesy of the Bibliothèque Nationale, Paris.

Introduction

The anthropological colleague who recently asked me whether I had any intention, in the future, of embarking on comparative research may find the title of this collection of papers inappropriate. The range of data adduced from societies other than my own and that of ancient Greece is evidently limited. But all these studies are comparative in the sense that they have been written in awareness that we can only grasp the specificity of any culture by seeing it against a comparative background, whether implicit or explicit; in awareness, also, that any interpretation of social and cultural phenomena is inevitably limited by the horizons of the interpreter's social experience and academic training – however much one may try to extend these.

The pursuit of Radcliffe-Brown's vision of a comparative sociology, a 'natural science of society' (Radcliffe-Brown, 1952, 1957) had by the beginning of the 1960s brought social anthropologists into a morass of definitional arguments (cf. Leach, 1955; Lewis, I.M., 1965). Cultural historians began to focus on similar problems, in France, at about the same time. Starting in piecemeal tinkering with relatively substantive notions like marriage (Leach, 1955), childhood (Ariès, 1960), madness (Foucault, 1961), or purity (Vernant, 1956; Douglas, 1966), the critique of the concepts which had hitherto formed the accepted basic currency of comparative studies rapidly developed into a programmatic cultural relativism, based on structuralism, in which it is maintained that every culture has its own way of dividing up and categorising reality, and that differences in the organising principles on which such classification systems are based make a unified 'science of culture' impossible. Key statements of this viewpoint can be found in D.M. Schneider's work on kinship (1972), Foucault's *Histoire de la folie* (1961) and *Archéologie du savoir* (1969), and Dumont's work on individualism (1967a, 1967b, 1975, 1977). Thomas Kuhn (1963; cf. also Chalmers, 1976) applied a similar approach to the concepts of the natural sciences. An attentive reader of my last collection of papers

(Humphreys, 1978) might have noticed a progressive development in relativism there, in which, for example, the notion of a separation between 'social and economic history' and 'political history', taken for granted in 1967 ('Archaeology and the social and economic history of classical Greece', Humphreys, 1978, pp. 109-29), had been discarded, as an obstacle to understanding, by the time of the latest paper in the book, 'Homo Politicus and Homo Economicus' (1978, pp. 159-74).

The present collection pursues that orientation, in stressing the problematic character of such apparently 'natural' phenomena as gender, the family, and death. But the problems involved are not merely problems of conceptualisation and comparison. These categories are deeply embedded in our social experience, and comparison will not take us very far unless it leads back to a more searching analysis of the position from which it started out. The anthropologist's claim that one of the reasons for studying other cultures is to escape from the illusion that our own cultural classification system corresponds to the structure of 'reality' is beginning to look a little naive. Comparison undertaken with this aim in mind was not an innocent activity in ancient Greece (below chapter 3, Appendix I), nor when Fustel de Coulanges tried simultaneously to prove that private property was as old as culture and that the notion of individual freedom was a modern invention (below, chapter 6); nor is it today. We may (to a limited extent) choose our perspectives for comparison, but cannot escape from taking responsibility for the choice and for the values and interests which motivate it (Weber, 1904; in the present craze for the history of ideas, both anthropologists and historians are showing themselves a great deal readier to criticise the choices of others than to face the reasons for their own). Any choice implies an exclusion of other points of view. The apparently formal and universalistic perspective of 'Death and time' (chapter 7 below) might well appear both obtuse and perverse to a theologian.

A formal approach may be useful at some stages in research, as a way of stimulating the systematic collection of data, but it is not an end in itself. The attempt to formulate a scheme which will serve for all cultures inevitably misses the illuminating sidelights which come from the idiosyncrasies of particular cultures. It is not having outlines of all the world's cultures on file, but knowing the details of a few particularly rich developments, which stimulates awareness of latent possibilities or of the alternatives excluded by a particular set of categories and institutions – as Lukác's comparison of Greek tragedy with the modern historical novel (1955), or John Jones's comparison of Greek and European tragedy (1962), shed light on both.

Thus I have chosen, in a large group of the studies in this book (chapters 1-5), to look at the society of classical Athens from the point of view of a principle of cultural categorisation particularly elaborately developed and at the same time problematic in modern western culture - the division of social life into public and private spheres. My hope is to have shown that a basis for comparison exists, in that the Athenians were beginning, in a tentative way, to classify social experience along these lines in the fifth century BC; and to have shown that awareness of the way in which elaboration of the distinction has proceeded in our own culture, and of the ambiguous reactions which it elicits, may be useful in shaping questions to ask the Greek sources and sensitising us to the ambiguities in values which they too hold within them. I am of course aware of the dangers of 'modernism'; but to replace an unthinking assumption that the characteristics of modern society are to be found universally with an equally unthinking belief that 'the others' are different from us, that non-modern societies lack social conflict, competition, difficult choices, scepticism and people with feelings of restlessness, frustration and alienation, is scarcely progress. If we want to explore the problems, incoherences and ambiguities of other cultures - rather than regarding them as perfectly functioning systems - the problems which interest us are going to be those of our own culture, and it may be as well to make the comparison explicit.

Some further clarification of my use of the terms 'public' and 'private' sphere seems to be required here. In its application to modern society (cf. especially Arendt, 1958; Sennett, 1977), the contrast is grounded in the social experience of the individual. In modern complex societies, it is argued, interaction in the public sphere is (ideal-typically) based on limited acquaintance and an assessment of persons not by the totality of their background and life-history but by a limited set of characteristics which they themselves help to select and emphasise. The fact that functional justifications in terms of the requirements of the 'public interest' may be advanced for some aspects of the selectivity of the public sphere - for its emphasis on achieved rather than acquired status, so that knowing a person's 'background' is unnecessary, or for its emphasis on the use of explicitly rational argument (cf. Connor, 1971; de Romilly, 1956) - is from this point of view treated as secondary. The question of public interest is only incidentally relevant:

what concerns us is the difference between the interests and world-view an individual derives from his or her intimate life in the private sphere and those which he or she derives from interaction in public. Interests based on interaction in the public sphere may or may not be justifiable in terms of *the* public interest. Nor is it particularly important, from the point of view being put forward here, whether the 'public sphere' is that of state politics or of some minor organisation, provided that the organisation is run in a relatively bureaucratic and impersonal style, and its personnel does not overlap too much with the private circles of acquaintance of its members.

Although the extent to which relations within any organisation or social context are impersonal or personal can be studied from an objective point of view (cf. chapter 2, below, and chapter 4, pp. 61, 65, 68), discussion of the problem has been (and is here) very much bound up with the question of individual consciousness of a dichotomy between the two spheres. The aim is not to decide where to place any given society on a continuum stretching from an ideal-typical fusion of public and private interests to an ideal-typical dichotomy, but to assess the weight attached to the boundary between public and private spheres in actors' classifications of social experience. In modern western society, it is argued, most working adults experience a sharp disjunction between public and private life, and tend to see them as competing, not only because they may well make conflicting demands on the actor's time, but also because the intensity and totality of relationships in the private sphere make those of the public sphere seem super-ficial, distorting and unsatisfactory, while the challenges of the public sphere – its competitive nature and assumption that actors are con-cerned with something beyond their own well-being and that of a hand-ful of other individuals – make private life seem tame and trivial. There is a disjunction in scope and power between the two spheres. Private life offers plenty of opportunities for the exercise of power (and correspondingly intense power struggles), but its scope is very limited. Public life is much wider in the scope of affairs with which it deals, but in most cases the individual can wield little power in it. A choice appears to present itself between a significant part in an insignificant sphere or an insignificant part in a significant sphere.

Attic tragedy appears to face the same problem, and to deal with it by conferring a world-shaking quality on intrafamilial power struggles – partly by choosing its themes from the stories of mythical kings and their families, partly by clothing them in language associated with the public sphere, and lastly through the role played by the gods.

Here is one of the most significant differences between classical Greece and the twentieth century. It is only in a secularised society that the dichotomy between private and public spheres can be formulated in the terms in which it has been presented above. In the past, the history of individualism and of the value attached to private life has been deeply influenced by Protestantism and the increased feeling of a personal relation between the individual and God which it fostered. But for many people in the modern western world this feeling has now ceased to be important in conceptions of personal identity. It has been replaced by ideas of 'development of the personality' through leisure interests and personal relationships, which were quite unknown in classical Greece – except, in a sense, in the limited circles of the philosophers. What classical Athenians thought about the gods is extremely hard to assess, and there is no doubt that there was wide variety both in belief and in practice. There were moments in which a strong feeling of a collective relation to the gods overtook them (as on the occasion of the mutilation of the Hermae). But there were also beliefs that each person's fate was individually determined; there were gods at every level of social grouping, in the household and village as well as on the Acropolis, and rites for every stage in the life cycle and every contingency; one could go to a temple of Asclepius for healing or become an initiate of the mysteries to gain spiritual insight; the power of the gods over individuals manifested itself whenever anyone fell in love, or went mad, or even got drunk (Vernant, 1966; cf. also Dodds, 1973). A determined effort had been made to eliminate divine intervention from the public sphere (Humphreys, 1978, pp. 252–7), but this, by diminishing the authority of priests, only left a wider field for initiative in the private domain. Certainly the classical period was not an age of startling religious innovations – while it was, on the contrary, a period which produced one or two startling manifestations of scepticism (Alcibiades' parodying of the Mysteries, Kritias' suggestion, Diels-Kranz, 1935, B 25, that the gods were invented by rulers as a way of keeping people in order). But most people still took the reality of the gods for granted. They were not expected to appear and walk among men, as they did in the Homeric poems, but their intentions, hard to ascertain, and their potential capacity for intervention in men's affairs formed a frame round human activity just as their appearance in prologue and epilogue framed a Euripidean tragedy.

Thus, in comparison between ancient and modern society, an

awareness of similarity leads on to an awareness of difference: there is a constant movement back and forth between the two, a constant need to consider and compare different perspectives. These essays are published in collected form in the hope of stimulating further expressions of different points of view: they are not intended to stand as a definitive statement.

1   *Oikos* and *polis*

Oikos and *polis* — household and city — are two of the Greek words which ancient historians are most prone to avoid translating. It is a charitable, and I think also a reasonable, inference that the concepts have a central and problematic position in the Greek scheme of values. Plato thought that a perfect city could only be created by abolishing the private household and family. He also admitted that the idea was impracticable and would seem shocking to a Greek audience. Sophocles' *Antigone* is a play about the conflicting values of city and family; Plato was certainly not the only Athenian to feel the conflict.

This poses an interesting problem of method: how can we relate the rather abundant evidence on values to institutions and social structure? I am restricting myself in this paper to Athens, and especially the Athenian urban elite from whom most of our evidence comes. What I want to do here is, taking the conflict in values as given, to look for its institutional correlates — the interferences, discontinuities and lack of articulation between public and private spheres of interaction - and the effect of these on the ideology of the *oikos*. After discussing briefly the part played by kinship in Athenian politics, I shall look successively at four other fields - law, economics, religion, social life. Finally, I shall try to say something about Attic tragedy, asking why, in the main cultural expression of values in fifth-century Athens, the *oikos* seems to be more important than the *polis*.

The contrast between public and private life in classical Athens was sharp. Public life was egalitarian, competitive, impersonal. Its typical locus was the open arena - assembly, market-place, law-court, theatre, gymnasium, battle-field. Monumental architecture clearly differentiated public buildings, religious and secular, from private houses. Oath-taking was extensively used to mark the transition from private status to public role - magistrates, councillors, jurors, boys entering the citizen body took an oath to fulfil their public responsibilities and disregard private interests.

The *oikos*, by contrast, was a closed space, architecturally functional rather than ornamental. Its relationships were hierarchic: husband–wife, parent–child, owner–slave. (Only the relation between siblings was egalitarian, and it seems to have been rare for adult male siblings to live together even when they owned property in common.) Women, children and slaves had no formal place in public life except for the part played by women in some public religious festivals. Division of labour was strongly marked in the *oikos*, much less so in the *polis*, where rotation of office and collegiate forms of organisation were dominant. On entry into the *polis* the oath of citizenship could be taken as representing a voluntary contract (Socrates takes it this way in the *Crito*). Entry to the household emphasised the control of its head – he decided whether to rear a child or not, purchased slaves, and arranged marriages.

These differences in the organisation of space and social relationships are commonly acknowledged, yet we are far from agreement about their significance. Assessments of the role of kinship and private ties in Athenian politics differ widely. Prosopography is an enjoyable game. The political elite was not large and at any time ties of kinship and affinity between its members are not hard to trace. Nevertheless, to predict political alignments on the basis of such ties would be rash. Athenian aristocrats believed that ambitious upstarts could gain political power by winning the favour of the *demos* in assembly – not by marrying a powerful man's daughter. It is easy to find texts which stress the impersonal disregard of private interests and loyalties expected of the man playing a public role – yet in others it is taken for granted that loyalty to friends and loyalty to the *polis* are equally characteristic of the just man.

A comparison between Athens and Rome may help to put the question in perspective. In the much more hierarchical and geronto-cratic political institutions of republican Rome, kinship, patronage and friendship had a well-recognised place. The young Roman's progress up the *cursus honorum* depended to a considerable extent on support from senior politicians who had the power to give him a favourable position in the public eye or keep him in the shadow. This type of control did not exist in Athens. For the Roman, if political alliance did not spring from friendship, it should at least lead to it (Brunt, 1965). Roman politics constantly required the mobilisation of 'action-sets' (Mayer, 1966). In the whirl of these 'kaleidoscopic combinations', as Brunt has called them, the language of *amicitia* could be used both to persuade the ally of the moment that he was more than a tool, and to clothe conflict and opposition with dignity. The advocate who spoke in defence of a notorious reprobate could plead friendship as his excuse. To cite private enmity as a justification for prosecution was rarer and less approved. In Athens the reverse was true: prosecutors dilate on their personal grievances, while the defendant's friends emphasise their long-standing knowledge of his circumstances and character rather than the obligations of the relationship. In Athens, friendship is stressed in the courts because advocates who do not speak out of friendship speak for money, as habitual sycophants or professional orators. Antiphon, always cited by those who believe in the predominant role of *hetaireiai* in Athenian politics, was mistrusted by the *demos* not for his friendships but for his rhetorical skill (*deinotēs*). But his career shows that personal connections and *hetaireiai* became of central importance in Athenian politics only in moments of conspiracy. References to private loyalties were tolerated in the courts (the lies inspired by friendship being thought less dangerous than those devised by sophistry), but were entirely out of place in the assembly. Whatever the real reasons which prompted Athenian politicians to support one policy or another, they were expected to justify their decision in terms of moral principle or the advantage of the city.

Kinship and friendship did not predetermine political choices either in Rome or in Athens. In both cities the fulfilment of obligations to kin outside the household was to a considerable degree optional, and the interrelations of the political elite were such that in any conflict a man was likely to have kin and friends on both sides. In both cities the ambitious politician pursued his own advantage while debating matters of public policy. The difference perhaps lies in the fact that the Roman political elite in the first century BC were seriously concerned at the divisive effects of political rivalry within their own body, while the political elite of classical Athens had to address themselves to an assembly which was suspicious of any sign of class solidarity among its leaders. The Romans feared violence, the Athenian elite feared the wish to please the *demos*; so the symbol of upper-class solidarity was friendship in Rome, rationality in Athens.

The ties of kinship outside the *oikos* could be used in politics, but did not seriously conflict with the norms of disinterested behaviour in public roles. What about conflicts between the claims of the *oikos* itself and those of political life? Disagreement on political questions between fathers and sons was perhaps becoming a possibility in the later fifth

century – general complaints of lack of filial respect are common – but
there is little sign that it was seen as a serious moral problem. Civic
duty and *oikos* ties conflicted most obviously in matters of war. We
must beware here of reading modern attitudes into ancient texts.
Success in war was still, in fifth-century Greece, one of the main criteria
by which cities and men were judged. The contrast between *oikos* and
polis could easily slide over, here, into a contrast between women and
men, as it does not only in the *Lysistrata*, but also in the *Trojan Women*.
As Vernant has pointed out, while the adolescent girl prepares for
marriage, the adolescent boy prepares for war. The Spartans believed
that the austerity and all-male company of the *syssition* were partly
responsible for their military success. Normal *oikos* life was 'softening'.

Nevertheless it was impossible to maintain that only women wished
for peace and suffered in war. When Aristophanes associates peace with
family festivals – the marriage and Apatouria of the *Peace*, the Rural
Dionysia of the *Acharnians* – it is the longing of the Attic countryman
to return to his home village which is uppermost in his mind. If it is
characteristic of Attic tragedy to see in the death of Iphigeneia an
excuse for Clytemnestra, the tragic choice was still Agamemnon's
decision to sacrifice his daughter for the sake of the expedition against
Troy.

Despite the undercurrent of criticism and questioning in tragedy, to
which we shall return, the masculine world of politics and the *polis*,
power and honour, ostensibly took first place in Athenian values.
Consequently, to look for recognition of the values of the *oikos* in the
heart of public life can take us only a limited way. We must turn now
to spheres in which *oikos* and *polis* were articulated with each other on
a more equal footing; and in the first place, to family law, in which the
city both recognised the *oikos* as a social unit of fundamental
importance and at the same time regulated its structure.

Attic law impinged on the *oikos* in four ways. First, the law of
citizenship and of slavery regulated entry to the *oikos* and defined the
categories of persons eligible to be full *oikos* members. Since in practice
marriage and legitimate filiation also applied to the free non-citizen
population (who could not marry citizens, but could marry within their
own category) the law also created, by distinguishing between citizens
and non-citizens, a category of quasi-*oikoi* which differed also from
citizen *oikoi* in that they lacked landed property, although they *could*
own slaves. Property, and especially landed property (*phanera ousia*)
played an important part in the conception of the citizen *oikos*, and the

law of inheritance regulated its transmission. Furthermore, the law defined certain rights and obligations within the *oikos* and offered means of legal redress in cases where the *oikos* head was incompetent or exploited his position of authority unjustly. Finally, an important consequence of this intersection of *polis* and *oikos* in the legal sphere was that the law courts of the city became a theatre for the expression of what may perhaps be called the ideology of the *oikos*: idealising statements about the nature and foundations of the *oikos* and the norms of behaviour within the household and between members of closely related households.

One of the norms frequently emphasised is that quarrels between kin should be settled without recourse to the courts – while quarrels within the nuclear family should not happen at all. Thus a contradiction is immediately apparent between the ideology of the *oikos*, which stresses the need for amicable regulation of the affairs of *oikos* and kindred inside the private sphere, and the provision by the city of mechanisms for settling their disputes in the public sphere. One consequence of this contradiction was that the laws offering protection from exploitation within the *oikos* were often completely ineffectual. The principle was admirable: in cases of ill-treatment of orphans and heiresses, incapacity of the *oikos* head to manage his affairs, failure of sons to care for aged parents, wrongful enslavement, and adultery by a woman (as 'a safe-guard against the complaisant husband', Harrison, 1968, p. 35) any citizen was allowed to prosecute through the *graphē* procedure. In practice, however, it was often impossible for women and children exploited by their legal guardians and protectors to find a man outside the household willing to champion their cause. In the five cases of which we have detailed record in which guardians were indicted for their handling of their wards' property (Isaeus vii, Lysias xxxii, Demosthenes xxvii-xxviii, xxxvi, xxxviii) the cases were brought by the wards themselves when they became adult and acquired full citizen rights. No one took action to stop the misconduct at an earlier stage, while the wards were still children – though at least one of the wards, Apollodorus (Isaeus vii) had a friendly stepfather who helped him when the case finally came to court. Only in one case (Dem. xxxviii, 23) do we hear of a denunciation of the guardian during his wards' childhood for not leasing their *oikos* out (a safeguard against mismanagement); and in this case the guardian (father's brother) 'persuaded the court to allow him to continue to manage the *oikos* himself'.

Another consequence of the feeling of opposition between the norm of the *oikos* and the processes of law was that kin who *had* quarrelled might try to take advantage of the full letter of the law in their disputes. We shall have to return to this point after discussing the place of arbitration, both private and official, in the Athenian legal system.

Arbitration helped to mediate the contradiction between *oikos* norms and law. It was customary for kin to take their disputes first to private arbitrators. In Lysias xxxii, Diogeiton's daughter - married to her father's brother and deprived with her children of his estate, after his death, by Diogeiton - persuades her daughter's husband to summon Diogeiton and a number of kin and friends of the family to a family council at which she denounces her father (§ 11ff). It is only after the failure of this démarche that the matter is taken to court. Similarly, in Isaeus ii, Menekles and his brother had quarrelled because Menekles, who was childless, had adopted his wife's brother and thus deprived his brother's son of the chance of inheriting his property. Friends of both parties were asked to arbitrate and persuaded Menekles to give up some property to his brother - which did not prevent the latter from contesting the validity of the adoption when Menekles died. In Isaeus vi, after Philoktemon had prevented his father Euktemon from presenting a boy of slave descent to his phratry as a legitimate son, they came to a private agreement that the boy should only get a small piece of land as his share of Euktemon's estate, after which Philoktemon withdrew his opposition and the phratry duly accepted the boy (an interesting example of the power of rich families over their phratries). After the deaths of both Philoktemon and Euktemon the boy was able to use his acceptance by the phratry as a basis for claiming the whole of Euktemon's estate. This case illustrates well a point which frequently appears, that where kin make an illegal compromise in order to avoid open enmity, the illegality of the agreement often provides an excuse for a later piece of double-crossing (cf. Isaeus v, [Demosthenes] xlviii).

When private arbitrators failed to provide a solution, the procedure in many types of case sent the disputants next to the men in their sixtieth year who served as public arbitrators for their tribe. Only if these men, too, failed to suggest a compromise agreeable to both parties did the case come to court; and a considerable part of the speakers' argument was devoted to questions of equity rather than questions of law - at least in those speeches which were considered worth preserving for posterity. (However, Isaeus xi, the speech of the unpleasant Theopompus in the Hagnias case, is an exception - and we do know that the highly tendentious technical arguments used in it were successful.) Both the arguments addressed to the jury in preserved speeches and Aristophanes' portrayal of jurors' attitudes in the *Wasps* indicate that jurors considered it their function and their prerogative to decide what was the most equitable solution in each case. They were not restrained by any authoritative instruction on points of law from a judge, nor by any doctrine of precedent. The whole ethos of the process was opposed to any form of legal systematisation.

The weaknesses of this type of law were first that the written code served to create disputes as often as to prevent them, especially in the field of inheritance where the order of succession laid down by Solon was frequently challenged by remoter kin who felt that in equity they had a stronger claim than the next-of-kin designated by law; and, second, that when cases were no longer settled by well-informed public opinion in a village community, but were heard by a large jury in the melting-pot milieu of the city, jurors found themselves compelled to rely for their judgment of the facts of the case on what the disputants chose to tell them and on their assessment of the speakers' character. From these two weaknesses, in turn, arose the peculiar strength of Attic law. It may not have been a very equitable or a very conclusive way of settling disputes (we know of several cases which were reopened time and again), but it did provide the Athenian public with a lively presentation of models of correct behaviour and examples of moral delinquency. It was the Athenian equivalent of the television soap opera; and one of the roots from which New Comedy grew.

By the fourth century (which of course is the only period for which we have evidence) there is a noticeable tendency for family law cases to turn on a contrast between natural feelings and legal regulations. The law that an adopted child severs completely his relationship to his natural father is one example of the type of technical legal rule which disputants often tried to circumvent (Isaeus x, [Dem.] xliv). The law that matrilateral half-siblings could not marry each other, and inherited only if there were no claimants on the father's side traceable as far as second cousins, often ran contrary to patterns of affection and associa-tion within the family; since Athenian women married much younger than men (women at about 15, men at about 30), many widows married twice and brought up two families in the house of their second husband. We find several manoeuvres structurally equivalent to the forbidden half-sibling marriage: adoption of the half-sister's son (Isaeus vii); alleged posthumous adoption to her second husband of a woman's son by her first marriage (Isaeus viii. 40-2); we also find an alleged will in favour of a matrilateral half-brother (Isaeus xi). Many inheritance cases turn on the opposition between the next-of-kin as defined by law and the use of a will (with or without adoption) to transmit property instead to an heir who was closer to *de cuius* in loyalty and affections (Isaeus ii, vii). Opponents, of course, claim that such wills are forged or that adoption has been made while *d.c.* was of unsound mind, being under the influence, of a woman (Isaeus ii). In Isaeus i, the speakers, who were sister's sons and next-of-kin of *d.c.*, Kleonymos, claim that the will in which he left his estate to more distant relatives had been made while Kleonymos was on bad terms with their father's brother and guardian, Deinias; after Deinias' death Kleonymos took them into his *oikos* and treated them with the warmest affection, and quarrelled with some of the beneficiaries of his will – but died before having a chance to cancel it and make new arrangements for the disposal of his estate. 'He made the will when he was in a rage and not thinking straight; when in his right mind he tried to cancel it' (§ 43). On these grounds the jury are asked to ignore the will.

New Comedy provides further evidence for the opposition in Athenian minds between natural affections and legal rules. Menander's *Aspis* makes much play with the situation of the young heiress forced to marry the greedy old uncle who was entitled to claim her by law (father's brother being her next-of-kin). Young Athenians of good family in New Comedy are always falling in love with penniless *hetairai*, freedwomen or slaves whom they cannot legally marry. In comedy, of course, the girl always turns out in the end to be of impeccable citizen parentage, but real life did not provide such happy endings. Demosthenes lix and Isaeus iii and vi deal with attempts to pass off liaisons with *hetairai* as proper marriages, or accusations of doing so. It is important to remember that the evidence from law-court speeches concerns only the stratum of society which had enough property for legitimacy to be worth arguing about. The number of illicit unions among poorer citizens is likely to have been a good deal higher.

Athenian society changed radically between Solon's reforms and the age of Demosthenes and Menander; family law remained unchanged except for Pericles' ban on marriage with non-citizen women. Flexibility was preserved by the freedom with which juries administered the law; but this freedom was itself the proof that Attic law had developed in a way probably unforeseen by Solon, in a direction to which the existence of a written code was an irrelevance if not an obstacle.

If we can judge from the evidence in Hesiod and Homer, legal

disputes in archaic Greece were settled by a ruling from one or more
basileis, the community as a whole doing no more than express its
opinion informally from the side-lines. *Basileis* could be influenced by
bribes, and laws were at first written down principally to guard against
this. The loss in flexibility implied by codification was less regrettable
than corrupt and arbitrary judgments. However, in classical Athens the
danger of bribery was guarded against by the use of large juries allotted
to courts only just before the day's trial began – which Solon can scarcely
have foreseen. The problem was that they were still asked to play the
role of the Homeric judge – to articulate the opinion of the community
on a question of equity – when they no longer had the small-scale
community's knowledge of its members' affairs. It is notoriously
difficult for us to tell who is lying in an ancient lawsuit; it was difficult
also for the jury.

Out of this contradictory situation comes the tendency of so many
disputants to buttress their case by presenting themselves as model
oikos-members. Instead of being the operating theatre in which a
diseased *oikos* submits to the healing hand of the *polis*, the law-court
becomes one of the city's windows into the *oikos*: a theatre for the
dramatisation of an ideological view of the *oikos*. Fifth-century tragedy
no doubt contributed to this development, which in its turn contributed to the development of New Comedy. The restraining influence of
kin and community which should have been able to enforce a settlement of *oikos* disputes was all too often, in the increasingly impersonal
milieu of the classical city, replaced by an unmediated juxtaposition of
oikos as actor and *polis* as spectator.

In politics, the effacement of the local communities which had once
mediated between *oikos* and *polis* was a necessary condition for the
smooth working of democracy, but in law this weakening of the bonds
of kinship and local community left a vacuum which the city's institutions could not entirely fill.

Let us turn now to the economic sphere. It was here that the
opposition between public welfare and private interest was perhaps
most clearly and frequently formulated. One great difference between
classical Athens and the modern world should, however, be noted here:
conspicuous consumption in Athens belonged very largely to the public
and not to the private sphere. Wealth was displayed by erecting statues
and public monuments, equipping warships, financing dramatic performances, making sacrifices at which the meat was publicly distributed,
and so on. Many of these liturgies were compulsory (they were one of the

main forms of taxation – citizens did not pay any regular direct tax) but they still had a potlatching aspect – there was competition to display more generosity to the city than was strictly required by law.

But this happy integration of consumption into the values of the city was not matched by any corresponding theory of production or exchange. Certainly, trade in the harbour and market grew, and its importance was recognised: warships were sent out to convoy the fleet, procedure in commercial law-suits was speeded up and distinctions of civic status in these suits were abolished. But as Weber said long ago, the Athenian was *homo politicus* and not *homo œconomicus*. The *oikos* tradition of economic activity was one of careful supervision and management, self-sufficiency, production for private consumption, mortgaging land if necessary to raise money for liturgies, for loans to friends or for family expenses such as dowries and funerals. The work was done by slaves. The market for agricultural products grew; urban versions of the *oikos*-economy were also developed – slave workshops making furniture, weapons and so on. But interaction between the market and the *oikos* as production unit was always impeded by the reluctance of *oikos*-heads to involve themselves in market transactions, the limited legal capacity of slaves and the almost total absence of free men willing to be employed as foremen or managers. To be a permanent employee was too much like a slave's life. Transactions in both land and labour were still largely governed by non-market patterns centred on the status categories and social relationships of the *oikos*. Land and slaves belonged to the *ousia* – 'being', the identity of the *oikos*. Money and goods exchanged in the market were *chremata* – 'things', transitory possessions. Transactions in the *oikos* sphere were part of a lasting pattern of social relationships – kinship, affinity, friendship. Market transactions were contractual and ephemeral. Frequent use was made of the distinction between 'visible' and 'invisible' property. Visible property – especially real property – was related to openly acknowledged social position and commitments. Its owner's wealth and status could easily be assessed, he could not evade tax obligations, his kin knew what they could expect from him. With 'invisible' property in cash and loans a man could conceal his wealth and evade social obligations: it was difficult to 'place' him socially. Hidden wealth meant hidden power, suspicion, unease. Some men were rumoured to be fabulously wealthy, yet turned out at their death to have very moderate means – or so their heirs claimed. On the other hand, a rich miser might pretend to own much less than he had.

There are two ways of looking at the contrast between *oikos* and *polis* in the economic sphere. The modern analyst is likely to see the growing importance of the market-place in Athenian economic life as part of a general process of urbanisation and role-differentiation which can equally be traced in the growth of the institutions of the democratic *polis*. He will focus – as I have done – on the difference between the traditional patterns of behaviour of the *oikos* and the new patterns of the market. Market relations in a sense reproduced the typical characteristics of public interaction in the political sphere – they were egalitarian, impersonal, competitive, achievement-oriented. *Polis* and market stand together in contrast to the *oikos* as formally rational against 'traditional' types of interaction. Indeed, the most precise and rational accounting and organisation of contracts was to be found in city finances, where record-keeping and the separation of public and private funds were taken for granted. (In private economic enterprise business capital could not be kept separate from domestic property and expenses – there were no limited liability companies.) It looks like a simple case of parallel development of the same type of rationality in both fields.

Such an analysis is misleading, because it ignores the relation between the Athenian economy and Athenian politics. Politicians and generals made money out of empire and war: ordinary citizens were paid for jury duty, assembly meetings and above all for service in the army or fleet. Tribute money used to pay the fleet was spent in the market: traders came because there was money in the market and because the fleet made trade safe. Production for export was fairly unimportant in the Athenian economy; essentially the city throve as the largest market in the Mediterranean world. If the state's funds ran low, the whole system was in danger, and the influence of personal ambition and economic interests in politics became immediately clear; there were always politicians and generals seeking prestige and wealth, and rowers to vote for any overseas adventure which would put them in pocket. Such was the experience of the period of empire and the difficult years which followed Athens' defeat in the Peloponnesian war – an experience which left an indelible impression on those who lived through it. Demosthenes' reasons for urging his audience to disregard economic considerations were different (see Jones, A.H.M., 1952) but his point of view was the same. Economic interests were seen as essentially private, egotistic forces opposed to rational political decision-making, in which only the good of the city as a political entity should be considered.

Although at any particular moment in time voting decisions were affected by many factors, among which the level of the city's revenues was certainly of considerable importance, it is clear that from a structural point of view seapower, war and empire served the interests of the market-place and had a disruptive effect on the *oikos*. Fifth- and fourth-century warfare no longer respected the labour needs of the peasant household, and often made heavy claims on the income of the *rentier*. The same was true of radical democracy. The introduction of pay for military and political service implied the assumption that one day's and one man's labour was equivalent to another. But the farmer's tasks could not always be postponed, and the long campaigns of fifth-century warfare required a rowing force of men who could not in all cases count on slave labour to replace them at home.

It is in this situation that the *oikos* was given a central place in the economic ideology of the upper class. *Oikos*-economy – *oikonomia* – was defined as production for use, aiming at self-sufficiency; the ambitions of the *oikos*-head were limited by his needs, and he could therefore – it was claimed – be expected to take a responsible and public-spirited attitude in political discussions. The economy of the market-place – *chrēmatistikē*, the art of money-making – was based on exchange and oriented to a pursuit of profit to which no bounds were set. Those involved in this section of the economy were (supposedly) incapable of setting aside their own economic interests in favour of the true good of the city. This ideology defined those whose economic interests inclined them to favour peace and a relatively oligarchic form of government as the only citizens capable of taking political decisions without considering their own economic interests. The concept of the *oikos* as the only sound economic basis for a well-governed state lent itself also to further elaboration based on the fact that only citizens could own land, and based also on tensions between the political ideal of equality, which concerned only citizens, and the tendency of the market-place economy to blur status distinctions between citizens, metics and slaves. (Slaves who produced goods for the market often lived outside the owner's *oikos* and in practice contracted freely as well as building up property of their own.) Since only citizens could own land, it could be argued, let metics and slaves deal in invisible wealth and occupy the unstructured world of the market – let them pursue private economic interest, since they had no place in political decision-making; but citizens should maintain their political integrity and their status difference by keeping to the traditional pattern of the landed *oikos*. This view identified the interests of city and *oikos* only by completely denying the realities of Athenian economic life. Xenophon's idealisation of *oikos*-life in the *Œconomicus* as the solution to Greece's peacetime problems was probably written on a large estate in an underdeveloped part of the Peloponnese. By the 350s, when he wrote the *Poroi* in Athens, he had changed his views.

Oikos in economic contexts as in legal contexts is therefore an ideologically loaded term (it may be no accident that *oikos* in the sense of property or economic unit is not attested between Homer and the fifth century). Greek discussions of economics which present 'the *oikos*' as the natural economic basis of the city-state have an obvious bias. Since there was no concept of economic policy to provide a framework within which the economic interests of citizens as individuals could be recognised as having a legitimate claim to consideration in discussions of public affairs, it was open to each class to accuse the other of pursuing private advantage at the expense of the city. Hence it was in the economic sphere that the citizen's duty to subordinate private interests and responsibilities to the claims of the city was most insistently proclaimed.

In religion, too, *oikos* can be a tendentious word. Fourth-century orators writing speeches for inheritance cases make much of the religious duty to 'preserve the *oikos*' of the dead man, and Roman analogies have led historians to take Greek domestic *sacra* perhaps more seriously than they deserve. In considering the religion of the *oikos* in relation to the city, three aspects have to be examined: first, the cult of the dead; second, the religious observances of the household; third, the place of the household in the cults of the city.

The cult of the dead was a memorial-cult, rather than ancestor-worship: there was a customary obligation to commemorate the family dead but they were not expected to protect their descendants or intervene in their lives. The All Souls' Day of Athens, in the festival Anthesteria, when the dead were supposed to return, was a festival common to the whole city and fixed in its religious calendar. There was no individual invocation of the dead in relation to particular household crises - except where the dead man was unburied or unavenged, where he still had unfinished business of his own to attend to, so to speak. A dead man could only become a protecting power as *hero*, recognised by a whole community and often worshipped at a tomb in the centre of the city - whereas ordinary men had to be buried outside the city walls.

Assertions of the wealth, prestige and alliances of the *oikos* through the medium of funeral ceremonies were restricted by Solon's laws. Attendance by women was restricted to close kindred and women over 60 ([Dem.] xliii 62), grave-gods were limited, cattle could not be sacrificed, the praises of the dead man could not be combined with eulogies of famous ancestors. Mourning cut the household off from public life – it was polluted by death – and in the privacy of the *oikos* grief could be given full expression; but its public manifestations had to be controlled. The *only* exception to the limits on participation in funeral processions was the public funeral of all those killed in the year's campaigns in war. Here all the kin and friends of the dead could join freely in the ceremony; but it was inevitably an expression of the solidarity of the city rather than that of the individual *oikoi* concerned.

The tendency of the public funeral, which can be seen at work in the history of this public cult offered to those who died in war (starting with the battle of Marathon, if not before), is to democratise the commemoration of the dead, and it is the state's assumption of the responsibility for commemoration in perpetuity which makes this democratisation possible. When we find, from the later fourth century onwards, growing evidence for individual commemoration ceremonies both in Athens and elsewhere, the obligation is laid on a corporate kin group, professional association, temple or other public body, and secured by an endowment of property to provide for sacrifices and feast the 'congregation' which is an essential element in the rite (cf. Kamps, 1937). Before the law reached the stage of development which made these foundations possible, continuity of cult was dependent on the degree of cohesion and common interest felt by each man's descendants, and such cohesion tended to crystallise only round concentrations of power and property. Even the continued use of the same family burial ground – and the importance of this already indicates the effect of social inequalities on the workings of familial piety – would not in itself ensure a regular performance of commemoration rites. Greek tombstones do not in fact address themselves to the descendants of the dead. They say *O parodita* – 'you who pass by'. Even tombs on private estates in the country are set beside public roads. They allude to the civic virtues of the dead or their common human lot rather than their family relationships. Despite all the pathos put into the idea of 'continuing the *oikos*', the *oikos* in fact divided in each generation and in general a man was lucky if his commemorative cult continued after the death of his own children (cf. below, ch. 5).

The dead belong to the sphere of Hermes - god of frontiers and thresholds, but also of public places - the crossroads and the market. The central *oikos* deity was Hermes' opposite, Hestia, the goddess of the hearth. In the cult of Hestia the city was a macrocosm of the household - it too had its sacred hearth. The young *ephēboi*, candidates for admission to citizenship, sacrificed at the city hearth at the beginning of their two years of military training, just as newborn children, brides and slaves were admitted to the *oikos* by a ceremony at *its* hearth.

There, however, the resemblance seems to end. The ceremony of bringing new fire to the hearth of the city from Delphi was not in Athens extended to the hearths of individual *oikoi* - the city hearth replaced them rather than reinforcing their importance. The city hearth was above all a place where the city publicly entertained guests - foreign embassies and so on. But in the private context 'to sacrifice to Hestia' was proverbial meanness; it was a sacrifice to which no outsiders were invited. It is perhaps arguable that distribution and commensality played such a central part in Greek religion that a sacrifice in which there was no sharing of food outside the everyday family circle could barely find a place in it. Even in the Anthesteria, the Attic festival which is most clearly a festival of *oikoi*, the central day of the three-day ritual comes to a climax in a drunken revel in which the relationships of the *oikos* are set aside; the fact that on this day (the *Choes*) each man brought his own wine and drank it himself, without any exchanges, was considered to need special explanation.

It is significant that some of our best information on other religious ceremonies of the household comes from Theophrastus' description of the superstitious man. The household was the context in which the Athenian learnt folk beliefs - nurses' versions of myths, and bogey-tales; sacred snakes, ithyphallic herms, bisexual Hermaphroditai; agrarian rites carried out in the family fields. The educated man was not expected to take all this very seriously. Household sacrifices and *rites de passage* were, however, important as occasions for gathering together kinsmen and friends. The social life of the family as a united group took place almost entirely in a religious context.

Theophrastus' Superstitious Man would also go off every month to the priest of the Orphic mysteries to get purified, taking with him his wife or, if she was busy, his children and their nurse. The mystery religions were probably almost the only non-household cults in which the whole *oikos* could participate as a unit. Women and slaves could

be initiated as well as men. The robe worn for initiation into the
Eleusinian mysteries might be preserved and used as swaddling-clothes
for the next child born into the family. Both because they offered a
promise of immortality from which the rest of the family could hardly
be excluded, and because they ignored the status divisions of the city,
mystery religions gave more place to the family than other public cults.

The festivals of the city's religious calendar, with the exception
of the Anthesteria, tended to divide the *oikos*. Some were only for
women, some only for men, some for boys. It would be false to speak
of conflict between city and *oikos* in the religious sphere, but there
were distinctions and discontinuities. *Oikos* religion tended to be rustic
and naive or secret and salvationist: it mobilised round the *oikos* a
personal network of kin, friends and neighbours. *Polis* religion was
ceremonial, public and often aristocratic in culture and organisation.
Hereditary priesthoods, complicated religious lore known only to
experts, fine sculptures, competitions in music, poetry and athletics,
played an important part in it. It expressed the formally recognised
sub-groups and status-categories of the city. The occasional recognition
accorded to the *oikos* among other social units was scarcely porportion-
ate to its importance in Attic society.

Women seem to have been regarded as keener in religious observance
than men, and one can see why. There were few other forms of entertainment open to them. The behaviour of women in tragedy, which has
sometimes been cited as evidence that Athenian women led active and
eventful lives, in fact provides quite a lot of evidence for the opposite
view. The 'womanly women' of Greek tragedy are constantly shrinking
from public appearances and producing excuses for being out of the
house; only desperate circumstances can bring them to talk to strange
men. The rules of modesty for unmarried girls were particularly strict,
but even a married women would never appear at a dinner party or
entertain strangers in her husband's absence.

The separation of men and women in social life meant that in a
sense the public world of the city reached into the house. One of the
boundaries between public and private life ran between the *gynaikeion*,
women's quarters, and the *andron*, the men's dining room, where
banquets and symposia were held. A man's dining and drinking
companions were the friends with whom he associated during the day
in assembly, market-place and gymnasium – many of them age-mates
with whom he had gone to school, been initiated to phratry and deme,
served as a soldier. But there was still a marked distinction between

public interaction and meetings in an *oikos*. Political meetings held in private houses were always associated with conspiracy. The symposium was not the place for serious talk about politics or even about philosophy. Plato's *Symposium* is presented as an unusually sober meeting at which all the guests have hangovers, but the subject of discussion is love. Xenophon's *Symposium* indicates other suitable topics for conversation: dancing, perfume, the education of women, drinking too much; there are speech-making competitions on subjects like 'Who has the most to be proud of?' or 'Who is the best-looking?'

The competitive aspect of *polis* life was strongly present in symposia, and it was accompanied by the formal procedures of the city: secret ballot to decide the result of a speech-making competition, election of a president for drinking contests. The gymnastic contests in physical agility which were so much part of public life were represented by competitions in maintaining physical control when drunk - dancing with full wine bowls balanced on different parts of the body, flipping wine-dregs at a target. As Alcibiades and his friends parodied religious rites in their parties, so the ordinary symposium parodied the life of assembly and gymnasium by challenging the participants to display their rhetorical and physical skills on frivolous subjects and in grotesque and erotic dances.

The dining couches of the *andron* also served as the locus for non-marital sexual activity - affairs with prostitutes, who were often invited to symposia, or with boys. Both friendship and romantic love - which in Athens meant homosexual love - belonged to this liminal context ambiguously placed between *oikos* and city. Between being a child in one's father's *oikos* and being head of one's own family came a period in which gymnasium and *andron* were the main centres of action. A boy was first *erōmenos*, the object of romantic passion, introduced into adult society by an older lover who took his father's place as a model of adult behaviour; later he became a lover and educator of younger boys in his turn. He would not drop out of the life of gymnasium and *andron* until some time after marriage, when his own sons were beginning to grow up. This was regarded as the normal sequence of sex roles - mockery of homosexuals in comedy is directed only at those who deviate from this norm. Plato, while deploring the consummation of homosexual love - which was probably commoner than he implies - valued it for its function in education and socialisation. But already by the late fifth century the Athenian *jeunesse dorée* seem to be increasingly socialising each other by this means into the attitudes of an exclusive, rebellious and alienated elite. The transitional sphere of friendship and homosexual love, which Greek sources some-times present as providing a bridge between the public values of the city and those of private life, tended rather to lead to the elaboration in a closed circle of behaviour patterns which reversed the norms of both.

I started this paper by suggesting that the elaboration of political roles, procedures and contexts of interaction in classical Athens created a contrast between the public life of the *polis* and the private world of the *oikos*. We have looked at four spheres of action in which both *polis* and *oikos* have a part: law, economics, religion, and the social life and socialisation of citizens. It remains to look at the main symbolic form of classical Athens - tragedy. The *oikos* is accorded in tragedy a dignity and significance which one hardly expects in a society where public activities were so dominant. Only *one* extant tragedy (the *Philoctetes*) has no female character.

I start from two statements by Aristotle: 'Tragedy is an imitation of action,' and 'Character in a tragedy is that which reveals a moral choice.' Jean-Pierre Vernant has provided this commentary:

> In the tragic perspective action implies a double nature: one aspect is to take council with oneself, to weigh up pros and cons, and to foresee the priority of means and ends; the other aspect is to wager on the unknown and the incomprehensible, to hazard oneself in an inscrutable situation, to enter into the play of supernatural forces, which may, in entering the game with you, be preparing your success or your ruin. The most thoroughly considered action of the most far-sighted man retains the nature of a hazardous appeal thrown to the Gods, the worth and meaning of which one will learn only by their response and most often to one's undoing. It is at the end of the drama that actions reveal their true significance and that the agents discover, through what they have already accomplished without knowing it, their true identity (Vernant, 1969, p. 119).

The research on the relation between concepts of 'action' and 'character' in contemporary American society by the social psycho-logist Erving Goffman (1967) seems to me of some relevance here. In the first place he argues that:

> Because persons in all societies must transact much of their enter-prise in social situations, we must expect that the capacity to maintain support of the social occasion under difficult circumstances

will be universally approved. Similarly, since individuals in all societies and strata must perform tasks, the composure that this requires will everywhere be of concern.

No one, I think, would question that men in classical Athenian society were constantly subjected to tests of their physical, social, intellectual and emotional control, poise and agility. The frequency of the play on the opposite qualities in comedy is equally evident. Goffman further suggests that 'character' is the capacity to continue to display these qualities under pressure, in 'fateful moments' in which the actor risks something of extreme seriousness to him. 'Action' is a general term for sequences of events which have these characteristics, and it can be divided into four phases:

(1) 'squaring off', in which a challenge is faced;
(2) 'play', during which the issue remains in suspense;
(3) the revelation of the outcome;
(4) the 'pay-off', the settling of accounts in which the actor faces the full consequences of the sequence of events in which he has become involved.

From a comparative point of view, Goffman perhaps lays too much stress on the qualities of self-control and calm. Some societies may require their heroes to display the ability to dominate stressful situations, not merely to bear them with poise; and in the dramatic representation of action and character a degree of emotional abandon may be permitted which would be less tolerable if it were not, as an artistic creation, the product of a very high degree of control. Also, different societies and indeed even different Attic tragedians vary in their conception of the role of the gods in 'action'. But it seems to me that Goffman's analysis, though not designed as a tool for comparative literature, is capable both of casting some new light on the construction of Greek tragedies and of raising new questions about their relation to values and social institutions.

On the first point I can only indicate briefly here the potentialities of the model of the four-stage action sequence as a tool for comparing dramatic technique: Aeschylus' architectonic combination of past, present and future action-sequences; Sophocles' variation of the normal pattern by the use of pseudo-action, in which the actor is deceived into believing in danger or disaster, or dramatic irony, in which he fails to perceive the fatefulness of his acts; the fragmentation of action sequences in Euripides and the extent to which the emphasis has shifted, in his tragedies, from challenge and play to outcome and pay-off. Goffman's concept of 'fateful' events and actions as those which decide the fate of the actor, whether or not he is aware of it at the time, shows the problem of choice in Greek tragedy in a new perspective: it is the form of the whole action-sequence which retrospectively confers on some of its episodes the quality of a moral choice.

If Goffman's analysis of the form of action-sequences is a valuable approach to Greek tragedy, his analysis of the sociological bases for the high value set on character-revealing action is equally valuable as a comment on social institutions. There was plenty of 'action' in Athenian public life. War was a constant reality. A political career was spent in commanding in battle and public speaking, and there was very little possibility of building up a solid position and permanent basis of support – the Athenian politician constantly had to prove himself afresh. Besides the major drama of the assembly there were the perpetual sideshows in the law-courts. Recreation was almost invariably competitive. Physical and mental alertness, agility and balance were highly prized and constantly challenged. Gambling – dicing and cock-fighting – was also popular. Even in the economic transactions of the agora there was a considerable gambling element in overseas trading and a sense of 'action' to be sucked from price fluctuations.

But why, in this case, is the *oikos* so often and so memorably presented as the scene of action, the context in which fateful decisions are taken and qualities of character are revealed under crushing tests? Tragedy comments on the action of public life by setting it in a wider context. The various arenas of public life, exacting as their demands might be, were governed by well-understood rules of procedure and decorum; their dangers and triumphs belonged to the delicate balance of shame and honour, not to the utmost limits of control and endurance. Tragedy presents situations in which the kind of determination, courage, reasonableness and power of persuasion needed for success in public life are shown to be inadequate. The gods do not abide by the rules of the *polis* (except, perhaps, in Aeschylus). Nor do women; and one reason for the frequency of female roles in tragedy is, perhaps, that women were allowed, in Greek culture, a wider range of emotional expression than men.

It will hardly do, however, to suggest that the *oikos* appears in tragedy only with the secondary function of indicating the limitations of the *polis* and its norms. The *oikos* could not have fulfilled this function if Athenians had not been prepared to consider the betrayals and loyalties, the loves and hatreds of the *oikos* capable of affecting man's fate more deeply than the hazards of public life. The tragedians leave us in no doubt that Athenians did think this. (Thucydides' account of the plague could be added if further evidence were required.) But there is still a tension between the position of the *oikos* and the claims of public life. The tragic heroine may be totally absorbed in the claims of the *oikos*, but a male character needed to have a public role to give him substance. Single-minded concentration on the *oikos* is far more convincing in Electra than in Orestes. When Euripides begins to comment openly, though still polemically, on the superficiality of public life, the end of tragedy is perhaps already in sight.

It may seem to us almost inevitable that in a society which develops differentiated norms, roles and institutional contexts for different functional spheres, the intimate relationships of private life and the family will be felt to involve the whole personality more deeply than activity in contexts with more specific functions. But the society of classical Athens was only at the beginning of the process of differentiation leading to the complex modern societies to which this kind of analysis belongs. The Athenian elite still lived in a social world small enough for political, economic and personal circles of relationships to overlap. The norms of the assembly, the sacrifice or the market gave ritual emphasis to the change from one role to another without necessarily implying a change of personnel (cf. Gluckman, 1962). And I have tried to show that the norms of public interaction in different functional spheres had much in common. It seems to me that the elaboration of this related set of norms for behaviour in public, together with increases in urbanisation and mobility of residence and social position which made the *oikos* more isolated, made the Athenians newly conscious of *polis* and *oikos* as being separate and different. Increasing mobility tended to sever the *oikos'* links with wider social circles which had earlier mediated its relations with the developing *polis*; but neither social techniques nor ideologies capable of creating a new type of integration had yet been developed. The Attic tragedians and Plato were grappling with the beginning of an opposition which has perhaps been as fundamental in western civilisation as that between nature and culture: the opposition between public and private life.

2 Public and private interests in classical Athens

The fifth century saw a double development in the relation between public finance and private resources. On the one hand, the dependence of the state on the generosity of ambitious rich men was limited; conspicuous spending was channelled, routinised and above all over-shadowed by the disbursal of state funds in the spheres once dominated by the Athenian nobility: religious festivals, public building, war. This separation of the activity of the state from the activities of its leading citizens helped to prepare the ground for the debate on the rival claims of private and public loyalties analysed in W. R. Connor's *The New Politicians of Fifth-Century Athens* (1971). On the other hand, the concentration of the decision-making process in council and assembly and the central position of war and the profits of empire in the Athenian economy meant that decisions taken in the public sphere affected the private life of Attic families as never before – especially during the Peloponnesian war, when far larger numbers became wholly dependent upon the urban economy. Hence the tensions over the introduction of Demos' private interests into assembly debates reflected in Aristophanes, Thucydides and above all Plato.

In other words, the Athenians in the fifth century discovered two of the major problems of western political theory: the relation between public and private interests, and the relation between politics and the economy. It seems worth trying to take a closer look at the institutional roots of these pervasive and entangling ideological growths.

I start with three situations which can usefully be contrasted with that of democratic Athens.

1 In Homeric Ithaca important political decisions were taken in the *oikos* of Odysseus or some other *basileus*. The struggle for the succession was carried on in Odysseus' *oikos* in the form of competition for his wife and exhaustion of his estate by persistent demands for hospitality. Telemachus' attempt to transfer the scene of action from his *oikos* to the assembly was unsuccessful. Ithaca's contribution to the

war against Troy was sought by Agamemnon and Menelaus, who stayed in the *oikos* of their guest-friend Amphimedon (*Odyssey* xxiv 115-19), and tradition represented the decision as taken by Odysseus alone. In Phaeacia, Alkinoos and his fellow-*basileis* make gifts from their own stores to Odysseus (while announcing their intention to recoup their outlay later by collections from the *demos*); there is, of course, no public store-chest in the Homeric state. Only the public sacrifice which Nestor and his sons are conducting by the shore in Pylos when Telemachus arrives, for which each of the nine segments (*hedrai*) of Pylian society had contributed nine bulls, hints at the development of the finances of the state which was to come in later centuries.

2 A glance at any collection of Hellenistic inscriptions will show the dependence of the ordinary Greek city on its rich men, both for the routine expenses of city life and, more particularly, in facing any emergency. In many cities the concepts of political office and of liturgy – which in Athens were perfectly distinct even if ostentatious performance of liturgies increased one's chances of election to office – had completely merged. In crisis years it was difficult to find anyone to stand for office. The mechanisms of the economic grip which these oligarchs had on their cities need further investigation (one suspects that many of the commodities which they gave were produced on their own estates, cf. Van Bremen, 1983), but we are clearly in a different world to that of Athens in the second half of the fifth century.

3 The subordinate segments of Athenian society, demes and phratries, though they borrowed all the forms of public procedure in the assembly, lacked its revenues and remained often under the sway of private resources and private interests. Private loyalties and, on occasion, conflicts were bound to be sharp in small patrilineally recruited groups. A rich and powerful man could successfully oppose the admission to his phratry of a boy presented by a father as his son by a second marriage, on the grounds that the boy was of slave descent, and could subsequently have the decision reversed after he and his father had come to a private compromise (Isaeus vi).

Demosthenes lvii presents the story of a conflict between two rival deme notables one of whom, Euxitheos, is appealing against the decision of the deme taken in the term of office of the other, Euboulides, as deme representative on the council of 500 (and perhaps also as *demarchos*), to remove his name from the list of deme members and so deprive him of citizenship. Euxitheos himself has served as *demarchos* fairly recently and has made himself unpopular during his term of office by trying to exact arrears of rent from members of the deme who held sacred land on lease (§ 63). He and Euboulides had competed for the deme priesthood of Heracles (§ 48). Euxitheos had dedicated armour in a local shrine of Athena and had an honorary decree passed by the deme on his behalf (§ 64). His father had held office in the deme; Euboulides' father had been demarch. A hereditary family rivalry for the honours of a group of only about eighty members. Note that it was a commonplace of Athenian politics - ably deployed in § 57 ff. here - that small demes were easy to bribe and irregular in their conduct of affairs.

Compared to these three sketches of the interlocking of public and private affairs in more archaic, poorer or smaller communities, there is no doubt that Athenian democracy in the fifth century achieved quite a substantial disengagement. Nevertheless, in studying Athenian kinship I have had to ask whether Athenians manipulated ties of kinship and marriage in political contexts, and what importance the *oikos* still had as a power-base. Davies' *Athenian Propertied Families* (1971) has made it very much easier to ask such questions; but the harvest for the later part of the fifth century is meagre. Connor's attribution of a decisive hardening of the public/private boundary to Perikles seems to me to be confirmed by Perikles' repudiation of his citizen wife in order to set up what was evidently a widely known and stable relationship with a foreign woman, just in the years when his own law had made marriage with foreign women impossible. The dogmatic separation of public and private life which led to Perikles' citizenship law (to prevent families based on international dynastic marriages from using their private relationships to manipulate foreign policy) led also, taken to extremes in Perikles' own private life, to a repudiation of all personal relationships to which a political significance might be attached, and therefore to the choice of metics as his personal associates. The reverse implication of the drive to eliminate private ties from public life was freer association between citizens and metics in the private sphere; this was especially marked in the philosophical circles to which Perikles, Aspasia and Perikles' friend and adviser, Anaxagoras, belonged. (Attacks in comedy and courts showed, however, that the Athenians saw that Perikles had merely exchanged one kind of private life for another, in which the possibility of determining political decisions in extra-political contexts remained.)

Marriage and divorce have their inconveniences as modes of political manipulation. The conditions in which one would expect to find marriage playing an important part in political alliance seem to be as follows: (1) where political power rests largely on inherited patrimony and control over persons of a feudal or patrimonial type, and these can be owned or transmitted by women. This possibility was for the most part precluded in Athens by the law of inheritance and epiclerate. (2) As a means of making alliances outside one's own state. The marriage of Agariste is the classic example of the importance attached to such alliances in sixth-century Greece; Iphikrates' Thracian marriage in the 380s is an interesting fourth-century case. But in general such marriages were excluded after 451 by Perikles' citizenship law. Hereditary guest-friendship had always existed as an alternative to marriage in forming foreign alliances, and persisted right through the fifth century. Archidamos of Sparta tried to play on his *xeneia* with Perikles to damage the latter politically (the negative side of personal ties, as usual, comes uppermost where Perikles is concerned), while Alkibiades in Sparta exploited his family's hereditary friendship with that of the ephor Endios. Hereditary *xeneia* was often also transformed into a relation to the whole state of the personal *xenos*, as proxeny (consul-ship). (3) Marriage was also a useful mechanism for public proclama-tions of political alliance within one's own state, as in the case of Peisistratos' marriage to the daughter of Megakles. The ordinary network of political ties between men in a small city-state scarcely ever divided itself neatly into distinct opposing groups. Everyone had connections in different camps (for Rome, see Brunt, 1965). But marriage provided a means of making a dramatic ritual gesture of alliance which was lacking in the wholly male sphere (though Solon had restricted the display of wealth in marriage-processions, he had not placed any limits on attendance). (4) Finally, politically conditioned marriages occur when those who occupy an isolated political status marry close kin because they can find no equals to marry. The paradig-matic Athenian case is the marriage of Themistokles' children Archeptolis and Mnesiptolema (patrilateral half-siblings) after their father's disgrace. If Kimon married his half sister Elpinike he did so for the same reason. These marriages which occur when a leading political family has suffered disgrace are formally the same as the sister marriages of Ptolemaic kings (and royal families in other societies).

It is not quite clear to me whether the dynastic marriages of Kimon and Isodike and Kallias and Elpinike in the 480s should be placed in category 3 or category 4. The three families involved all seem to have been under attack at this time. Kimon and Elpinike had been brought to disgrace and financial ruin by the condemnation of their father, Miltiades, in 489. Isodike belonged to the Alkmaeonid family who were suspected of trying to betray Athens to Persia in 490; repeated attacks were made on the group and their associates (such as Perikles' father Xanthippos, married to an Alkmaeonid wife) in the 480s. (It is normally rash to deduce political affiliations from kinship, but where a concerted campaign is waged against a whole lineage, they have little choice but to act in concert.) Kallias was the victim of gossip and at least one attack, in the courts, for having acquired a great deal of wealth about the time of the battle of Marathon (490) in suspicious circumstances. The marriage of Kimon and Isodike can be seen as a dramatic political gesture only if it took place after the battle of Salamis when both families were again on the rise. Kallias' use of his wealth to save Kimon and Elpinike from debt must belong to the 480s and was at best a somewhat ambiguous gesture in the circumstances.

Inside Athens, although marriage could be used as a means of making public statements about alliance, it presupposed alliance rather than creating it. Appeals to ties of kinship through marriage had no special status distinguishing them from appeals to ties of friendship. When we find that men associated with each other as *hetairoi* are also connected by marriage – as in the case of Andocides, Kallias, son of Telokles, and Eukrates, the brother of Nikias, in the affair of the Mysteries – there is no way of telling which of the two relationships came first. For political alliance inside Athens it was not necessary to penetrate into the inmost private sector of the *oikos*, the women's quarters: the companionship of gymnasium and symposium was enough. It was therefore in relations with other states, which inevitably implied hospitality and used a concept of friendship which went back to the Homeric days when the *oikos* was a political centre, that personal ties acquired their greatest weight.

The procedure by which ambassadors were nominated in Athens is not well known, but it is clear that 'private' qualifications often determined their selection. Ambassadors were expected to be rich (and to supplement the official travel allowance from their own pockets in order to travel in fitting state); their political sympathy with the policy they were asked to negotiate often had to be considered; they might be chosen for their ties of hereditary proxeny or other personal links with the state to which the embassy was despatched. Xenophon (*Hellenica* VI, iii. 4ff.) has given us a brilliant parody of an ambassadorial speech at Sparta by Kallias III, *daidouchos* of Eleusis and hereditary proxenos of the Spartans in Athens. The combination as ambassadors to Dionysios I of Syracuse in 393 of Konon's associate Aristophanes, Eunomos, 'friend and *xenos*' of Dionysius, and the rich Eurippides of Myrrhinous excellently illustrates the qualifications required of ambassadors - in a period when private means and private relationships were more than usually important, owing to the low state of Athens' finances. (Aristophanes' marriage, which is exceptional in being explicitly ascribed by our sources to political patronage, belongs to the same years.) The re-entry of Persia into Greek affairs also brought with it a new twist to the concept of hereditary guest-friendship, the 'token' of friendship which could be passed, presumably, from father to son. (It would not be surprising if something of this kind lay behind the choice of Hagnias of the Bouselidai as ambassador to Persia in 396 at an early age - if the identification is correct.) One of the reasons for the continued importance of personal relationships in foreign affairs was the personal style of politics in many of the states with which Athens was involved. The more patrimonial and personal power relations were in a foreign state, the greater the importance of the private resources and connections of the ambassadors sent to it.

Within Athens, personal ties could be forged in the semi-private, semi-public masculine world of the symposium and gymnasium without recourse to marriage. The culture and the traditions of the *hetaireia* are more important than dynastic marriages. The cries of 'Conspirators, conspirators!' which Kleon voices in Aristophanes' *Knights* whenever he sees the chorus - typical members of the upper-class gymnasium/symposium set - were justified in 411 and 404. What made the *hetaireia* a revolutionary element in Athenian politics?

It is remarkable that Kleisthenes, who is generally credited with the creation of the institutional basis for fifth-century democracy, should also be credited with the introduction of ostracism. I am not concerned here to discuss whether Kleisthenes' contribution would have developed as it did if the financial resources of the Athenian state and consequently the numbers and importance of the decisions taken by council and assembly had not grown so dramatically at the time of the Persian wars. Nor am I concerned with the precise date of the introduction of ostracism. What I want to underline is that in the 480s and for the rest of the first half of the fifth century the major political issues in Athens were still very largely settled outside the assembly, without speeches, by votes mobilised, in all probability, on personal as much as ideological grounds with the help of canvassing by the supporters and enemies of the principals. The problem of sixth-century politics had been that the support built up for use in elections by political leaders had grown too powerful for the peaceful working of a system of rotation of office. Ostracism harnessed this machinery developed for winning elections to the fear of tyranny by providing for its use in anti-elections designed to rid the city of potential tyrants.

Two elements seem to be involved here: the *hetairoi* who actually canvassed for their friend and the members of the demos persuaded to vote on his side. Both were recruited through the private sphere. The links between *hetairoi* were forged in the young men's world of the gymnasium and symposium - a prepolitical world, in the sense that its members were not expected yet to take an active part in politics, yet one which had its own traditions of political opposition (the tyrannicides in Athens, Alkaios in Lesbos, Damon and Phintias in Syracuse . . .). The gymnasium was a scene of play war, and its homo-sexual loyalties were celebrated as the basis of solidarity on the battle-field and in internal political conflicts; the symposium by the late fifth century had become a place of play oratory, where the conventions of the assembly were both practised and mocked. Whatever Kleon might say, symposia were not meetings of political parties. But the world of the symposium and gymnasium provided a network of friends whose support could be drawn on in later years, a set of values which stressed daring and loyalty, and a social milieu in which political business could be transacted ouside the official contexts without attracting attention.

So much for the *hetairoi* - friends who would lend you money if you were short of liquid funds for political expenses, speak for you in courts, drum up feeling against your opponent if you were threatened with ostracism. It was a fairly egalitarian relationship. There were few opportunities for patronage in Athenian politics. The three chief archons each had two *parhedroi*, whom they appointed themselves, to accompany them (*Athenaion Politeia* 56); but the post was powerless. There were rather more openings in the military and diplomatic spheres. A naval commander selected the trierarch whose vessel he would use as flagship, and chances of singling out individuals for favour must presumably have arisen whenever small detachments were sent off to operate independently (a study of Greek warfare from this point of view would be useful). But the frequency of collegiate commands gave the Athenian general less scope than the Roman proconsul.

In so far as patron-client relationships, or something analogous to

them, existed in Attica, the 'clients' were collective rather than
individual. The support of demes, phratries, *genē*, tribes, neighbours,
could be won by generous spending. In Plutarch's story of the contrast
between Kimon's use of his own wealth to build political support and
Perikles' use of the funds of the city and empire, there is a difference
not only of quality but of range. Perikles spends the city's money for
the city as a whole, whereas Kimon's gestures tend only to reach a
limited group: fellow demesmen and neighbours, gymnasium-users.
Although when rich men in law-courts boast of their liturgies they
speak of their generosity to 'the city', the principal beneficiary in the
case of the older liturgies (choregia and trierarchy as against eisphorai,
proeisphorai, epidoseis, etc.) was always a smaller group. A generous
man could do a great deal for the well-being of the crew of his trireme,
the poorer hoplites from his deme, a tribal team or chorus.

The presupposition of the use of private resources in politics was
that the *demos* voted for people rather than policies. At its best,
Athenian democracy in the second half of the fifth century was a
political system in which it was more exciting to be one of the judges in
a debating contest on which two orators were staking their prestige
than to vote in an election or ostracism. Thucydides' reports of the
Mytilenean debate and the debate in which Kleon was given the
mandate to take charge of operations at Pylos show how exciting confrontations in the assembly could be. At its worst, it was a struggle over
the level of public expenditure and employment in which the least
scrupulous could easily get the advantage. Conditions in the Peloponnesian war increased the need for state employment in military service,
since many Athenians were cut off from their land, and made it easy
for Kleon to play openly on the *demos*' economic interest in assembly
decisions.

The sanctions his tactics aroused were sharp. By the 420s, evidently
a considerable proportion of the upper class had internalised the
Periklean boundary between public and private spheres, although it had
originally been directed against their own use of private resources. The
long supremacy of Perikles gave him ample opportunity to develop the
dignified and didactic style of political oratory which Thucydides
admired. Financial affairs – and the greater part of the assembly's
business had some financial aspect – were handled in a sophisticated,
efficient and impersonal fashion. The hereditary ties of Kimon's family
with Sparta, and the name of his eldest son, Lakedaimonios, gave
plenty of opportunity for reminders that private loyalties should not be

allowed to interfere with public interests. It was easy enough thereafter
to turn the accusation of importing private interests into public
business against Kleon, by accusing him of appealing to the (meta-
phorical) pockets of the *demos*. This became a stock accusation against
demagogues and, in time, the basis of the oligarchic political theory
that *banausoi* could not be trusted with political power.

It might be thought that the impersonality of the public sphere as
experienced in the assembly and council would be contradicted by
experience in the law-courts, where private interests were emphasised
rather than concealed. But our sources suggest that in the later fifth
century attention was concentrated on the figure of the sycophant as
scapegoat for the sufferings of the rich and prominent in the courts.
Prosecutions undertaken for purely financial motives were much more
feared than prosecutions undertaken for political motives; and the
typical victim of the sycophant was thought to be the rich quietist or
ally rather than an active member of the political elite. Sycophants
were classed as another manifestation of the monetary greed of the
banausos rather than as an example of the use of friendship in politics
(cf. the very idealistic and apolitical picture of Krito's 'friendship' with
Archedemos in Xenophon *Memorabilia* ii. 9). Personal friendship or
enmity was stressed as a motive for appearance in court in defence
against the accusation that the speaker's motives were economic, that
he made a living either as a sycophant or as a professional speech-
writer. It was acknowledged that *hetairoi* played an important part in
court cases, but their role was thought of as purely defensive and not in
any way programmatic. In the fourth century matters were different.
Private alliances both inside Attica and with foreign powers were of
great importance, as were private resources. A successful general had to
be able when necessary to pay his own troops, make his own alliances
with foreign rulers and maintain good relations with leading politicians
at home in Athens. When the difficulties of the immediate postwar
period were over, the *demos*' enthusiasm for military service began to
be damped by the frequent irregularities of pay, and their economic
interests in the assembly were increasingly focused on the Theoric
fund from which payments for attendance at festivals were made – a
ritual symbol rather than a key element in the Athenian economy. For
Demosthenes, those who put private before public interests are those
who prefer peace to war: the tax-dodgers. Whereas fifth-century radical
democrats had striven to limit the excessive use of private wealth in
liturgies and similar expenses as a way of acquiring political power,

Demosthenes contrasts the good citizen who spends his money in this way with the egotist who avoids all forms of political activity and spends his money on private pleasure.

My interest in the development of the distinction between public and private realms in classical Athens has been two-fold. On the one hand I wanted to know how Plato had managed to persuade himself and his public that the economy of Athens had in principle nothing to do with politics, why he remained blind to the economic implications of imperialism. It seemed inadequate to say simply either that his view of economic matters was that of a conservative trying vainly to put the clock back in an age of economic development (the empire had been in existence for 50 years by the time he was born!), or that it reflected the view of the oligarchic opposition in the later stages of the Peloponnesian war, who felt that they were being bled dry by taxation in order to pay for policy mistakes made by irresponsible demagogues and a greedy *demos*. The latter view is correct as far as it goes, but does not explain the appeal of Plato's analysis among both Greek and modern readers. It is only when we have taken into account the historical reality of the process of defining the boundary between the public and private realms in fifth-century Athens (bearing in mind that some of the external trappings of Athenian democracy were spread throughout the empire and beyond, and handed down to the Greek cities of later ages even when the real distribution of political power was very different) that we can see how easy and persuasive it was to turn the weapons of radical democracy against itself.

My second concern with the relation of public and private spheres comes from work on kinship and is more difficult to define, let alone to satisfy. Anthropologists have developed great skill in analysing kinship systems as maps of social relationships. The phratry, tribe, deme, *genos*, *anchisteis* and wider kindred all fit easily into this framework. The unit which I find really problematic is the *oikos*. Part of the difficulty comes from the highly tendentious statements made about the sacred duty of continuing the *oikos* by fourth-century orators. But this is a superficial problem. The real trouble is the difficulty of discovering from ancient sources the meaning of family life to an ancient Athenian. Tragedy and comedy seem to show an increasing concern with the personal relationships of the *oikos* during the course of the classical period (it is difficult to date the change in comedy, but *Ploutos* already has a domestic atmosphere, though we have to wait for Menander to find the full development). Orators' speeches are full of lively domestic detail; the professionalisation of speech writing led to concentration on *ethos* and the dramatic aspects of case presentation, and not to interest in technical points of law. Philosophers' discussions of friendship stress the pleasure of the company of a like-minded friend rather than the need for friends to help in political or financial difficulties - friendship is seen as an essential complement to the contemplative part of the personality, part of the *theoretikos bios*, as well as being an ingredient of action and the *bios praktikos*. We seem to be approaching something like the modern western notion of private life. But there are dangers of ethnocentrism in this view. I should like to throw open to general discussion the question of the effects on private life of the claim that in a democracy politics must be concentrated in specifically political and public contexts, from which private interests and loyalties must be excluded.

3   Women in antiquity

'Women in antiquity' is a vast subject and a complex one. It includes goddesses and slaves, wives and prostitutes, Greeks and Romans and the societies which they conquered, pagans and Christians, myth, cosmology, biology, law and everyday life. The study of women is furthermore complicated by the fact that we have to study them almost exclusively through statements made by men. This is not an accident of source preservation; making statements in writing was with very rare exceptions an exclusively male activity. The framework through which women are presented to us is therefore male both at the level of the individual point of view and at the level of the cultural conventions through which it is expressed. Our sources, inevitably, select and emphasise the particular aspects of women which fit their interests at the time of writing. We have no account of a woman's life as a continuous biography. The situation which Marylin Arthur analyses in Hesiod's *Theogony* (Arthur, in press; cf. Arthur, 1982), in which male gods are successively presented as actors controlling the cosmos, while a shifting constellation of female deities round them represent and receive different, fragmented aspects of power over gods and men, encapsulates in narrative form a discontinuity in the perception of women virtually universal in our sources. The richness of the mythological data on women from ancient Greece is surely in part due to the tendency of men to use women 'to think with'.

As Roger Just points out in our opening paper (1975), the sources on women relate to several different levels of reality and although they are often interconnected we must not expect a simple correspondence between them.

The papers by Pembroke (1978), Arthur, Loraux (1978) and Zeitlin deal with the role attributed to women in theories of human evolution, the first concerned with the theories of the late eighteenth and the nineteenth centuries, the rest with some of the Greek texts most often cited by modern scholars to support their theories: it is only recently, indeed, that these Greek texts have been analysed as statements of evolutionary theory in their own right rather than as representing, supposedly, the preservation of genuine memories of primitive stages of social organisation in the Greek peninsula. The treatment of cosmo-logical myth by Marylin Arthur also has links with the myth of parthenogenesis analysed by Detienne (1976) – which in its turn demands consideration of biological theories and of ritual – and with the late uses made of the ethnographic myth of the Amazons, in Rome, studied by Giampiera Arrigoni. Froma Zeitlin's analysis of Aeschylus' *Oresteia* shares with Loraux' paper (1978) an interest in Greek misogyny, but also provides a parallel and contrast to Dominique Gérin's study of Euripides' *Alcestis*: in both tragedies a dominant woman takes the place of a male as *oikos*-head, but whereas Clytemnestra acquires her position by villainy, Alcestis wins hers by heroism.

The implication of these analyses of role-reversal in tragedy is that the perception of the relation between husband and wife as one of dominance and subordination was taken for granted in the upper-class intellectual milieu of classical Athens. But K. J. Dover's 'Eros and Nomos' (1964) reminds us that attitudes may have varied with social class. In the upper class, homosexual activity also was firmly stereo-typed into an 'active' role for older males and a 'passive' one for boys and youths. However, in homosexual affairs a greater equality between the participants was introduced by the convention that boys were expected to resist their lovers' advances, and that the older partner mitigated the strong implications of dominance associated with sexual penetration by an extravagantly submissive style of courtship.

The contradiction between the dominant position of men and their vulnerability to sexual desire was, of course, a recurrent theme in the literature of heterosexual encounters from the seduction of Zeus by Hera in the *Iliad* to the women's sexual strike in Aristophanes' *Lysistrata* and the infatuation of young men with *hetairai* in New Comedy. There are indeed contradictions at many levels in ancient conceptions and treatment of women. Lloyd's paper shows that Greek doctors were sometimes caught between a professional ethic which required them to treat all patients alike and to pay careful attention to the patient's own account of his or her symptoms, social conventions inhibiting the free examination of women patients, and a tendency to believe that women were too uneducated and superstitious to give a rational account of themselves. Nevertheless, they did often succeed in transcending both the conception of women as the untouchable property of other men and the view that they could not be rationally interrogated. Indeed, one of the valuable aspects of the medical writings is that they allow us a rare glimpse of interaction between men and women of a strictly practical nature, recorded by observers who had a professional commitment to accurate reporting.

The sources for the Hellenistic period, discussed by Claire Préaux (1959), give further evidence on what women actually did. Especially in Egyptian papyri, we see them owning-property, making contracts, arranging their own affairs. A Greek woman, unlike an Egyptian woman, had to have a male guardian with her for any officially registered transaction, but it is clear that his presence was often a mere formality. Here the contrast with classical Athens is sharp: in Athens women could only act through men, even though they may sometimes have been adept at persuading men to do what they wanted.

Finley's article (1965), like those of Dover (1964), Lloyd and Préaux (1959), deals mainly with the behaviour expected of women, extracted from laws, moral judgments and documented events, but emphasises that 'law codes are never automatic guides to the actual behaviour of a society' and that behavioural norms are likely to have varied from class to class. Roman sources contain both idealisations of women (seen in an extreme form in the case of the Roman Amazons of Arrigoni) and violent attacks on them. But we have no idea what the women themselves thought.

The papers discussed here cover a chronological spread of-roughly a thousand years and deal with myth, fiction, rationalistic theory, law, ideology and everyday life. In choosing them, no attempt was made to cover the history of women in the Greco-Roman world in a systematic way. The material for that task scarcely exists as yet. Rather, they present a variety of problems and approaches which can signpost the way to directions for further research. Above all, the study of women in history is not viewed as a specialised topic which can tranquilly be left in the hands of feminists, but as an integral part of any study of society and culture. Any theory about what women are is also, implicitly if not explicitly, a theory about what men are. As Roger Just says, it is 'necessary to see in what way women were thought to be different from men in order to appreciate the meaning of those characteristics which men attributed to women'.

Each of the authors whose works I consider has his or her own point of view and it is neither my business nor my wish to try to impose uniformity on them. Diversity is essential to the enterprise. The more detailed discussion of the individual papers which follows is, therefore, merely a personal view of the sometimes unexpected links which emerge from treatments of different themes, and of the questions for further research which they have suggested to me.

Just's article (1975) emphasises the shift which has taken place in recent years from concentration on the value-laden question whether women were 'well' or 'badly' treated in antiquity- to the study of conceptions of women (and men) as cultural constructs. In particular, he makes the important suggestion that male virtues and masculine psychology in classical Athens are centred round the notions of self-control, rationality and the capacity not to give way to emotion. Women, by contrast, were considered psychologically unfree, incapable of controlling themselves. This, he argues, is a key which can help us to understand both the ideological bases of the social, political and jural subordination of women and their portrayal in myth and drama as powerful and dangerous creatures.

This paper was originally published in 1975, and several of the points made in it have been independently developed more fully since that date by other scholars. The place of the Amazons in a whole spectrum of exotic societies conceptualised by the Greeks as lacking or reversing fundamental characteristics of civilisation is discussed by Michele Rossellini and Suzanne Said (1978); the raw-meat-eating and cannibalism of the *Bacchae* is situated more fully in the context of Greek conceptions of society and its rejection or antitheses in Marcel Detienne's *Dionysos mis à mort* (1977). The fruitfulness of an anthropological approach to the study of the associations of women with different symbolic codes (plants, spices, etc.) has also of course been brilliantly demonstrated in Detienne's *Les Jardins d'Adonis* (1972).

Just's article ends with a paradox which is worth underlining, because it directs attention to an aspect of women's life to which this collection - due to unavailability of suitable studies - devotes insufficient space. Athena, the patron deity of male-dominated Athens, was female yet 'androgynous, asexual and purely rational'. The reasons for this conceptualisation are no doubt complex. As Marylin Arthur's paper shows, Zeus and his wives and daughters can be isolated as a sub-system of the Greek pantheon in which some of the implications for the social order of the supreme power of Zeus are concretised by the embodiment of aspects of it in deities whose subordination to Zeus is clearly marked by their status as female members of his household.

As the daughter of Metis, Athena has a special position here, as J.-P. Vernant and Marcel Detienne have shown (1974). Another clue, however, may be provided by one of Athéna's cult titles, *Ergane*, the craftswoman or weaver. Weaving, with its doubling-back of threads and shifting play of colours, seems to be an activity full of *metis*. It was also a woman's most important contribution to the domestic economy.[1] Seen as a female goddess among others, Athena represented woman as worker – her least erotic, most rational and responsible role.

As I have already indicated, the rejection by twentieth-century anthropologists of the myth of primitive matriarchy has led both to the recognition that evolutionary and ethnographic myths existed in antiquity as well as in more recent times, and to a closer interest in the production of such myths, or mythicising theories. Both in ancient and in modern times reversals of normal society are located either in the borderlands of ethnography or in the earliest stages of social evolution – or in the utopias of the future. This double process of trying to account for the exotic while simultaneously reflecting on the familiar (which of course has parallels in the attempts of the sexes to conceptualise each other) is the subject of Simon Pembroke's paper on 'The early human family: some views 1770-1870' (1978). The double standard applied in considering 'primitive' and 'civilised' thought is nicely illustrated here by the juxtaposition of Adam Ferguson's view that 'when traditionary fables are rehearsed by the vulgar they bear the marks of a national character' with John Millar's belief that 'when illiterate [western] men, ignorant of the writings of each other and who, unless on religious subjects, had no speculative systems to warp their opinions, have, in distant ages and countries, described the manner of people in similar circumstances, in proportion to the singularity of any event, it is the more improbable that different persons, who design to impose upon the world, but who have no concert with each other, should agree in relating it' (Pembroke, 1978, pp. 275, 280). In other words: the traditions and myths of primitive peoples can be studied, without reference to their historical accuracy, as evidence for cultural patterns, but the travellers' tales of the 'civilised' nations, if not deliberate fictions, must be taken as true reports.[2]

The developments in the history of ideas which Pembroke analyses may help us to understand the different representations of women in different fields of discourse in ancient Greece. To expect to find a single, monolithic 'attitude' to women in the works of Aeschylus, Herodotus, the Hippocratic writers, Aristophanes and Plato is as absurd as to expect a similar consistency from novelists, ethnographers, doctors, students of comparative law and utopian socialists in the nine-teenth-century. That the nineteenth-century was too complex for such a uniformity may seem obvious, yet in some ways it was not all that much more complex than the society of classical Athens. R. G. Latham was during the course of his life a professor of English, a practising physician and a expert on ethnography; he was also just as much involved in asserting the freedom of these domains from the influence of religious belief as Hecataeus, Thucydides or the author of *On the Sacred Disease*. Fields of research were differentiated and had their own assumptions about the questions to be asked and the ways in which answers should be sought, but there was plenty of communica-tion across disciplinary boundaries. Furthermore, the same theory could appeal to different men for very different reasons. The myth of primitive promiscuity or primitive matriarchy could find a place both in the logical evolutionary schemata of McLennan and in the utopian fantasies of Fourier.

The theme of the place of women in speculations about social evolution is pursued in Marylin Arthur's re-examination of the view that Hesiod's *Theogony* represents a process of evolution from 'matriarchy' to 'patriarchy'. The situation is, as she shows, far more complex. The history of the events leading, on the one hand, to the establishment of the supremacy of Zeus in the cosmos and, on the other hand, to the separation of men and gods plays on a number of contrasts which must be present in the reader's mind, as they were in the poet's, throughout the poem. A temporal situation of conflict and struggle, symbolised by the need for each ruling god to acquire his power through conflict with his father and other enemies, and by man's need to work to keep alive and his dependence on women to produce children to sustain him in old age, is contrasted with the timeless fixity of the rule of Zeus on Olympus; this eternal order is opposed both to the chaos which preceded it and to the imperfectly ordered life of men. The order which Zeus represents is also that of just dealings between men, symbolised especially by oath-keeping and 'straight' speech, and it is contrasted with the trickery and guile to which Gaia resorted in saving her children from Ouranos, which is perpetuated in human society through the gift of Pandora, first of the race of women. The contrast between these two modes of behaviour is bridged in the narrative by the patterns of interaction which characterise Zeus' rise to power, from Rhea's appeal to her parents for help against her husband to Zeus' assignation of status and functions among his daughters and allies. The manipulation of alliances within family groups, the use of a stratagem with no destructive physical consequences to persuade Kronos to relinquish his authority in favour of his son, the division of inheritance between Zeus' daughters and the recognition of the claims of more distant kin (Hekate), lead gradually outwards from the informal procedures by which disputes are settled within the family to the fully public exchanges by which Zeus rewards his allies (Styx) and deals with his last opponent (Prometheus).[3]

At one level, therefore, the poem presents a process of evolution from purely domestic interaction, in which women may get the upper hand and an ordered stability cannot be achieved, to the rational world of male-dominated public life. This process starts from the situation in which women have greatest control over men – Gaia's trap for Ouranos when he is overcome with sexual desire – and culminates in the situation in which men have greatest control over women – when Zeus gives Pandora, a woman produced under his control, to Epimetheus, as a father gives his daughter in marriage. At the same time, however, the *Theogony* also presents a progressive division of the characteristics of women among the different daughters and helpers of Zeus (although these characteristics are partly recombined, in the person of Pandora, in the final episode of the narrative). It may be worth noting here, in view of the obsession with plant fertility so liberally attributed to ancient and primitive peoples by nineteenth-century anthropologists, that the *Theogony* has nothing to say about divine responsibility for plant growth.[4] Hekate has power to influence the prosperity of herds (ll. 444-7), but even this power is associated with human management rather than with natural processes.[5] From this point of view the *Theogony* well illustrates Robin Horton's remark (1967, especially pp. 64-6) that 'primitive' peoples may well consider social relationships and human behaviour more worthy of theoretical concern than natural processes.

While he stigmatises the efforts of women to act without or against males, Hesiod in this section of his poem allows them a very wide sphere of action as helpers of males. Hekate's range of powers gives her an influence over almost all the activities of men which her functions as *Kourotrophos* barely seem to justify, while the relation between the Muses and the human poet seems almost to parallel that between a male sperm-giver and a female child-bearer. It seems possible that the apparent absence of any firm model for co-operative relations between males in Hesiod's peasant society has encouraged an emphasis on the possibilities for co-operation and support for men from women which later Greek sources rarely reveal. One may compare also the relation of Athena to Odysseus and Telemachus in the *Odyssey* and the interventions of Athena, Hera, Thetis and Aphrodite in the *Iliad*. (By contrast, Hippolytus' devotion to Artemis in Euripides' *Hippolytus*, a not dissimilar relationship, is presented as unsuited to an adult male – and not only, I think, because of the choice of deity.) The co-existence of men and gods created permanent possibilities of duality in the conception of male-female relations: the idea of male dependence on women could be denied in human relations while simultaneously accepted in relations with goddesses.

Nicole Loraux' paper 'Sur la race des femmes et quelques-unes de ses tribus' (1978) picks up Hesiod's thoughts about women at the point where Marylin Arthur's analysis ends. In the *Theogony* the characteristics of women, united in Gaia, were distributed among her offspring and then finally reunited in Pandora; in the *Works and Days* the 'race of women' inaugurated by Pandora is split up again, into different types, when Hesiod gives advice on the choice of a wife – a passage which Loraux links with Semonides' poem on the different types of women. Behind the comic abuse lie two serious questions. One, which still preoccupied Aristotle, is whether women and men should be considered one species or two; the other concerns the asymmetry between the way in which men were classified by the Greeks – in terms of their political affiliations in the *polis* and its sub-divisions or, especially later, their occupations – and the classification of women, which (unless derived from a relation to father or husband) tended to rely on personal characteristics with no social-structural significance.[6] Paradoxically, it was because women were structurally all the same that Semonides' radical division of the *genos gynaikōn* into separate subspecies identified with different animals was possible.

Froma Zeitlin, in 'Male-female polarities in the *Oresteia* of Aeschylus', shares Loraux' concern with Greek manifestations of misogyny, and Just's interest in the associations between men, *polis* society and self-control as opposed to women, the world of nature and lack of control. She reads Aeschylus' trilogy as embodying a theory of social evolution from woman's rule to male-dominated society parallelling that in Hesiod's *Theogony*. Aeschylus' account, however, is both more anthropocentric and more optimistic than that of Hesiod. The disorder produced by Clytemnestra's rule in Argos and the female Furies' championship of her cause is replaced by a new order symbolised by the patronage of Athena over justice in Athens, the triumph of Apollo and Orestes in court, and the incorporation of the Erinyes into the cults of the *polis* as benevolent minor deities. The issue of the biological nature of women, only hinted at by Hesiod, plays a key role in the argument of the *Oresteia*; whereas Hesiod stresses that women are essential to men because of their role in reproduction, Aeschylus justifies women's subordination by the claim that the father provides the seed while the mother merely serves as a receptable for it. The introduction of this theme not only reveals the new medical interests of the fifth century, but also suggests a greater consciousness on the poet's part of the homology between the different symbolic codes he is using, a more deliberate construction of a set of parallel contrasts – although it is often difficult to draw a sharp line between mythic patterns of opposition or association and conscious antithesis. If the portrayal of the Furies, in Zeitlin's words, 'draws on the deepest fantasies of buried masculine terrors', at a different level of thought there is contrast between 'lower' and 'higher' elements in Greek religion, and this is then linked through Apollo's use of biological argument to an opposition between mythical and rational argumentation. Clytemnestra's defenders are monstrous; they belong to a world of crude superstition; they are incapable of the type of discourse appropriate to the institutions of the *polis*.

The reversal of roles between Clytemnestra and Aegisthus which symbolises the diseased state of society in the *Oresteia* occurs again in a very different setting in Euripides' *Alcestis*, analysed by Dominique Gérin ('Alceste ou l'inversion des rôles sexuels'). Euripides, considered a misogynist in antiquity if Aristophanes' *Thesmophoriazousai* is to be believed, has been hailed in modern times as a poet with an exceptional interest in and capacity for presenting situations from the woman's point of view. But Gérin shows that this view is too simplistic. It is true that Euripides made a greater effort than his predecessors in tragedy to get inside the skin of each of his characters, both male and female, and make their actions credible as those of real men and women. But Gérin shows that the framework of normal social life, in which the all-male, public world of the *polis* contrasts with the domestic milieu of the *oikos*, and in which the *oikos* is dominated by a male head, is constantly presupposed. The criticism of both social and mythical-dramatic conventions which Euripides mounts takes place *within* this framework, by exploiting discrepancies between the traditional plots of myth and the conventions of *polis* and *oikos* – here, the incongruity of a woman, Alcestis, dying heroically to save a man. By accepting Apollo's gift of the right to substitute another's death for his own, Admetus disrupts all the relationships which surround him; Euripides, as often, takes an unimaginable situation and translates it into believable human action. Alcestis must dominate the situation; in so doing, in realising Apollo's gifts, she takes on towards Admetus something of the role of a protecting goddess. Thus the portrayal of the grief of both Alcestis and Admetus at their separation, which modern readers may be inclined to see as evidence that something like companionate marriage existed in classical Athens, if read with a close eye to the culture of the time shows Alcestis movingly, but fundamentally unsuitably, behaving like a heroic male about to die, and Admetus mourning like a woman, unable to produce an effective male solution to the dilemma he has brought upon himself. Indeed, Admetus displays, it seems to me, the kind of ineffectualness exposed in conventional Athenian gentlemen by the cross-questioning of Socrates; when faced with a situation for which his code of manners and morals (he is *hosios*) provides no ready-made prescription, he is helpless. He is unable to face either his own death or that of Alcestis, and he cannot learn; all Heracles' intervention can do is to restore Alcestis to him in a proper state of wifely subjection.

Gérin points out that the story of Alcestis was used by Plato in the *Symposium* (179b-180b) as a model for the self-sacrifice of a male lover to save his *erōmenos*; this parallel emphasises the anomaly both of Alcestis' act, heroic self-sacrifice being associated usually with the male sexual role, and of the element of romantic devotion in Admetus' relationship to her, which again was more commonly associated with homosexual than heterosexual love. No discussion of the position of women in the ancient world can be complete, from the point of view of the values of our own civilisation, without consideration of the extent and effects of the association of romantic love with homosexuality. These seem to be most marked in the Greek city of the sixth to fourth centuries, but this is certainly not the only period in which the relation between homosexual and heterosexual relationship has to be considered: in *P. Tebt.* 104, a marriage contract of 92 BC, the husband promises not to keep either a concubine or a boy. Consequently, I include Sir Kenneth Dover's 'Eros and Nomos' (1964) in this discussion. It is an essential point to remember, in dealing with ancient attitudes to women, that although the male/female dichotomy was

strongly emphasised in behaviour patterns, civic rights and psychological typification, the ancients regarded bisexuality as normal and did
not regard sexual dimorphism as fully established until a man had
grown a beard and was old enough to take a full and active part in
political life. The distinction between males and females was partially
overlapped by a distinction between 'active' and 'passive' male sexual
roles which ideally corresponded to the distinction between bearded
and beardless males.

On the foundation of this assumption that youths were as attractive
to men sexually as women and not dissimilar to them – which stretches
from the myths of Achilles hiding among the maidens and of the
Amazons to Trimalchio and the rules excluding young boys from
Egyptian monasteries – varying cultural elaborations were developed by
different groups. The Spartan and Boeotian patterns are only dimly
discernible. In Athens, as Dover has shown, an upper-class sub-culture
developed based on a game of flirtation more sophisticated, long-drawn-
out and uncertain in its outcome than would have been possible with
the strictly controlled well-born girls of classical Athens. It helped to
fill in the time before young men could persuade their fathers to give
them property on which to marry; and from the father's point of
view, flirting in the gymnasium was likely to be safer, and cheaper, than
running after *hetairai*. Homosexual love reinforced shared male interests,
whether these were the specialised intellectual concerns of Plato and his
friends or the athletics, horse-racing, horse-play and political and
military training of the average upper-class youth; although homosexual
love and the milieu of the *hetaira* overlapped in the symposium, the
former was not intrinsically opposed to the norms of the *polis* and
oikos as was the latter. It was those classes who lived most fully in the
male-dominated public sphere of *polis* affairs that looked to their peers
rather than to women for satisfaction in close personal relationships.
In this sense there is indeed a relation between the separation of the
sexes in classical Athenian society and the minimisation of their
differences as sexual partners; and both are related to the degree of
separation of public and private life.

The attitudes of the philosophers towards homosexuality and
women develop explicity some of the ambiguities latent in this situation. Plato idealises ('platonic') homosexual love, depicts the flirtations
of symposium and gymnasium with sympathetic vivacity, excluded
Xanthippe from the last moments of Socrates (the contrast with
Alcestis is interesting), and by surrounding himself with like-minded

disciples and friends in a small-scale, less formalised version of the Pythagorean community created a lasting model for the social setting of the *bios theoretikos*. Nevertheless, he stated firmly in the *Republic* that the weaknesses usually attributed to women were, like those of the left hand, due more to culturally prescribed lack of training than to natural deficiency, and he proposed that in the ideal state women should be educated to form part of the Guardian class with men. The Cynics also believed in the equality of men and women, and there were women among the pupils of both Crates and Epicurus. Thus there was a strong tendency to carry over the educational element which played such a strong part in Plato's conception of homosexual relationships into relations with women also. This is seen particularly clearly in Xenophon's *Oeconomicus* where Ischomachos, while strongly emphasising the subordinate status of his young wife, at the same time considers her capable of being educated to run the household in a rational way. In a sense, of course, all Athenian husbands relied on the rationality of their wives in this sphere; what is striking is that the formal expression of the principles of *oikos* management in writing implied that the wife has to learn how to do her woman's work from her husband, instead of learning it from her mother as was presumably more usual.

Greek thought thus seems to oscillate between a separation of men and women so radical that communication between the two seems scarcely possible, male substitutes being found even for the role of women in sexual intercourse, and an equally radical identification which either conceptualised women as inferior copies of men (rather than inferior and antithetic) or else accentuated the separation by representing women as equal to men and self-sufficient, as in the myth of the Amazons and related themes.[7] In 'Potagerie de femmes, ou comment engendrer seule' (1976), Detienne discusses one of the myths belonging in this field, concerning Hera's procreation of children without Zeus in revenge for the birth of Athena. This version of the myth of independent procreation is more radical than those concerning Zeus: Athena is born from Zeus' head after he has swallowed her mother, Dionysus reborn from his thigh after a normal birth from Semele, but Hera produces Ares and Hebe solely with the aid of plants and the goddess Flora.[8] The magical flower which engenders Ares has no botanical identification, but Hebe is born after Hera has eaten a lettuce, and this plant links the myth to the myth of Adonis, to the ritual of the Thesmophoria and to Greek theories of medicine and biology. Adonis' death was associated with a lettuce and the plant was believed to cause impotence in males; at the same time it has held to be good for women, promoting both lactation and the flow of menstrual blood. The latter characteristics are found also in the *agnus castus* on which women slept during the Thesmophoria – a rite which promoted female fertility but demanded chastity from the participants during its enactment.[9] The key to the dual implications of the lettuce – sterility for men but fecundity for women – is found in the Greek belief that sperm, blood, milk and menses were all formed from a single substance 'cooked' to different degrees, and in the belief of some theorists[10] that women contributed sperm, as well as men, in normal procreation and could, like birds, produce 'wind-eggs' without being fertilised by a male.

Geoffrey Lloyd's paper on 'The treatment of women in the Hippocratic corpus' takes up from a different angle both the theme of theories of female biology and the question of the capacity of women to accommodate themselves to the new forms of rational communication developed in the classical period. The question, of course, is two-sided: were women considered rational enough to reach the standards demanded in 'scientific medicine' both from physician and from patient, and was Greek medicine 'scientific' enough to overcome the limitations or distortions introduced by circumscribed interests, lack of the personal experience which a doctor could derive from himself possessing the organs with whose functioning he was concerned, conventions restricting access to women's bodies, low estimates of women's intellectual capacities and *a priori* assumptions about the inferiority of the female sex?[11] Cultural stereotypes and social constraints might have discouraged Greek doctors from any attempt at understanding women's bodies in non-mythical terms, or might have led them to practise 'veterinary medicine' on their female patients without any attempt to gather information by cross-questioning as well as by examination. In fact this did not happen, and while the influence of various forms of cultural bias can certainly be seen in the medical texts, they also provide, for the classical period, almost the only source we have for communication between women and unrelated men on strictly practical matters.

The situation with regard to sources changes considerably in the Hellenistic period. As Claire Préaux points out in 'Le statut de la femme à l'époque hellénistique' (1959), we have relatively abundant material about what women actually did, especially from Egypt, and much less evidence for male ideology as expressed in philosophical and literary works. Numerous papyrus contracts make it quite clear that, although Greek women who wanted their contracts officially registered had to have them signed by a male guardian (*kyrios*), *de facto* they are conducting independent transactions secured on their own property and persons. The intervention of the *kyrios* is a mere formality. There is a very marked difference here between Hellenistic Egypt and classical Athens in the capacity of women to control property. How far the greater freedom of women in Ptolemaic Egypt is due to native Egyptian influence (perhaps underrated by Préaux), and how far it is merely a continuation of the customs of Greek communities which had always been less repressive than Athens, remains uncertain (cf. Schaps, 1979). But a general increase in the amount of property owned by rich women is perhaps suggested by the fact that they appear in several cities in the Hellenistic period as holders of public offices in which the obligations of the office-holder were essentially liturgic.[12] Property-owning also, as Préaux points out, brought women into contact with the machinery of the state as tax-payers.

A particularly interesting type of document found in the papyri, which still has not received the full attention it deserves, is the contracts and agreements made on the occasion of marriage and divorce. Marriage contracts regularly specify not only the financial arrangements occasioned by the marriage, but also the reciprocal moral obligations of the spouses. The husband undertakes to support the wife economically – this obligation is implicit in the Greek conception of the dowry as a fund for the wife's support which has to be repaid if she returns to her family of origin – and not to have children by another woman or keep alternative sexual partners in the marital home. The woman generally promises in vaguer terms to do nothing to shame her husband. Disputes over alleged breaches of these conditions are to be entrusted for settlement to arbitrators (always male!) agreed upon by both parties. Both have equal right to initiate divorce – although, as Préaux points out, a woman might have difficulty in enforcing her rights without male assistance.[13]

An especially noteworthy document from the first century BC (BGU 1104) shows a woman making formal acknowledgment to her deceased husband's mother that her dowry has been returned to her and that she has no longer any claims on her husband's family; it is specified that 'since Dionysarion [the wife] has become pregnant, she is not to return for childbirth on the grounds that this gives her stronger claims; she may expose the child and give herself in marriage to another husband.' Although the two women concerned both appear with male guardians, it is clear that they are taking their own decisions and if need be can invoke the law in defence of these.

The evidence of this kind offered by papyri is abundant and still very much under-exploited. It can yield important information on family relations (and in particular the continued relation of married women with their families of origin), women's economic activities,[14] or their relations with officials and with the judicial machinery of the state. The increased freedom of widows to live alone and manage their own affairs shown in the papyri suggests another theme for research. Influential widows can be detected already in the records of some fourth-century Athenian inheritance cases in which widows seem to be trying to unite the estates of their first and second husbands to the profit of the children of both marriages: the mother of Hagnias (Isaeus xi) must have had an influence on the (alleged) will in which his maternal half-brother stood to inherit if his full sister's daughter died before the age of marriage, as indeed she did; Diocles (Isaeus viii.40) claimed to have been adopted in the will of his mother's second husband; Apollodorus (Isaeus vii) adopted the son of his matrilateral half-sister, in recognition of his stepfather's help when he was claiming his inheritance from his guardians, who were patrikin. The women behind these cases were, however, remarried widows.[15] A widow living by herself and managing her own affairs was more obviously autarchic: as Julian Pitt-Rivers has pointed out (1977, pp. 44-5, 80-3), widows are structurally male in many respects and therefore anomalous and dangerous. Pitt-Rivers's Spanish widows, indeed, seem to take on almost the proportions of a Clytemnestra in their anomalous mas-culinity. But the same recognition of widows as a disruptive force is already emphatically present in St Paul's letters (*I Timothy* 5).

The position of women in early Christian communities is an important topic to which too little attention has yet been paid.[16] Like other alternative communities detached from political and military life (such as those of the philosophers), the Christian group offered oppor-tunities for new configurations to emerge in both social and conceptual relationships between men and women. These had their own contradic-tions. Being more secluded than men from pagan society, women could live a more consistently Christian life; being weaker, their heroism in martyrdom was more conspicuous. Yet at the same time inherited patterns of thought and practical problems of male choice associated them, in the antithesis between flesh and spirit which played a major role in Christian doctrine, with the side of the flesh. Not surprisingly, Christianity also produced its own versions of separated all-male and all-female communities.

For precursors of the female saints and martyrs, outside Jewish tradition, we have to look to Rome rather than Greece. Romans were much more ready than the Greeks to admit that women could make a valuable contribution to the proper functioning of society or show virtue by legitimately resisting the misuse of authority. This propensity to idealisation, comes out both in descriptions of the high moral standards of early Roman society (cf. the contrast between Rome and Greece in Dion. Hal. ii. 24-5) and in later encomia such as the *Laudes Turiae* (*ILS* 8393, 9-10 BC). Lucretia's heroic suicide had its place in the story of Roman resistance to the Tarquins,[17] while the senatorial resistance under the early emperors had its Arria and Fannia (Pliny, *Letters* iii. 16, vii. 19). But 'The silent women of Rome', as Finley calls them (1965), are only allowed to say what men wanted to hear from them. When they did not conform to the ideal, they risked being censured, satirised and represented as female monsters.

One minor point in Finley's article is particularly worth noting: he is one of the few scholars who, in discussing women in the ancient world, has attempted to provide any data on their life expectations. Since this is clearly one area in which social experience has radically altered since antiquity, both in relation to life expectations and to age of marriage, we obviously risk being seriously misled by our own assumptions here unless we examine them critically.[18]

The final paper in our collection both continues the theme of the idealisation of Roman women and links it to the Greek world by showing how the myth of the Amazons – at first sight hardly promising material – was adapted to serve it. 'Amazons' appear among the conquered enemies in Roman triumphs and on sculptured monuments commemorating imperial victories; but they also appear as consorts, confirming the tendency of Roman culture to appropriate to the service of the established order examples of androgyny which originally had a more subversive and hostile air. Not only did theatrically-minded emperors such as Nero, Caligula and Commodus appear with their mistresses in Amazon costume – perhaps suitable for women of such ambiguous status – but also an ordinary husband in Rome, in the second or third century AD, proclaims (in Greek) that his dead wife had 'the beauty of the Amazon' (Penthesilea), a beauty which made her even more lovable when dead than she had been while alive.[19] In the story of the love which sprang into being when Achilles' eyes met those of the dying Penthesilea - or, in other versions of the myth, when he saw her dead face - the tension between men's admiration of women for possessing masculine qualities and love for them as weak and inferior creatures is perfectly balanced, but it was not a balance easy to maintain.

In view of the tendency of much of the past literature on women in antiquity to try to arrive at unitary conclusions, it is perhaps not superfluous to emphasise the ambiguities in ancient attitudes to women which these studies reveal. They were held to be irrational, educated only haphazardly, yet expected to be fully rational in their own spheres of activity, despised for being 'like women' and admired, yet feared and often disapproved of if they behaved like men, capable of a heroism which threatened to turn the world upside down around them; hotter than men in the folk theory of sex but colder in Aristotelian biology; like men by nature for Plato, unlike them by nature for Aristotle; powerless in the *polis*, yet as goddesses subordinate only to Zeus, and then only in the last instance (perhaps in a position like that of the mother and her female slaves, in relation to the household head, as perceived by a child); like Pandora, a dubious gift of the gods.

This contradictoriness must be to some extent a product of the nature of our sources, which are heavily dominated by cultural theories in which women are seen through a grid designed to fit men. We can only dimly glimpse from time to time the social experience which contradicted the theories: the experience of the child in the power of women in his early years, of the families managed by strong-minded widows, of the priestesses who had an honoured and active role in the religious affairs of the city, the successful *hetairai*, the working wives, freedwomen and slaves, the property-owning women of Sparta[20], the queens and princesses, the saints, the aristocratic women of societies in which politics was carried on in the private houses of the elite as much as in public places. Much more work is required to establish the degree of variation in social structure and social experience from one period and area to another, as well as more detailed studies of the complexities and contradictions of ideology in different fields of discourse. But perhaps what we need more than anything else is to begin to study ancient *men* in the way in which the authors of the papers discussed here have studied ancient women.

Notes

1 It is specifically mentioned as such in the provisions of the Law Code of Gortyn on divorce, II. 45-55; cf. also Schaps, 1979, pp. 18-20.

2 The influence of legal thinking and law-court experience on the criteria for judging the reliability of historical sources is well illustrated by Millar's remark, and the contrast with Ferguson shows just what is missing in this approach.

3 My account differs slightly here from that of Arthur in that I differentiate more sharply between 'gifts' to daughters or other female dependents – which, like dowry, can be seen as a form of anticipatory inheritance – and gifts to outsiders which form part of a sequence of reciprocal exchanges.

4 Demeter is of course mentioned in association with corn in the *Works and Days* (32, 300, 393, 465-6, 597, 805), especially in the formulaic phrase *Demeteros hieron akten*, and Dionysos is mentioned as giver of wine (614).

5 The association of Hekate, Kourotrophos and Artemis Hekate in the sacrificial calender of Erchia (Sokolowski, 1969, no. 18 B7-13) may suggest a closer association with natural processes of reproduction, but this is very far from certain.

6 I do not think it is accidental that the classification of men by character does not appear as a literary *topos* until the fourth century, by which time political affiliations had, at least in some milieux, considerably decreased in importance.

7 Vidal-Naquet, 1970. For the ritual representation of an autarkic society of women in the Thesmophoria see Detienne, 1979.

8 For Homer Ares is the husband of Aphrodite, an embodiment of adult male virility, but Detienne argues convincingly here that his association with Flora marks him as an adolescent like his sister Hebe – perhaps a significant characteristic for children produced by parthenogenesis. Greek armies of course included both adult and adolescent males.

9 Sexual activity was considered to have a bad effect on lactation: contracts for wet-nurses (*e.g.* BGU 1107) require the nurse to refrain from intercourse while suckling.

10 Aristotle rejected this view, his assumption that women were 'colder' in nature than men (by which he explained their inability to produce sperm), also ran counter to the views of other theorists (*On the Generation of Animals*, iv. 765 b 19-20).

11 Cf. Rousselle, 1980.

12 Pleket, 1969. My colleague Riet van Bremen is working on a doctoral thesis for the University of Leiden on this topic; cf. Van Bremen, 1983.

13 The documents show considerable variation in whether they treat divorce purely as a matter of individual choice or whether they present it as a penalty for breach of the marriage agreement. Sometimes the right to divorce is specified as one of the clauses of the marriage contract itself, sometimes a divorce is laid down as a sanction for breach of contract. But the dilemma here was perhaps more formal than substantive.

14 Schaps, 1979, deals only with mainland Greece and the Aegean islands.

15 Note, however, the striking picture of the widow of Diodotus arguing for her children against her father, also her deceased husband's brother, in Lysias xxxii.

16 Stählin, 1974, and McNamara, 1979, do not contribute much.

17 Contrast the role of homosexual love in parallel Greek stories of resistance to tyrants: Damon and Phintias, Harmodius and Aristogeiton.

18   Judith P. Hallett, in a forthcoming study of the position of women in
      Roman society (Hallett, nd.), makes the valuable point that, because women
      married much younger than men, the father's sister was a figure of consider-
      able seniority and authority, while the mother's brother was only some
      fifteen years older than his nephew – a much younger and more companion-
      able personage than the father or his brothers.
19   *IG* XIV. 1839. Cf. Moretti, 1979, no. 1268. The reference to the wife living
      according to God's law has suggested that the couple may be either Jewish
      or Christian, but this is far from certain.
20   Redfield, 1978, shows that the difference between Spartan men and the
      males of the ordinary Greek *polis* generated parallel displacements in con-
      ceptions of Spartan women.

APPENDIX I   GREEKS AND 'OTHERS'

As has been said before, the 'other' in human societies is a cultural, not a natural,
fact; and this implies the possibility of an ethno–anthropology, a comparative
study of the ways people in different cultures perceive each other. Building on the
questions formulated by our own culture, what I am asking here is:

1   How do people perceive other societies as structured systems?
2   How are such perceptions linked to social experience in one's own society?
3   What kind of general views about humanity are implied in such perceptions?

My examples are taken from the Greeks, with some references to other ancient
societies and to modern anthropology; my interest is in discussing some aspects
of the influence of the ancient world on later ideas about race and the understanding of other societies.
     The Greeks had a concept of ethnicity rather than of race in the strict sense
of the term; there is no stress on physical differences. Herodotus defines the
Greek *ethnos* by descent, religion, language and culture. He notes that the Carians
do not admit to their religious ceremonies those who speak Carian but are not of
Carian descent (i. 171). The Eleusinian mysteries, on the contrary, were open to
all who spoke Greek. But the Olympic games were only open to those of Greek
descent.
     As is well known, Greek ethnography – like much of the ethnography of more
recent periods – is difficult to disentangle from myth and utopian fantasy. From
the point of view of the Greeks themselves there was certainly a difference:
ethnography was (generally speaking) a part of history and as such clearly distin-
guishable – in theory, at least – from myth. But mythical elements were apt to
creep into both. And in practice Greek historiography tended to differentiate the
diachronic history which could be written about civilised peoples from synchronic
descriptions of primitive societies, whose history was difficult to discover. This
created a preliminary distinction within Greek ethnography between other
societies implicitly recognised as civilised and those regarded as primitive –
although the same term 'barbarian' was used for both.
     The sociological understanding of other civilised societies was based on the
two notions of *politeia* and *paideia*: the political institutions of a society and the
process of socialisation required to keep them functioning without serious
conflicts. A *politeia* has a history and undergoes changes: the Aristotelian *Constitution of Athens* consists of a historical account of changes in the Athenian
constitution followed by a synchronic account of its form and functions in the
writer's own time. Every *politeia* required an appropriate *paideia*: thus Plato's

Republic lays down both the political structure of the ideal society and the appropriate processes of socialisation. Herodotus and Xenophon use the terms *politeia* and *paideia* in reference to the Persians, and in the early Hellenistic period Hecataeus of Abdera described the *paideia* of the Egyptians. But in accounts of primitive peoples these terms are not used: instead, ethnographic accounts present their culture and institutions as a collection of unsystematised 'customs' (*nomima*). The observer may detect underlying patterns in these ethnographic sketches, but the Greeks themselves lacked a clear conception of a type of social system which could not be described in terms of centralised political institutions.

More specifically, they failed to develop the study of kinship and kin groups as a tool for understanding acephalous societies. This is somewhat surprising, since they used genealogical models in representing the relation to each other of different Greek sub-cultures (Dorians, Ionians, etc.) and of descent groups within cities (the eponymous 'ancestors' of the four old Athenian tribes were brothers, sons of Ion). Aristotle gave an account of social evolution in which social structure evolved from family to *genos* (patriclan), from *genos* to phratry (his pupil Dikiarchos said that phratry began as the union of two intermarrying *genē*), from phratry to tribe and from tribe to city. Plato gave a similar account in the *Laws* (680-1). But such a conception of social structure – which of course has been immensely influential in later times – is in fact very rare in Greece before Plato and Aristotle. In early Greek literature societies are conceptualised in terms of quite different forms of social organisation: oppositions between nobles and commoners, rich and poor, men and women, the old and the young. Herodotus does mention the clans of the Persians and Scythians, it is true, but he does not base his accounts of Persian and Scythian society on their kin groups.

In so far as the Greeks in the fifth century thought of primitive societies as coherent entities, they organised their ideas not round kinship but either in terms of a common life-style (e.g. that of nomads) or through analysis of family structure and marriage rules (cf. Rossellini and Said, 1978, for parallels between diet and family structure). They also used a sort of notion of caste, or at least of hereditary occupational differentiation; this idea was one which aroused a great deal of interest in the fifth and fourth centuries: it is used by Plato, and by Herodotus in his account of Egypt, before the ethnographic writers who accompanied Alexander applied it to the Indians (FGH 715 F. 19). Finally, they also conceptualised other societies in terms of different sex/gender systems and differences in the position of women. Here we are obviously close to myth and utopia; the Amazons appear in ethnography as well as in myth, as the ancestresses of south Russian tribes who were believed to live like Amazons, and in Plato's *Republic* women are to receive the same education as men.

Both in relation to 'castes' and to the position of women, there is a tendency to consider Sparta and Crete as Greek societies which could be used as models for understanding barbarians.

The men's houses (*syssitia*) of Sparta and Crete reappear in Greek ethnography: Antiochos of Syracuse, in the fifth century, attributed their invention to the Oenotrians of southern Italy. But the conception of a society organised in occupational or sex-based groups was also linked to Greek choral poetry, in which choruses of young women or of warriors played a prominent part, both in archaic lyric poetry and in Old Comedy.

In this short sketch of Greek ethnographic thought two themes stand out which were to continue prominent for a long while: the tendency to perceive other societies in terms of the structure of one's own society, and especially in terms of the problems of one's own society (occupational and sexual roles were certainly under discussion, and undergoing change, in fifth to fourth-century Athens), and the tendency to use reflection about other societies as a kind of mental experiment in utopian thought. There is a striking coincidence between ethnography and utopia in Herodotus' description of a classificatory kinship terminology among the Agathyrsoi (iv. 104) and Plato's construction of a similar terminology for his ideal city in the *Republic*.

Examples of the influence of contemporary social experience and preoccupations on ethnography are of course easy to find in more modern times. Family organisation plays a great part in nineteenth-century discussions of primitive society (cf. Pembroke, 1978). Maine transplants the Victorian patriarchal family into primitive Indo-European Society; Bachofen, on the contrary, sees primitive society as a reversal of the family structures of his own day; Le Play sees family structure as the key to the social problems of his own day. There is an interesting change at the end of the nineteenth century, when western society appears to lose confidence in the family as the basic social unit; at this period both the problems of modern society and the structure of other societies tend to be seen more in terms of the division of labour, of associations (men's houses in primitive society), or of the development and functions of the state.

To return to the Greeks, it seems to me that Herodotus' descriptions of barbarian societies reveal not only the influence of Greek social organisation, but also an implicit recommendation not to have too much to do with other societies. The context of his famous affirmation that 'law is king of all' (*nomos panton basileus*) is as follows. Herodotus says that for each society in the world its own laws are best, but this does not make him a relativist, as is shown by the story he uses to illustrate his point. The Persian king Darius had asked some members of an Indian tribe in which dead parents were eaten whether they would like to cremate them, like the Greeks. The Indians reacted to the proposition with horror – just as the Greeks did, when Darius asked them if they would be willing to adopt the Indian custom. So, says Herodotus, in every society it is law which rules, and for every man the laws of his own society are the best. It is surely implicitly suggested also that the laws of other societies are repulsive and unacceptable. Herodotus' ethnographic reports contain numerous examples of burial and marriage customs which Greeks would have found unacceptable.

There was a tendency in Greek thought to treat mixed marriages (between members of different ethnic groups) as if they were unions between different species. Cyrus, for example, child of a Persian father and a Median mother, is referred to in an oracle as a mule. In Herodotus the marriage of the Egyptian king Amasis to a Greek woman was on the point of collapse because he was impotent with her and accused her of sorcery, until Aphrodite intervened to save the day (ii. 181). Although many families claimed descent from the union of a god with a mortal woman – at worst Heracles, the only child of such a union to be admitted to the society of the gods, is called a bastard (*nothos*: Aristophanes, *Birds*) – Ixion's attempt to mate with a goddess led to disaster and to the birth of a race of monsters, the Centaurs. There was evidently some speculation about the genesis of mules: some believed that they could only be produced in specific regions (Herodotus iv. 30). But the idea that the products of interspecific breeding were sterile was not part of common culture in the way that it has been in more modern times – when the question whether the different human races were different species or not was hotly debated and it was claimed, in support of the theory that they were, that 'mulattos' were sterile.

One can distinguish two main lines in Greek theories of social evolution, one based on the family and the other on a sort of 'social contract'. Both refer explicitly to models taken from animal life. In the *Laws*, Plato says that even birds have families, and so did the earliest men. The 'contract' theory sees the earliest form of human society as a herd ruled by its strongest male member. Since men had reason they would eventually decide that it would be better to be ruled by the wisest member of the herd rather than the strongest (cf. Cole, 1967). There is a current in Greek thought for which thinking of mankind in general is more or less equivalent to thinking of men as animals; this is particularly clear in Cynic philosophy, for which the basic common element in humanity is man's animal nature: there is nothing specifically human.

In the Hellenistic period, it is true, there is a universalistic conception of humanity, but it still has little to say of or to the barbarians. From this point of view modern ethnography is very different. It started off with an evolutionary schema which explicitly legitimised the acculturation ('civilisation') of primitive peoples by classifying 'savages' as children or as survivals of an early stage of human history. This perspective appeared to give western society the right to change other societies and (for a time) prevented the formulation of the view we find in Herodotus that for every society its own laws are best. In modern times, the emergence of relativism implies a loss of confidence in western society.

It does not seem to me that the Greeks really cared about hellenising other societies. They certainly had a concept of Greek culture, but not a mission to impose it on others. The Romans, on the other hand, did have an idea of romanisation as a developmental process prerequisite for the grant of Roman citizenship to communities under their control. It seems to be characteristic of the Greeks that, believing in their own superiority, they did not really bother much about other societies (cf. Momigliano, 1975). They did not want either to change them or to get mixed up with them, but only to use them as a basis for reflection. Other societies were 'bonnes à penser' rather than 'bonnes à manger'.

One might say that modern western society has a threefold inheritance from the ancient world: the intellectual imperialism of the Greeks who used other societies as material for thought, the territorial imperialism of the Romans who wanted to change other societies in order to exploit and govern them more easily, and the monotheism of the Jews for which the defence of one's own religion implied that the religions of other peoples were erroneous. An awkward combination of legacies.

APPENDIX II   GREEK SEXUALITY

K.J. Dover, *Greek Homosexuality*, London, Duckworth, 1978.
Paul Friedrich, *The Meaning of Aphrodite*, Chicago and London, University of Chicago Press, 1979.
Different as they are, there is an interest in considering these two books together. They are in some respects complementary, their subjects are, in my view, closely related; they indicate the variety of approaches which can be applied in studying the history of Greek sexuality, and the number of avenues which remain to be explored in an area which until now has received scanty attention.

Both writers start quite consciously from a view of the relation between our own society and Greek culture. For Friedrich the Greek poets and Greek myths (along with the *chefs d'oeuvre* of other cultures) represent part of a collective human wisdom dealing with central concerns such as sexuality and emotional relationships; to understand the Greek conception of Aphrodite may help us to deepen our own understanding of female sexuality. For Dover, the importance of sex and of intimate personal love-relationships in our own society makes it essential for us, if we are interested in Greek society, to understand what they meant to the Greeks; the fact that in classical Greece intense personal sexual relationships tended to be homosexual rather than heterosexual implies that we must make an effort to overcome inherited Christian prejudices in studying Greek society – and this in turn may suggest that greater tolerance of diversity in sexual behaviour would be salutary in our own society too.

These divergences in orientation lead Dover rather to emphasise the different-ness of the Greeks, while Friedrich is more concerned to empathise with their emotions. Dover is at pains to stick as far as possible to 'hard' data. His book starts with a detailed analysis of the evidence supplied by Aeschines' prosecution of Timarchus for the Athenian law on homosexuality and the normative state-ments on the subject considered appropriate for a law-court speech, together with parallel evidence from other sources (emphasising particularly the lack of associa-tion between homosexuality and effeminacy in Greek culture and the entire absence of any censure of 'active' as opposed to 'passive' homosexual behaviour). From this discussion of behavioural norms he passes to the study of affirmations of homosexual love in graffiti, *kalos*-names on vases, the evidence of vase-paintings and comedy for the physical features homosexuals admired in a boy and the ways and positions in which they hoped to achieve satisfaction, and the general presentation of homosexuality in comedy on the one hand and philo-sophical writings on the other. There is a short section on 'women and homo-sexuality' (where the story of Harmodius and Aristogeiton might have been brought into connection with female beauty contests, p. 181), and a valuable final chapter on the evidence for different attitudes to homosexuality in different Greek cities and for changes in attitudes over time. Finally, we have a catalogue of the vases mentioned in the book, drawn from a much larger catalogue of representations of sexual activity, sexual symbolism, etc., on vases. One can only hope that Dover will exploit this material further himself, since a selective catalogue which fails to indicate provenience, subject, and shape is not much use to the reader who wishes to ask further questions about, for example, the shape and functions of vases decorated with such subjects, their distribution (trade areas; dedication in temples?), the proportion of heterosexual to homosexual motifs, or the relation between mythical and non-mythical scenes.

One of the most interesting sections of Dover's book is his discussion of the 'steady importation of homosexual themes' into Greek myth in the archaic and early classical periods (pp. 196-200). He does not discuss religion (e.g. cult of Hermes in gymnasia), but it is clear in any case that homosexuality was not deeply rooted in Greek beliefs about the relation between men, nature and the gods. Friedrich, in dealing with *The Meaning of Aphrodite*, has in this respect a much more difficult task. Leaving aside the connections mooted in his initial chapter between Aphrodite and a range of prehistoric deities from ur-European waternymphs to the Sumerian Inanna, he has to deal with a figure who represents both the ideal embodiment of feminine seductiveness and the psychological force which possesses a man or woman in love. The contradictions inherent in the combination of the two ideas are already felt by the poet of the probably seventh-century Homeric hymn, who represents Aphrodite as succumbing to her own power, in some embarrassment, when she seduces Anchises (see Bickerman, 1976).

Friedrich's best chapter is that on Sappho, in which he shows excellently how Sappho's relation to Aphrodite is patterned on a girl's homosexual relation to an older woman who teases, pets, and looks after her (compare the teasing tone of Socrates when he pretends to flirt with the young beauties of the gym-nasium; we know little of the *oaristys* of men and women in ancient Greece, but I find it hard to think of any parallel in Greek heterosexual flirtations). Friedrich brings out very well here the combination of erotic and parental elements in

Greek homosexuality; it is a pity, however, that in his final chapter on the relation between female sexuality and maternity he forgets to distinguish homosexual and heterosexual relations. In fact Friedrich is perhaps altogether too easily inclined to take Sappho as representative of Greek women in general.

Greek men tended to divide women into three categories: virgins, wives, and *hetairai*. The opposition between wives and *hetairai* was symbolised, as Detienne (1972) has shown, by the opposition in cult and myth of Demeter and Aphrodite. Certainly Aphrodite also, especially in Homer, symbolises the sexual attraction of wives; but the evolution of the role of *hetaira* (which must be seen in relation to the development of male homosexuality, since *hetairai* participated in symposia, the term *hetaira* seems to be associated with the term *hetairos* and the type of the intellectual *hetaira*, such as Aspasia, can only be understood in this context) must have influenced conceptions of Aphrodite. Friedrich tries to extend Detienne's analysis by comparing Aphrodite not only with Demeter but also with Hera, Athena, and Artemis. But this procedure would only make sense if each goddess corresponded to a clearly distinguished social role, and if Greek worshippers related to their gods only as role-models. A full structural analysis of the place of Aphrodite in the Greek pantheon, along the lines which have proved so fruitful in the work of J.-P. Vernant and of Detienne, would have to consider her in relation to other deities concerned with sexuality, in particular Hermes (some initial indications in Laurence Kahn, 1978, ch. 3), and in relation to other deities who 'possess' humans as well as supplying role-models (Ares, Apollo, the Muses, Dionysus?). A study of the religious experience of women would have to include Dionysus, Asclepius, Zeus Ktesios, and even in some Greek cities Ares (an excellent article by Farnell, 1904, demonstrated the lack of correspondence in Greek religion between the sex of deity, officiants and worshippers).

There is probably no more difficult task for us, in trying to understand the Greeks, than to grasp the interconnections of religion and sexuality in their culture. Friedrich's book is important because it is an attempt to explore this very tricky area. The other problem which has to be faced, as Julian Pitt-Rivers has recently reminded us (1977), is the relation between sexuality and politics. Dover has gone some way in exploring this; he notes the close association between sexual penetration and domination, elucidates the reasons for the exclusion of the male prostitute from political life, and discusses the role of homosexual love in Greek military ethos. He suggests a connection between the importance of war and politics in Greek life and the integration of homosexual love into the values of the community: the male lover could embody the qualities valued by society and share political and military life in a way which a woman could not. Homosexuality satisfied 'a need for personal relationships of an intensity not commonly found within marriage or in the relations between parents and children or in those between the individual and the community as a whole'. Agreed; but a more detailed look at the political implications of homosexuality seems to be needed.

In general terms, the period in which homosexual love becomes accepted as a part of Greek sexual life and culture (seventh–sixth centuries) was also the period in which the political institutions of the city-state developed and political life moved from the *oikoi* of the powerful into the open spaces of the *polis*. This development of course reached its extreme in the 'Spartan revolution' with its concentration of social life in all-male 'messes'. In Athens – about which we have of course much fuller information – the development was complicated by tyranny, which in my view had a twofold effect on the cultural elaboration of homosexual love. On the one hand, the cessation of overt political competition left more space for the development of athletic competitions, the life of the gymnasium, apolitical court poetry dealing with themes of love and wine; on the other hand attempts to overthrow the tyranny gave the terms *hetairos* and *hetaireia* new revolutionary connotations and favoured the rise of *isonomia* as a political ideal for the upper class. Since, as Dover has well shown, sexual penetration was regarded as an expression of domination (cf. Veyne, 1978), there was a contradiction between homosexuality and the value attached to *isonomia*, mediated by the conventions of romantic love which encouraged the *erōmenos* to resist his lover's advances and the *erastēs* to indulge in extravagantly submissive behaviour. In the radical democracy of the fifth century, there was a further contradiction between the close personal alliances between upper-class citizens based on homosexual love and the idea that the use of private ties in politics was undemocratic (cf. ch. 2). Theoretically, the fact that Athenians could not hold political office until the age of twenty-nine, and were supposed to cease being *erōmenoi* when their beards grew and gradually lose interest in boys when they married and began to take a serious part in political life, should have prevented too much clash between homosexual devotion and political rationality. But it is clear that Alcibiades when he began to hold office as general still retained the charm and glamour of the successful *kalos*, and the hybristic and arrogant attitudes which the much sought-after *erōmenos* was led to develop; while the case of Kritias shows that the prolongation of life in the homosexual milieu of gymnasium and symposium encouraged by the development within it of serious philosophical interests could produce explosive results when combined with the revolutionary tradition of the *hetaireia*.

4 The family in classical Athens: search for a perspective

I Studying the family: between quantification and psychology

When I decided to study kinship in ancient Athens, I did so partly because of an interest in the family as a problematic component of modern society. It took me a long time to realise that the application of anthropological techniques for analysing the forms and functions of descent groups and kin networks was not producing any insights into the relationships of family members inside the household. This article is the product of that belated realisation.

The study of kinship is one of social anthropology's oldest and most successful enterprises. But it has always raised problematical questions about the location of the dividing line between the natural and the social, which have particularly affected the way the family has been viewed. In the nineteenth century Bachofen, Fustel de Coulanges, McLennan and Morgan were prepared to see even the nuclear family as a product of social evolution. Malinowski, in reaction against this view, asserted the universality of the nuclear family (1913) and suggested that the explanation of culturally variable forms of kinship terminology and behaviour should be sought in the extension to more remote kin of attitudes and patterns of behaviour learnt in infancy in the family circle (1929, 1930); under his influence, anthropological monographs included chapters with such titles as 'Personal relations in the family circle' (Firth, 1936). But thereafter the study of the family took two different directions : it has been split between, on the one hand, a positivistic preference in research methodology for data which can be measured and quantified, linked to a concentration on the variations, in different periods and societies, of the composition and external relations of the household, and on the other hand, a strong influence on studies of relationships within the family of Freudian theory, which makes claims to provide a universally applicable account of man's psychological 'nature' difficult for the anthropologist or historian either to accept or to refute. Malinowski was unusual both in his insistence on the importance to the anthropologist of 'imponderabilia', and in his readiness to tackle Freud head-on (1927). Margaret Mead's pioneer work on sex-roles and adolescence (1935, 1928) effectively showed the arbitrariness of western concepts of what was 'natural' in family life, but failed to suggest a basis for explaining cultural variation; the 'culture and personality' school which developed out of her work and that of Ruth Benedict has moved back into the Freudian orbit and concentrated heavily on the early socialisation of children. Meanwhile, the development of kinship studies has pursued its way with increasingly little concern for intrafamilial relations. Both the strengths and the limitations of this tradition are strikingly revealed in Elizabeth Bott's *Family and Social Network* (1957), in which contrasting types of family are analysed in terms of their relations with persons outside the household. (In one type families relate to other families as complete units; in the other, men interact with other men, women with other women and children with other children. Sex-roles are more stereotyped in the second kind of family than in the first.) Role theory and network analysis are excellently used here to show how social experience outside the family influences conceptions of family roles; but the disturbing underlying implication is that social experience inside the family is not only difficult of access for the researcher but also either too uniform or too random to be considered as an independent variable interacting dialectically with outside influences.

The situation in historical research is similar. The bulk of work on the history of the family is either strongly positivistic and quantitative, concentrating on demography and household composition, or else is psychoanalytic in orientation (cf. Stone, 1981). Concentration on 'hard' data sources has produced curious distortions: arguments on the history of sexuality based on records of illegitimate births, arguments about parental affection based on infant death rates and the employment of wet-nurses and swaddling clothes. Equally, psycho-historians have ignored variations in household composition and institutions. For example, the views of Slater (1968) on the significance of the absence of adult males at war in late fifth-century Athens fail to take into account the role of male slaves in boys' upbringing (which, of course, raises a number of specific and quite different questions), the organisation and functions of the gymnasium, and the differences between the modern American mother's conceptions of marriage and family life and those attributable to fifth-century Athenian women.

Recently, however, work has begun to appear which breaks away from this unsatisfactory division of perspectives on the family between psychological studies of a presumptively universal core unit and quantitative analysis of the composition and external relations of the household. Ariès' study of the history of childhood (1960) was the first attack by a historian on the assumption that the family was made up of 'natural' components, showing how radically the number of years assigned to childhood, and its cultural content, had changed over the centuries. In anthropology, Schneider (1972) opposed the view that the concept 'kinship' referred to a core cluster of phenomena common to all societies, to which variable 'extensions' might be added in different cultures: he maintained on the contrary that the boundaries and organising principles of each system of social categories had to be analysed without any *a priori* assumptions about 'core' elements. Leach (1955), had made a somewhat similar point about marriage, and by now the approach has been widely generalised in both cultural anthropology and history (cf. Introduction). The implication (not always recognised yet by historians) is that the first task in studying 'the family' in any society is to see how social units and relationships are classified, in order to decide whether something with connotations similar to those of our concept of 'family' exists, and what its place is.[1]

The new work to which I have referred includes a number of different approaches. The study of the relation between patterns of interaction and control within the family and those of the wider society was initiated by the Frankfurt School (Horkheimer, 1936; Adorno et al., 1950; cf. the critique by Poster, 1978, pp. 53-8), and also figured prominently in American studies of the Puritan family (e.g. E. S. Morgan, 1944). The Parsonian school of sociologists, rather than looking at the relation between parental and societal authority, stressed the contrast - heightened by the growing complexity of modern societies - between impersonal interaction patterns in the wider society and the intimacy of family relationships; out of this perspective developed both the explanation of the so-called crisis of the family in modern western society as due to the heavy functional load placed on marriage partners as supporters of each other's definition of reality (Berger and Kellner, 1964) and the critique of the 'privatised' modern family as incapable of socialising children successfully for participation in society at large (Sennett, 1970, 1977). The Parsonian view of the modern family, with its emphasis on intimacy and its restricted but highly valued functions, as a product of modern complex societies helped to generate historical research on the factors - demographic, socio-economic and religious - which shaped its development (cf. Stone, 1981). More recently, the idea that bourgeois family patterns spread to the working class through imitation or as an inevitable result of 'modernisation' has been sharply attacked by Jacques Donzelot (1977), who points out the way in which an ideal model of the proper functioning of the family has been used by the state in the nineteenth and twentieth centuries as an instrument of social control.[2]

The work of Berger, Sennett, and Donzelot - to which recent work in women's studies might also be added - is noteworthy particularly because it opens up possibilities of relating the internal structure of the family, the tensions and conflicts within it, to institutional and ideological developments in the surrounding society - the possibility of an analysis of structure and process within the family which is neither psychological nor purely biographical, but social and cultural.

A common theme running through such work on modern society is, as has already been indicated, concern with the separation between the public world of work[3] and private life. In chapters 1 and 2 (cf. also Humphreys, 1978, pp. 250-65), I already suggested that the separation of public and private domains was beginning to be felt in classical Athens. I want now to pursue this orientation further, to ask whether an approach to the Athenian family via the analysis of the relation between public and private life can help us to understand the data we have on interaction within the family - which of course come mainly from Attic drama.

II 'Modern' aspects of the family in classical Athens

First we must look in more detail at the resemblances and differences between the changes which took place in Athens in the fifth century and those associated with the development of the 'modern' family.

It may be noted at the outset that there is no reason to suppose that either a 'demographic transition' or a change in household structure took place in Athens during the period under consideration. Infant mortality presumably continued high[4], and neolocal marriage had probably been the norm already in the archaic period[5]. Households of course continued to contain slaves as well as nuclear family members throughout antiquity; and it is noteworthy that there is no ancient parallel to the movement to separate family from servants which accompanied the rise of the bourgeois family (Ariès, 1960; Donzelot, 1977, pp. 15-20).[6]

The composition of the family, then, is likely to have remained constant through the archaic and classical periods. Nevertheless there were significant changes in attitudes. The values of women, representing the interests of the private sphere, are contrasted with the male values of the public, political sphere in a new way, in the second half of the fifth century, both in tragedy (e.g. *Antigone*, *Trojan Women*) and in comedy (*Lysistrata*). The situation is a complex one which will be discussed further below, but the contrast with Homer is instructive. In book vi of the *Iliad* Hector meets Andromache before returning to battle: the inappropriate behaviour of the small boy Astyanax, who fails to recognise his father in his 'public' attire and is frightened by his helmet, makes both parents laugh. Andromache pleads with Hector to take care, and reminds him of what his death would mean to her and to the child; but she is not criticising war or the values which make it imperative for Hector to fight. She and Astyanax represent what Hector and the other Trojans are fighting for (cf. Redfield, 1975, pp. 123-5). Andromache is not a heroine; she is an appropriate wife for a hero, whose words emphasise the magnitude of what is at stake for him. The heroines of fifth-century tragedy are different: they are agents in their own right, acting in opposition to men or as substitutes for them [7].

It was not only in drama that new ideas about women began to appear. Along with other ascribed statuses, the status of women came into question among philosophers. Plato thought that women should be given the same education as men, just as the left hand should be trained as far as possible to do everything which the right hand could do.[8].

There were changes also in attitudes to marriage. Euripedes' *Alcestis*, which presents Alcestis as sacrificing herself to preserve a traditional vision of the *oikos* (Burnett, 1971, pp. 34-5), goes on to negate the sacrifice by showing that the meaning of life and *oikos* for Admetus was bound up with his relation to Alcestis. Husband's and wife's roles are here reversed; it is Alcestis who acts heroically on behalf of the traditional masculine view of the importance of *oikos* continuity, and Admetus who shows the total dependence on a single personal relationship more normally associated with women (Euripides, *Medea* 13-15; cf. Gérin, in press. This dependence of women, in tragedy, is often heightened by structural isolation from kin – Tecmessa, Medea, Andromache; Admetus replicates this situation by deliberately repudiating his parents).[9]

The wish of the young to choose their own marriage partners, which had become a stock motif of New Comedy by the end of the fourth century (cf. Fantham, 1971), seems already to have played a part in the plots of Euripides' *Andromeda* and *Aiolos*.[10]. In *Andromeda* the heroine's parents objected to the hero because he was poor; in general, the point was not so much that marriages must be founded on romantic love (the Greeks did not regard romantic love as either a guarantee of or a prerequisite for happiness), as that the young object to having their choices made for them on the basis of the external criteria of wealth, status or kinship. This Phaethon, in Euripedes' play of that name (Diggle, 1970), objects to the marriage planned by his mother and step-father because the bride is of superior status (cf. also Euripides, *Andromache* 636 ff.), a theme which is echoed in a number of *mots* about the disadvantages of marrying a rich *epiclēros*. The same attitude appears in reverse in Menander's *Aspis*, where the heroine is in danger of being married off as an *epiclēros* to her miserly old uncle (FB), when she is really in love with the boy next door. Many of the complications of New Comedy arise because the hero has fallen in love with a girl who appears not to be of citizen parentage, so that according to Athenian law he cannot marry her.

In comedy, such situations are usually resolved by the discovery that the girl is after all of citizen birth, but in real life the only solution for an Athenian attracted to a non-citizen girl was to keep her as a mistress. Attempts indeed might very well be made to pass off such liaisons as legitimate unions, but if the man had any property his kin were likely to refuse to recognise the children of non-citizen women as legitimate. Several cases of this kind turn up in the speeches of the Attic orators ([Dem.] lix, Isaeus iii, vi; in the latter case, where the father of the family had moved out to live with a freedwoman, his son agreed not to oppose the registration of her sons as his father's children provided that they were left only a small amount of property, but this illegal compromise – as often happened – led to more extravagant claims and eventually to litigation). It is noteworthy that the theme of the wife who finds herself faced with the prospect of sharing her household with her husband's concubine occurs several times in tragedy (Clytemnestra in Aeschylus' *Agamemnon*, Deianeira in Sophocles' *Trachiniae*, Hermione in Euripides' *Andromache).*[11] These situations are not essential elements of traditional mythical plots; they reflect fifth-century interest in and capacity to sympathise with the feelings of both the wife and the concubine. Andromache is in a particularly strong position because she has a son and Hermione, the wife, is childless;

that such plots are not mere fantasy, but reflect feelings which could issue in action, is shown by the Athenians' special grant of citizenship to Pericles' son by his Milesian mistress Aspasia when his two other sons had died in the plague. The tendency to disregard jural impediments which shows itself in the fifth century in this exceptional grant, and in drama, comes to the fore in the fourth century in struggles in the law-courts and by the Hellenistic period gives rise to open grants of citizenship to citizens' illegitimate children (Vatin, 1970, pp. 120-8). The Demosthenic remark, often quoted indignantly by feminists, that 'we have *hetairai* for physical excitement, mistresses (*pallakai*) to look after our day-to-day bodily comfort, and wives in order to procreate legitimate children and have a trustworthy custodian for the household' (lix. 122), is remarkable not so much for its separation of wife and *hetaira* as for its introduction of the middle term – the woman with whom one has a stable, lasting relationship resting not on considerations of status, alliance and property (and not on the desire for variety in sex), but on personal affection. Such a relationship was not necessarily a mésalliance from any point of view except that of citizenship: the mistress could be the social equal of the wife (Andromache, Iole, Aspasia). Its representation in tragedy and (potentially, until the problem is resolved by marriage) in New Comedy dramatises tensions between the family as a structure of rights – involving links with, and potential sanctions from, outside kin, especially the wife's kin – and the family as a web of ties of affection. The concubine, having fewer rights than the wife, might well be, literally, more 'attached'.[12] A similar desire for a more total attachment of the wife to her husband is suggested by Xenophon's advice (*Oeconomicus* vii. 4ff.) to marry a young girl and educate her yourself to run the household as you wish it to be run. Here the complex of connections between love, companionship, community of interests and education characteristic of the Socratic circle and the philosophical view of private life is transferred into the domestic sphere of relations between husband and wife, in one of those ambiguous moves which simultaneously raises and lowers the status of women; a closer communion between husband and wife is to be achieved by devaluing the knowledge which has hitherto been transmitted from mother to daughter. (Note that justifications of child marriage superficially similar to Xenophon's in China are concerned to avoid friction between son's wife and mother-in-law in an extended household, not with the relation between wife and husband.)

To a considerable extent, what may at first sight appear to be a revaluation of relations between men and women should rather be seen as a general revaluation of the relation between structure and sentiment, between people's statuses and what they 'really' are. The contrast between what people are by law or social convention and what they 'naturally' or 'really' are is found not only in the acceptance of metics as social equals (e.g. Cephalus' family in Plato's *Republic*) and in discussions of marriage and legitimacy (Humphreys, 1974), but also in lawsuits concerning adoption, where the legal rule that an adopted child loses all kinship with his original father is felt to be contrary to natural feeling and is often circumvented ([Dem.] xliv, Isaeus x; Hellenistic inscriptions regularly name both *pater* and *genitor*). More generally, it is found in the idea, emphatically presented in Euripides' *Electra* (367-90) that a poor uneducated man may be a true gentleman in his behaviour.

The most explicit formulations of these new ideas come from philosophical milieux characterised by emphasis on male friendship, but there is also evidence of other kinds which suggests a new value placed on family life as well as on *philia* between individuals. Art, and particularly funerary art (and funerary epigrams), shows a new interest from the late fifth century onwards in portraying children as children (rather than as miniature adults) and dwelling affectionately on their games, toys and amusing ways.[13] Funerary reliefs and inscriptions show a new concern to portray the family group in an idealised, timeless union (cf. below, ch. 6). The religious observances of Theophrastus' 'Superstitious Man' (*Characters* xvi) are concentrated round his *oikos* and his family. It was in the fourth century that philosophers first put forward the idea that the family was the earliest human social group (above, pp. 53f.), and began to incorporate the redesigning of the family into utopian schemes. The 'policing of families' began with the appointment of *gynaikonomoi* ('women-controllers') in fourth-century Greek cities (Wehrli, 1962; cf. Croissant and Salviat, 1966). The speeches composed for litigants in cases concerning inheritance and other family matters were published by their authors for an audience wider than the jury before whom they were initially delivered; courts and drama reciprocally influenced one another. An emotive rhetoric of familial piety developed in the courts;[14] and dramatists contributed an equally extensive repertoire of gnomic quotations on familial topics, often cynical in tone (Euripides' contributions to this stock were perhaps responsible for his unpopularity among Athenian women). It may also be noted that comedy loses the open bawdiness of Aristophanes during the fourth century, and turns to intrigues based on romantic love and the opposition between young adults (abetted by slaves) and their parents. For the philosophers, sex becomes problematic: an irrational bodily need which should either be repressed (Plato) or satisfied with the first partner who comes to hand (Cynics, Stoics). A change in attitudes to sexuality seems to be taking place, although much more exploration of the iconographic evidence is needed.

These sparse but convergent indications of a shift in the significance accorded to the family are matched by evidence for an increasing tendency to regard involvement in political life, or detachment from it, as a matter for choice. Of course, there had always been obscure, hard-working citizens in the villages of Attica whose political experience did not stretch beyond their own deme and phratry. But in the late fifth century members of the elite began to withdraw from politics by deliberate decision, and to defend their stance by a new set of terms clustering about the key-word *apragmosyne*,[15] which could be appropriated also to dignify the quietism of those who had no great political opportunities open to them. Although the most conspicuous, articulate and influential among those who chose to withdraw from public life were the philosophers, the pose of the man who avoids *pragmata*, the hassle of political life and the law-courts, was adopted by every litigant in the fourth century who could plausibly claim inexperience; for such ordinary Athenians, a life free from *pragmata* was spent in the *oikos* (which was also a unit of production, either agricultural or artisan).

The philosophers' contribution was, however, distinctive both in the explicit formulation of the *bios theōrētikos* as a lifelong occupation to be carried out in the company of like-minded friends, and in their influence on education, which made experience of this milieu of 'theory' part of the life of a considerable proportion of the Athenian upper class for a limited period. Greek males had always had a long interval between puberty and full adulthood; a man was not expected to marry until he was about thirty, unless his father was dead, and it seems to have been the norm for political office to be restricted to those over thirty also. The majority of youths had probably always spent the intervening period in military service, for their own state or as mercenaries, and travel (Humphreys, 1978, pp. 164-8).[16] When at home, upper-class boys were expected to prepare themselves for a political career in the manner described by Lysimachus and Melesias in Plato's *Laches* (179 a-e), who took their meals with their sons and told them about the glorious deeds of their ancestors to inspire them to emulation. But Lysimachus and Melesias already feel (the dramatic date of the dialogue is after 424) that this traditional education, plus the instruction in music and gymnastics which had always accompanied it, was not enough. Professional teachers were now offering lessons in hoplite fighting, just as others were offering lessons in the art of politics and public speaking. Instead of learning about war and government by accompanying their fathers on campaign and into political meetings, the young were to learn by practising, by taking part in mock fights or debates and by questioning what was done in the adult world. This in itself created a momentous dividing line between public life and self-conscious reflection on it. This domain of education – of which the *bios theōrētikos* was a lifelong prolongation – introduced discontinuity into social experience in a number of ways. While a child's time was spent entirely in the private sphere and that of an adult male was divided between public and private domains, this lengthy intermediate period was spent in contexts which occupied an interstitial position between the two.[17] The sexual relationships which characterised it, either with other males or with *hetairai*, were alternatives to marriage rather than being a preparation for it. The new education separated sons and fathers and created possibilities for the young of acquiring positions or life-styles different from those of their ancestors.

The opposition between the philosophic domain and the family should not, however, be exaggerated. The philosophers' schools took on some of the functions and characteristics of family groups, as is clear from the wills recorded by Diogenes Laertius – philosophers recruited their younger kin as pupils, arranged for the guardianship of orphans, and regularly commemorated dead teachers. The same words, *philos* and *oikeios* were used to describe the family and its close, intimate associates and to describe the philosophical group.[18] The conventional translation of *philos* as 'friend' suits the philosophers, but obscures the fact that *philos* is also regularly used for members of the family. Antigone, in insisting on burying her brother, is satisfying the claims of *philia*.[19] The term *philos* overrides the distinctions we make between love, family and friendship.

There is in fact no Greek word for 'family'. *Oikos* denotes property and slaves as well as members of the family household, and anyone who is on 'familiar' terms with the *oikos* can be termed *oikeios*. Whereas for us intergenerational ties play a very prominent part in family relationships, the ancient Greek distinction between intimates and the rest of the world seems more concerned with the claims adults can make on each other.

The opposition between *apragmosynē* and *pragmata*, and the importance attached to having trustworthy *philoi* and *oikeioi*, suggest that in the opposition between public and private spheres in Athens the emphasis was on the competitive and aggressive nature of interaction in the public sphere rather than – as in the modern case – on its impersonality. Nevertheless, the strains of the public sphere came partly from the exposure to mass audiences which it involved (several thousand in the Assembly, 500 in the Council, 201 in the smallest jury), and the style of argument developed in the second half of the fifth century proclaimed impersonal logic as its aim. (The writers of speeches for law-courts, who found their clients unable or unwilling to carry off this style, and juries suspicious of 'cleverness', justified their aberrations from the norm of rationality by reference to a science of the portrayal of character.) The 'new politicians' of the later fifth century made a polemical point of ignoring personal ties and loyalties in politics and concentrating only on the good of the *polis* (Connor, 1971): Sophocles' Creon in the *Antigone* carries this attitude to extremes (Knox, 1964, pp. 80-90).

The most notable differences in character – rather than merely degree – between the ancient and modern forms of the separation of public and private spheres are, first, that the public sphere in classical Athens, for those about whom the sources tell us, was the world of politics rather than a world of work, and secondly, that as far as we can see women played no part in defining the character of the private domain in ancient ideology, although male conceptions of femininity were involved in its definition.

The difference between ancient politics and modern work does not seem to me crucial from the point of view of the individual's social experience, although of course it is highly significant in other respects. If it is argued that access to opportunities for active participation in politics was unequally distributed in ancient Athens, one may respond that opportunities for significant achievement in the modern world of work are also restricted.[20] Similar ambiguities of attitude are involved: it was easier for an ancient Athenian to complain of the distasteful or frustrating aspects of political life than to break away from it completely or to respect those who did so. The *apragmones* were drop-outs – and adolescent drop-outs were tolerated more easily than those who made the decision a permanent one. Both in the ancient and the modern case, it seems to me that we can only measure the significance of a location of the central meanings of life in the family by considering the alternative, public domain which is thereby implicitly pushed into second place or, in extreme cases, rejected altogether (cf. Tolson, 1977, pp. 12-13, 129-33).

The difference in the position of women is far more difficult to deal with, and in order to explore it further it is necessary to turn to a fuller discussion of the evidence of Attic drama and the problems of interpreting it.

III Drama and the family

Attic drama concerns itself repeatedly with the relationships between husbands and wives, parents and (usually adult or adolescent) children,[21] and siblings; and drama is the most interactional of art forms. The emphasis in ancient drama on action and interaction rather than 'character' (Jones, J., 1962) might even be thought to make it, potentially, a richer source for the sociologist than the modern novel. But it is essential to remember that women played a far greater part both in the development of the novel and in the social changes which accompanied it than they did in the literature and society of classical Athens. The ideology of the bourgeois family presented women as more virtuous and self-controlled than men, and gave them a mission to 'civilise' society (Donzelot, 1977); the novel provided an outlet for the presentation of women's as well as men's views of society, so that at least in the two we have complementary distortions on which to base an analysis. In addition, novels were directed to a public of both male and female readers - the latter predominating - and this provided pressure to give the viewpoints of both sexes adequate representation. In Athens, though women have been able to attend theatrical performances (Pickard-Cambridge, 1968, pp. 263-5) there is no sign that their opinions carried weight. (As is well known, in the *Thesmophoriazousai* Aristophanes says that Euripedes - considered a sympathetic creator of female characters by modern critics - was unpopular with Athenian women.) Women symbolised the crystallising values of the private sphere, but their symbolic role was not linked to any increased influence either in the family or in society at large, and attitudes towards both women and the private sphere were more ambiguous than in eighteenth- and nineteenth-century western society. Women were seen as less controlled than men (Just, 1975), and the private sphere was seen as a threat to the norms of public life - the source of disruptive individual interests and ambitions - rather than as a basis for training in the co-operative virtues.

To claim that the prominence of the family in Attic drama is a response to an increasing awareness of separation between public and private spheres, and increasing sensitivity to their interrelations, is not to say that Attic dramatists set out with any intention of presenting a realistic picture of family life – although Euripides was felt to be making a deliberate attempt to present the traditional mythical plots in a way which would bring them closer to the experience of ordinary people (Aristophanes, *Frogs*, 959-1055). The separation of the public and private domains was not yet explicitly perceived as a dominant feature of social experience. It was recognised only intermittently and tentatively. What we have to look for is not explicit statements, but a subtle shaping of plots, interaction sequences and vocabulary by the writer's sense for tensions in his society.

Given that we are looking for patterns of which the Athenians themselves were not fully conscious, the quantitative abundance of the material – especially if the plots of lost plays are taken into account – might suggest that a statistical approach to intra-familial relationships is worth trying. Philip Slater – working only on fully preserved tragedies – has analysed 65 representations of interaction between parents and children in terms of the intensity of positive or negative affect they display (Slater, 1968, Appendix III). I myself carried out a similar but wider study including relations between spouses and siblings as well as those between parents and children [22] and utilising lost tragedies where their plots seemed sufficiently well established. The operation is worth carrying out, if only because one's ideas about the quality of relationships within the Athenian nuclear family may otherwise be too strongly influenced by the best-known myths. However, it is doubtful whether the method can produce solid conclusions. The assumption that Aeschylus, Sophocles and Euripides can be treated as if the relation between tragedy and contemporary social experience was the same for all of them is in itself highly questionable. Furthermore, it would be extremely difficult to devise a scoring method which all readers could apply in a uniform manner. In fact Slater considered same-sex relations between parents and children to be solidary, while cross-sex relations were found to be hostile or problematic; working independently, I considered same-sex relations usually hostile, the mother-son relation ambiguous, and the father-daughter relation more inclined to be solidary.[23] It is impossible to decide many of the questions which present themselves when such an exercise is attempted. Should hostility which is played out in detail on stage be given more weight than hostility expressed towards the absent (e.g. Oedipus' hostility to his sons in Sophocles' *Oedipus at Colonus*)? Or should we take the view that some forms of family conflict set up such deep-seated reactions in an Athenian audience that they could not be played out on stage? (Cf. the remarks of Xanthakis-Karamanos, 1980, on the modification of myths by fourth-century tragedians.) Is the avoidance of any hint of Oedipus' and Jocasta's incestuous relationship in their on-stage inter-action, in the *Oedipus Rex*, a sign of lack of interest (Vernant, 1967) or of repression? Are the relationships of a new figure introduced into a traditional myth in the fifth century (e.g. Electra) more significant for fifth-century attitudes than those which are essential to the plot of the myth as handed down? What is to be done about cases where potential tensions in family relationships are polarised out in drama by the use of parallel characters, one hostile and one co-operative (Electra and Chrysothemis in Sophocles' *Electra*; the two father–son pairs in Terence's *Adelphoe*)?[24]

Such problems are insoluble. It is better to abandon the hope of a quantitative approach and concentrate firmly on the quality of the interactions portrayed on stage. In some cases it may be justifiable to treat these as a fairly direct reflection of Athenian experience. It is hard not to feel that the society which produced and appreciated the joy of the recognition scene between Electra and Orestes in Sophocles' *Electra*, and the total absorption in plotting together of the same pair in the *Electra* of Euripides, was one in which the brother–sister relation was often close and affectionate. (Even in the plots of lost tragedies brother–sister conflict is very rare. Medea seems to have killed her younger brother, to save Jason, in Sophocles' *Kolchoi*, and Euripides' *Alcmaeon in Psophis* portrayed a wife who was loyal to her husband and hostile to her brothers (Apollodorus III, vii. 5-6). In extant tragedy, the Egyptian priestess Theonoe opposes her brother in Euripides' *Helen* but she is reconciled to him at the end of the play.)[25] Equally the rivalries of wives and concubines, already discussed above, have the ring of realism about them. But the situation is rarely so simple. Both tragedy and comedy, in different ways, concern themselves with deviations from the norm, and very often the action portrayed does not merely exaggerate the normal loyalties or frictions of family relation-ships, but transforms their structure in a more radical way. Several studies recently have adopted a structuralist approach to such trans-formations, emphasising the tendency for tragedians to portray strong female characters as quasi-masculine, and correspondingly to feminise the men who surround them (Zeitlin, 1978; in press; Gérin, 1974; Shaw, 1975). To play an active part in tragedy women had to depart from the norm which said that 'the greatest glory for a woman is to be as little spoken of as possible' (Thucydides ii. 45.2). But why were such figures so attractive to dramatists and audiences? Psycho-historians tend to ascribe their fascination to the Athenian male's subconscious fear of women (Slater, 1968; Zeitlin, 1978; in press). But I should like to suggest that such figures belong to the discourse on the relation between public and private life rather than to a discourse on relations between the sexes. Antigone, Alcestis, Jocasta in Euripides' *Phoenissae*, Hecuba, the Trojan Women – all stand for the values of private life. It is no accident that in Phaedrus' speech in the *Symposium* (179b-180b) Plato compares Alcestis to the homosexual lovers who have sacrificed their lives for *philia*. But such stories of the devotion of male friends belong back in the Homeric age or in the context of resistance to tyranny; it was much more difficult, in the fifth century, to represent a man in the situation of Antigone, making a heroic stand on behalf of private loyalties against Creon's claim of impersonal devotion to the public interest. (On the threefold relation between 'bush', *oikos* and *polis* in Sophocles' *Philoctetes*, see Vidal-Naquet, 1971.[26]) Similarly, one could not represent a husband sacrificing his life for his wife; it had to be Alcestis who took a heroic, masculine step to preserve the head of the *oikos*, and Admetus who was correlatively forced into the recognition that the masculine view of the *oikos* as linear transmission from fathers to sons was inadequate (Gérin, in press). Such heroines represent a way of exploring the implications of placing the central meaning of life in the private sphere, without arousing all the ambiguous reactions which the audience would feel if presented with a male hero taking this stance.

Even the passages in which the most strenuous attempt is made to see life from a woman's point of view turn out to suffer from what Evans-Pritchard has called the 'if I were a horse' syndrome. Medea's speech on the troubles of women (Euripides, *Medea*, 230-51) makes the following points: a woman has to 'buy' a husband with her dowry, and, worse still, the result of the bargain is to get a 'master of her body' (a particularly humiliating thought for a man, trying to put himself in a woman's position, to contemplate). Then she has difficulty in knowing whether she is getting a good husband or not (the corresponding difficulty was probably greater for males, given the seclusion of women and the fact that women married much younger), and finds it difficult to break off negotiations if the suitor turns out unpromising. She has to learn new ways in a new household (though marriage is neolocal, it is taken for granted that it is the wife who must adjust – cf. the reference above to Xenophon's views on the education of wives); and if things go badly at home she cannot escape to other company. Finally, it is conceded that childbirth may be more of an ordeal than fighting as a hoplite. The speech represents an Athenian man's view of what it would feel like, to a man, to be the kind of wife Athenian men wanted.

Medea is tragic because she *feels* like a man in this situation; she is totally dependent on Jason, he lets her down, and she reacts with the outraged *philotimo* of an Alcibiades threatened with a lawsuit which might destroy his relationship with the *demos*: she cuts off her nose to spite her face. Her repeated justification for killing her children is that she cannot bear Jason to laugh at her. She wants to prove that she can harm her enemies and do good to her friends (809) – a conventional definition of male *aretē* which was coming under scrutiny in the late fifth century (Dover, 1974, p. 180; Connor, 1971).

Although tragedy for the most part concentrates on a stark juxta-position of *polis* and *oikos* with few references to the institutional contexts which in contemporary life occupied an intermediate place between the two, it nevertheless interpenetrates *polis* and *oikos* in multiple ways: not only by using plots about mythical ruling families whose actions have political as well as domestic significance, but also by breaking down the boundaries between public and private speech and action. A woman defies the authority of the ruler in order to bury her brother; another woman kills her children in order to preserve her honour. Tragedy is private life 'raised' to the political level; both spheres are equally essential to it and the ostensibly hierarchic relation between them is, implicitly, constantly called into question.

But tragedy also has a third constituent. The plays which do not take place in a *polis* and/or an *oikos* are very often located on sacred ground (Wolff, n.d.); as well as dealing with public and private life, tragedy represents man's relation to the gods. The action is three-dimensional: relations between protagonists and *polis* (represented by the chorus and by references to anticipated reactions of public opinion), relations between protagonists and their intimate circle of *philoi*, relations between protagonists and gods (cf. Sophocles, *Ajax*, 456-65).[27] We are used to one-dimensional literary forms and it is hard to follow the score of this more complex genre.

Perhaps the best way to start is by close and careful study of the semantics of social interaction in the plays. Some work of this kind has already been done: for example, Gérin (1974) and Shaw (1975) have analysed Medea's use of the masculine language of courage, victory, arming oneself (1242, *hoplizou*, *kardia*), the honour of the family. Antigone too talks the language of patriotism (46, 'I will not be caught being a traitor'; 502, 'What could bring me greater glory?') and calls on the *polis* and its citizens to witness her fate (843 ff.), as well as justifying her actions in terms of loyalty to *philoi* and the unwritten laws of the gods. (Her treatment of Ismene is that of a political leader dealing with an unreliable ally; it entirely contradicts the principles of *philia* on which she otherwise insists.)

The introduction of the language of the political sphere into the mouths of women and the affairs of the family is only one of the fields which need study. There is also a language of exchange which can be used within the family as well as outside. In Aeschylus' *Choephoroi* both the old slave nurse and Clytemnestra, at different times, remind Orestes that they have suckled him (750, 896-928). For the nurse this reminder is simply a proof of devotion; there is no exchange between masters and slaves. But Clytemnestra expects repayment (the idea that children were expected to repay their parents for rearing them, with care in old age, is quite common in Greek texts). Tecmessa reminds Ajax of the pleasure she has given him in bed: one good turn deserves another (*charis* begets *charis*, Sophocles, *Ajax* 520-2); he should not desert her. There are vocabularies of domination, subordination, resistance, dependence (Creon cannot bear to be 'ruled by a woman', *Antigone*, 525). How do the vocabularies of power vary when applied to the gods, to political rulers and to control of the household? [28] It is only this kind of analysis which can form a basis for a study of the relation between the Athenians' experience of interaction within the family and their experience of interaction in the wider society.[29]

IV Epilogue

The loss of almost all of fourth-century drama (Xanthakis-Karamanos, 1980) makes it impossible to trace the development of representations of the family, and of the dialectic between public and private life, between Euripides and Menander. In the plays of the latter – a man who grew up in the moralistic climate of the Athens of Lycurgus and

of Demetrius of Phaleron, in a period when the political decisions
affecting Athens were mostly taken elsewhere, in the courts of
Macedonian kings - reference to the political world seems to have
disappeared almost completely, and even the concern over public
opinion shown by characters of the parental generation is presented in
a negative light. Study of the language of law-court speeches dealing
with family matters (cf. Thompson, 1976) may help to fill the gap.
Overall, what happens is that the discourse on private life which is still
regarded with ambivalence in the late fifth century, and is therefore
difficult to disentangle from the discourses on public life and on the
relations between men and gods with which tragedy interweaves it,
becomes legitimate and develops new forms of distortion: romanticisa-
tion in New Comedy, idealisation in law-court speeches, utopian
fantasies and moralistic legislation in the works of the philosophers
and the activities of reforming legislators like Demetrius of Phaleron.
The union of romantic plot, ridicule of the petty agonies of private
life, and serious reflection on the ethics of intimacy presented in New
Comedy gave it relations with four more limited genres which were to
outlive it: the ancient romance (cf. Perry, 1967, especially pp. 55-60,
72; Müller, 1981), the mime, the Cynic diatribe and a different type of
philosophical reflection, stemming ultimately from Plato (Hirzel, 1895,
I, pp. 350-1, cf. Wehrli, 1949, p. 60), on the relation between the *bios
theōrētikos* and the private life of the ordinary man. In writers of the
Roman period such as Seneca, Musonius Rufus and Plutarch the Cynic
and Platonic traditions merge; it is taken for granted that the philosopher will give practical advice on marriage, the education of children,
bereavement, old age and death (Bickel, 1915; Oltramare, 1926; for a
general view see Bevan, 1923). The situation was very different from
what it had been in the Athens of Euripides and of Plato's youth.
Two of these new genres were destined solely for private reading,[30]
and the other two were addressed to a public excluded from institutionalised political life by its low status. Public and private life were
more openly recognised as separate, and questions about the relation
between the two were put in different terms. Nevertheless, later writers
on the private domain were conscious of dealing with problems which
had been given their first formulation in classical Athens: the books
of Stobaeus' late antique anthology which deal with private life are
filled with quotations from Attic drama.

Notes

1 The starting point of the enquiry is determined by the researcher's interests, it is not a 'universal'. I could have decided to compare the Athenian family with the Roman or Polynesian family, but there is no Platonic idea of the family to which I can refer. Cf. Introduction.

2 The implications of legislation designed to reform society through acting on the family have also been discussed recently, in relation to Augustus' legislation at Rome, in a very acute article by Leo Raditsa (1980).

3 Arendt (1958, pp. 38ff.) points out that whereas in antiquity the public sphere is the political sphere, in the modern world the public sphere has become divided between political and 'social' domains (or, one might say, between the state and what used to be called 'civil society'), the primary contrast being between private life and social life. I do not here follow Arendt, however, in the further distinction she makes between 'labour' and 'work'.

4 Mortality was of course exceptionally high during the plague years 430-429 in Athens. It has been suggested (Fuchs, 1961, pp. 241-2; Stupperich, 1977) that contemporary changes in tomb monuments reflect an increased concern for the dead which arose as a reaction from the neglect forced on kin during the crisis; but the impact of such experiences is difficult to gauge and has not been much studied (cf. below, p. 168). Athenian families were always relatively small; there are three groups of five siblings in the genealogy of the Bouselidai (Davies, *APF* 2921), but this is uncommon; cf. the tables on pp. 109, 113, 118 below. Both contraception and exposure were practised (Hopkins, 1965).

5 The extended households of Priam and Nestor in the *Iliad* and *Odyssey* appear to be exceptional.

6 Cf., however, Plutarch *De liberis educandis* v-vii (*Moralia* 3c-5c). In view of Ariès's discussion (1960) of the spatial separation between family living area and servants' quarters, it is worth remarking that at Olynthus, a fourth-century site, bathrooms seem to open directly off the kitchen (Robinson and Graham, 1938, pp. 198-203). The ethical deficiencies attributed to slaves in antiquity – deceit and laziness – were recognised to be related to their structural position, and there was therefore no reason to suppose that they could contaminate the morals of free women and children (although they do figure as the natural allies of subordinate members of the family against authority, in comedy).

7 For this reason the argument of Mary Lefkowitz, 'Women's Heroism' (1981), seems to me to neglect essential chronological distinctions; but I have profited very much, in defining my own views, from reading this article in proof and from discussions with the author.

8 Plato's views on the education of women are a consequence of his attempt to generalise the *bios theōrētikos* into a way of life for a whole self-reproducing social class in the *Republic*.

9 Behaviour similar to that of Admetus on the part of the widow, Laodameia, was described in Euripides' *Protesilaos*, probably an earlier play: Vernant, 1962, cf. 1976, 1977.

10 Note too that Euripides' *Antigone* gave much more emphasis to the love of Antigone and Haemon than that of Sophocles, where this theme is only indirectly indicated by the choral ode on the power of love, and we are not shown Haemon as a young man in love (cf. Burnett, 1971, p. 3 on the use of choral odes to indicate complexities not developed in dramatic action).

11 It has sometimes been suggested that Medea was Jason's concubine, and not his wife; but she should be seen as a wife who is easily divorceable because she has no kin.

12 The situations of *pallakai* were of course very varied, and in real Athenian society many of them had more independence than the captive women portrayed in tragedy – although the seduction of slaves must also have been common in real life (cf. Lysias i. 12-13).

13 Stone (1977, p. 409) suggests an inverse correlation between 'structural' naming and emotional involvement with children as individuals. Structural naming was common in classical Athens, especially for boys; and the plot of the Greek original of the *Comedy of Errors* partially depends on it, the younger of the twin Menaechmi having been renamed (with the name of his father's father) when his elder brother was presumed dead (Plautus, *Menaechmi*, 'Argumentum'). But structural naming can coexist with the use of individual nicknames, and children's nicknames are attested in fourth-century Athens (below, p. 108). The interest in small children in visual art is not matched in literature except for an occasional funerary epigram.

14 Cf. above, pp. 7ff. The remarks of Sennett, 1977, pp. 39ff, on the problems of evaluating persons in a public context are very relevant to the situation of the jury in an Athenian law-court, and show how experience in the courts would generate interest in character types and in discrepancies between appearance and inner character, as in the virtuous *hetaira* of New Comedy or Euripides' noble peasant.

15 Lawrence Carter has just completed a PhD dissertation at University College London on *apragmosyne* which I hope he will publish soon.

16 Sparta had from the archaic period institutionalised a period of military training from the age of seven to twenty, followed by a further period of compulsory residence in men's houses, which definitively removed boys and younger men from the family context.

17 See above, pp. 16ff. In Spartan education and in a tradition of Attic thought which had early roots, although an institutional basis for it cannot be securely located, adolescence was associated with life 'in the bush', on the borders of the social world: Vidal-Naquet, 1968, 1971, 1974. But the marginal status of the upper-class youths of classical Athens was spatially expressed in locations between the public and private domains (*andrōn* on the outer edge of the *oikos*, the gymnasion on the outer edge of the *polis* between public *polis* and private *chōra*) rather than outside both.

18 Plato and Aristotle, particularly the latter, stress *philia*; but *oikeiotēs* became a technical term for the Stoics (Pembroke, 1971).

19 Cf. Knox, 1964, pp. 80-2. *Philos* can be derived from the reflexive pronoun **swos* (Hamp, in press) and still sometimes has this sense in Homer.

20 Cf. n. 3 above. Arendt's distinction between 'work' and 'labour' is relevant here, but I find her definition of 'work' too narrow.

21 Young children appear in several of Euripides' plays but do not really interact with adults; their part in the action is almost entirely passive. The children in the *Medea* are treated as if they could not understand the conversation of adults (70-105, 1040-1) although they are old enough to be instructed to take Medea's gift to their father's new wife.

22 Kin outside the nuclear family do not figure in drama often enough to provide a basis for generalisation, although Euripides and New Comedy provide some interesting cases.

23 Father–son conflict is frequent in comedy, both Old and New (not considered by Slater). It is not often portrayed in detail in tragedy (but cf.

Euripides, *Hippolytus* and *Alcestis*); nor, however, does tragedy provide representations of solidarity and collaboration between father and son to match those of the *Iliad* and *Odyssey*. The nearest we come to a scene of co-operation between father and son in extant tragedy is in the end of Sophocles' *Trachinial*, when Hyllos promises to burn his father Heracles alive and marry Iole who indirectly caused the death of both his parents. Slater starts out with the *a priori* assumption 'that drama concerns itself with issues and relationships which are problematic and conflict-laden, and which generate ambivalent responses. *One would therefore expect* to find that cross-sex parent-child dyads are treated more often, more thoroughly and with more emotionality than same-sex parent-child dyads' (1968, p. 406; my italics).

24   Based on a Menandrian original: cf. Fantham, 1971.

25   Historical evidence on brother-sister relationships in classical Athens is scarce, but the closeness of Kimon and his sister Elpinike was notorious. Plato was closer to his sister's son Speusippos than to his brother's son.

26   It may not be pure chance that the term *apragmon* is first attested – used by Odysseus, however, not by Philoctetes – in the *Philoctetes* of Euripides performed in 431 (fr. 193 Nauck[2]; cf. Dio Chrysostom *Orations* lvii and lix. I owe this point to Lawrence Carter).

27   Correspondingly, there are three bases for the Athenian's identity: the fate allotted by the gods, the public reputation won by action, and the associative status derived from *philoi* – parents, affines and friends. We have to remind ourselves that falling in love, for the fifth-century tragedians, had as much to do with the relations between men and gods as with the plane of interpersonal relationships (cf. Vernant, 1966).

28   Gérin (1974, p. 191 n.263) suggests 'deux schémas de recherche bien généraux: 1) l'interaction entre individus dans le cadre de l'*oikos*, 2) l'articulation entre pouvoir "despotique" et pouvoir politique.' As Gould (1978) has shown, analysis of the forms of speech in tragedy is also very important.

29   I am grateful to Christian Wolff for letting me see an early draft of an article on public and private spheres in Euripides (Wolff, n.d.).

30   The development of the letter as a literary genre – in which the reader is invited to eavesdrop on a private communication even more blatantly than in the intimate scenes of drama or the modern novel – also belongs mainly to the Hellenistic and Roman periods, cf. Sykutris, 1931; Städele, 1980.

5 Family tombs and tomb-cult in classical Athens: tradition or traditionalism?

I Modern perceptions of ancient practices

Fustel de Coulanges's thesis that ancient society was founded upon the cult of ancestral tombs (1864) has had, for a thoroughly self-contradictory argument, a remarkably successful career. Neither Fustel himself nor the many subsequent scholars who have quoted his view with approval faced clearly the difficulty of deriving a social structure dominated by corporate descent groups from the veneration of tombs placed in individually owned landed property. On the whole, historians have tended to play down Fustel's insistence on the relation between ancestor-cult and property and to exaggerate the role of the corporate kin-group. This tendency, which assimilates Fustel to Sir Henry Maine and other lawyers interested in the reconstruction of Indo-European institutions (e.g. Bonfante) has in my view considerably impeded understanding of the role of kinship in early Greek society; it also obscures one of the most individual aspects of Fustel's work which, thanks to the researches of Philippe Ariès (1977) on the development of the modern tomb-cult in the nineteenth century, can now be placed in its historical context.

Research on the treatment of the dead in Greco-Roman antiquity had been proceeding vigorously for some 300 years before Fustel arrived on the scene: Fabricius' *Bibliographia antiquaria* (1760) has an entry of 20 pages on the subject (1019 ff.). These antiquarians have nothing to say about tombs on private property and are not much concerned with the cult of the dead after burial. They are much more interested in the conduct of the funeral itself, particularly the elaborate funerals of important persons. They were well aware that - as Pauline Schmitt-Pantel (1982) has recently reminded us - non-kin as well as kin took part in these funerals and in the annual commemorative feasts which sometimes followed. Mourning involves the participation of professional dirge-singers; for a great man, a whole city may suspend its customary activities. Mourning is not necessarily a purely domestic affair. They also knew, from reading Roman legal texts, of the practice of manumitting slaves by will under the condition that they should tend the tomb of their deceased owner. They note that ancient tombs not infrequently ask the passer-by to pray for the occupant, and this interest in the prayers of strangers seems quite natural to them, since they themselves prayed in church for the surrounding dead in the building itself and the churchyard; they also saw the roadside tombs of the Greeks and Romans, like the church burials of their own day, as a salutary *memento mori.* From the beginning of the eighteenth century the ancient norm of burying the dead outside the city walls is cited with particular approval as a wise measure of hygiene: this is the period when medical concern over burial in city churchyards and churches begins to break forth, especially among Protestants who in any case were liable to be excluded from Catholic burial grounds.[1] Probably in relation to the same concerns, they note that multiple burials were rare in the ancient world: three or four to a grave at Megara, but single burials at Athens. John Potter, later archbishop of Canterbury, in his *Archaeologiae Graecae* (1699), adds 'only those that were joined by near relation or affection were usually buried together, it being thought inhuman to part those in death whom no accidents of life could separate'; he also tells us that 'each family had its own burying place', and mentions the role of kin in funerals rather more than most authors of his period – perhaps an example of the early development of new attitudes to family relationships in England (cf. Stone, 1977). But we are still dealing here with interest in the handling of the corpse (receiving the dying breath from the dead man's mouth, the final kiss, closing the eyes, etc.) or in reunion in the grave – both phenomena attested by Ariès for the eighteenth century – not with the cult of the tomb by surviving members of the family. It is worth noting also in this connection the interest shown in cremation in the seventeenth-eighteenth-century writers linked with the question 'How did they distinguish the ashes of the corpse from the ashes of the pyre, or the bones of the corpse from those of animals or slaves burned with him?'

Thus, as one would expect, dissertations on ancient burial customs reflect the practices, practical concerns and fantasies of the period in which they were written. Even the wilder fringes of this literature are clearly related to the social practices of their day: the pertinacious belief that the Romans had invented a miraculous liquid which would keep lamps burning in tombs for hundreds of years, supported by assertions of men who claimed to have seen such lamps excavated, still burning, from ancient tombs (see the sarcastic account of Octavius Ferrarius, *De veterum lucernis sepulcralibus*, 1699) is clearly related to the contemporary custom of lighting candles for the dead.

The same relation between contemporary concerns and interpretation of ancient sources can of course be seen in Fustel de Coulanges. Ariès (1977) cites at some length the project for the reorganisation of burial and the care of tombs submitted to the Institut in 1801 by one J. Girard, who was convinced that the best solution of all would be for each man to be buried on his own property: this would help to create a deeper sense of property and attachment to the land, which would have a stabilising effect on society. Girard's proposal is particularly striking in its resemblance to Fustel's ideas, but the idea was common at the time. The prize-winning essay of Amaury Duval in the same competition of 1801 also mentioned burial on private property with approval, while Chateaubriand (1802) attributes the custom of burying one's ancestors in private gardens to the Chinese, again in a clearly favourable tone. Chateaubriand's lament for the desecration of the royal tombs of St Denis during the Revolution (ibid.), and the fate of his own father's remains (1948. p. 140), indicate the background to this idea. Although, according to Ariès, the emptying of the cemetery of Les Innocents in the years immediately before the Revolution had not aroused much public reaction, the desecration of other cemeteries and funerary monuments during the Revolution, together with the disorder and lack of control in the newly created suburban cemeteries round Paris during the same period, had created considerable anxiety and concern. Projects for further removals of bones and bodies from churches and churchyards gave rise to concern for the rights of property of the dead, and a feeling that these could only be safeguarded if protected by the rights of property of their living heirs in privately owned land (cf. Chateaubriand's negotiations over his own tomb, 1948, App. iii). The Swiss pastor Edouard Hornstein (director of the seminary of Soleure), who published in 1868 a book on *Les Sépultures* which deals with ancient customs as well as modern issues, exclaims (p. 130): 'Si l'on s'obstine à rejeter les saintes prescriptions de l'épouse de Jésus-Christ, au moins qu'on respecte ses droits de propriété!' The question of the relation of civic and religious authorities in the supervision of cemeteries is one which concerns him deeply. It is axiomatic for him that all the peoples of the earth have a tomb cult and that this cult is carried on by the dead's descendants and associated with belief in immortality. He cites as 'well-known' the response of an American

Indian tribe when asked to cede some apparently unused land to the whites, 'Dirons-nous aux ossements de nos pères: levez-vous et suivez-nous sur une terre nouvelle?'

Thus, in a very short space of time, during the first half of the nineteenth century, the family cult of the tomb grew from being almost unknown in the modern world and largely disregarded in books on antiquity to become a massive phenomenon of contemporary life and a self-evident fact of history and ethnography. It is time now to examine this self-evident fact and see whether, in the case of the ancient Athenians, it will continue to remain solid after the custom which first drew interest to it has been largely abandoned by modern society.

II Athenian family tombs: the evidence

It must be admitted from the outset that the evidence is difficult to interpret. A tomb inscription bearing more than one name is at least a strong indication that kin were buried together, but it is impossible to prove the opposite from tomb stelai bearing single names, if not found *in situ*; family burial plots in the fourth century certainly included cases in which a number of individual monuments to members of the same family were placed in such a way that the visitor saw them as a family group. For example, *IG* ii² 6390 and 6391, commemorating two brothers and their wives, may have been set up together, but since the provenance of 6390 is unrecorded, certainty is impossible. For a full picture of Attic burial customs we need to combine evidence from cemetery excavations with evidence from inscriptions. Unfortunately, only one major cemetery has been excavated by modern methods and published in detail, and this is the Kerameikos, where the crowding of burials and mounds makes interpretation particularly difficult. A number of important sites which should have produced valuable evidence have been found in the Attic countryside, but so far none of them has been adequately published. The archaic mounds of Velanideza and Vourva were excavated by Stais in 1890, when techniques of excavation and dating were still crude. For an important group of archaic graves excavated at Vari in 1935-8 (Fig. 2) we have detailed publications of some of the vase finds (Karouzou, 1963) but only the briefest preliminary reports on the excavation. For the fourth century, a major family enclosure containing at least 17 burials stretching over five generations of the same family was excavated by

Papadimitriou at Merenda (Myrrhinous): the stelai have been published by Mastrokostas (1966), but he could find no information on the excavation. The current exploration of fourth-century family enclosures at Rhamnous is so far only known from brief reports (*Ergon*, 1975, 1976, 1977; Petrakos, 1977, 1978, 1980).

III The role of kin in death and burial at Athens

Death, as it affects the members of a kin-group, is a long and complex process which begins with will-making or other preparations for death, and only ceases when the dead and his tomb are completely forgotten and neglected. An enquiry into family tombs and tomb-cult must therefore examine the role played by kin in the whole sequence of events. As we shall see, the grouping of the tombs of the same family in a single place over a long period of time has a crucial bearing on the duration of the process, and on the range of kin participating in it. We can, however, take it for granted from the outset that the obligations and interests of kin in relation to death extended bilaterally, as did rights of inheritance. We are not concerned here with the corporate, named agnatic *genos* as a group holding hereditary rights to priestly office.

Obligation to perform burial rites was closely associated in Attica with inheritance. By a law cited in [Dem.] xliii 57–8 (post-Cleisthenic in form, possibly passed as a result of the experiences of the plague in 430?), the heirs or next-of-kin had a statutory obligation to bury the dead and could be called upon to pay the costs of burial by deme officials if they did not carry out this obligation with sufficient promptness. How this law worked in practice in the case of the poor we cannot tell; the consequence among the well-to-do was that a man who intended to put in a claim to an estate tried also to take charge of the deceased owner's funeral.

In Isaeus iv, a speech concerning the two-talent estate of one Nicostratus who had died abroad, the speaker's side claims to have buried Nicostratus' remains (26), whereas the opposing claimant Chariades, although serving as a soldier with Nicostratus when he died, neither cremated him nor took charge of his bones (19). The speaker also alleges that because the value of the estate was high and because, Nicostratus having been abroad for some time, there was some difficulty in establishing who his kin were, 'everyone in Athens' was cutting their hair and putting on mourning in the hope of being able to put in a successful claim (7). In Isaeus vi, Euctemon of

Kephisia had died as an old man in the house of a mistress whose sons tried to claim his estate; the speaker, Euctemon's daughter's son and adopted son of Euctemon's deceased son Philoctemon, asserts that his opponents had tried to prevent Euctemon's wife and daughter from entering the house where he had died to prepare his body (40 f.). In [Dem.] xliv, concerning the estate of one Leocrates of Otryne who had been adopted out of his family of origin, the speaker's family tried to take possession of Leocrates' corpse as well as his estate, but were prevented by his natural father Leostratus. In Isaeus viii (21-7, 38-9) the speaker explains that he went with a patrilateral cousin (as witness) to fetch the corpse of his maternal grandfather Ciron to his own house for burial, but was persuaded by the widow (Ciron had remarried after the death of the speaker's grandmother) to conduct the funeral from Ciron's house. The widow's brother, Diocles (acting as her *kyrios*) allowed this but claimed reimbursement for his own expenditure on burial preparations; later however he refused to accept this repayment, on the grounds that he had already been repaid by a rival claimant to the estate, Ciron's brother's son. The speaker, 'in order that they might gain no advantage over me by alleging to you [the jury] that I bore no part of the funeral expenses, consulted the interpreter of sacred law and by his advice paid for at my own expense and offered the ninth-day offerings in the most sumptuous manner possible'.

In order to prevent undignified squabbles over his corpse, the prudent Athenian would try to make firm arrangements for the disposal of his property before his death, either in a written will or by oral expression of his wishes. In either case, he would be wise to see that all potentially interested parties were present, plus one or two disinterested witnesses in addition. The content of a written will was read out to witnesses before the will was sealed and deposited (preferably in more than one copy) with trustworthy friends.

Wills, of course, might be made at any time and were quite often made by young and healthy men about to go to war (Isaeus vi 3, 8; xi 8). The most usual form of will was the conditional testamentary adoption of an heir by a childless man (Gernet, 1920). There were many details which wills did not regulate. A dying man would summon his friends and kin, would give instructions about burial (Plato *Phaedo* 115b-c), and would solemnly conjure his heirs or trustees to pay any outstanding debts; Socrates' last words, 'Crito, I owe a cock to Asclepius, please pay the debt for me', express an unconventional attitude to death in an entirely conventional manner (*Phaedo* 118, cf. [Dem.] xli 6-9, 16-17). It is, of course, characteristic of philosophers that friends take the place of kin in this scene of death; compare the role of friends as trustees in the philosophers' wills transmitted by Diogenes Laertius.

So far, the evidence considered has all come from the fourth century. For an idea of death in the archaic period we have to turn to Solon's legislation forbidding ostentatious funerals.[2] The body was to be laid out for the last greetings from family and friends (*prothesis*) within the house ([Dem.] xliii 62). Burial must take place before sunrise on the day following the *prothesis*, the third day from the death. Women under the age of sixty were not allowed to attend *prothesis* or funeral, or enter the house of the dead after the funeral, unless related to the deceased as *anepsiadai* or more closely (first cousins once removed or second cousins: Thompson, 1970); women were not allowed to lacerate themselves or wail (*kokeuein*: Cicero *de Legibus* ii 59ff., Plutarch *Solon* 21). No one was to lament for persons other than the man or woman being buried; no ox was to be sacrificed at the graveside; no corpse was to be buried with more than three garments (*himatia*); no one was to visit the tombs of non-kin except for a funeral (Plutarch *Solon* 21).

Similar controls were imposed by the phratry of the Labyadai at Delphi in c.400 BC (Hainsworth, 1972, no. 3; Buck, 1955, no. 52; *SGDI* 2561; Sokolowski, 1969, no. 77; *SEG* xxv 574) and by the city of Iulis in Keos, probably under Attic influence, in the late fifth century (*SIG*[3] 1218). The regulations of the Labyadai say that after the lid (? *thigana*) is put on the tomb there is to be no mourning and wailing for those previously buried in the same place, but each man is to go home except for members of the deceased's household (*homestioi*), patrikin (*patradelphoi*), wife's kin (*pentheroi*), descendants (*esgonoi*) and affines married to women of his own family (*gambroi*). The amount of property to be buried with the corpse is restricted, the funeral procession is to go in silence, without stopping in the streets. At Iulis the procession is also to be silent, the bier is to be covered; the amount of wine, oil and cloth used in the funeral is limited, and the bier, bedding and vessels used in the funeral are to be returned to the house afterwards. A passage of uncertain interpretation says either that women must, or that they must not, leave the tomb before men.[3] After the burial no woman is to enter the house of the dead except those polluted – mother, wife, sisters, daughters and not more than five other women and two girls, 'children of daughters and of cousins'.[4]

These provisions give us, in intaglio, a picture of the type of funeral the legislators wished to prevent. A noble family wishing to make the maximum display in honour of a dead member would, in the first place, prolong the *prothesis* for as long as possible before decomposition set in. (In the *Iliad*, where the gods lend miraculous help in preserving corpses, Hector is mourned for 9 days, xxiv 785-9; in the *Odyssey*, xxiv 63-5, it is stated that Achilles' *prothesis* lasted 17 days).Boardman (1955) suggested that in the *prothesis* scenes shown on pre-Solonian Attic vases the *prothesis* should be thought of as set in a public place rather than the courtyard of an *oikos* (Ahlberg 1971, pp. 297-9, is more doubtful). The funeral procession would take place in daylight, when everyone was about to see it. The bier would be covered with rich and elaborately woven cloth (Kurtz and Boardman, 1971, p. 144; Euripides, *Troades* 1207 ff. The modest expense on cloth permitted by the Iulis law is 100 drachmai). It would be followed by numerous friends and supporters of the family, both male and female, with musicians and professional female mourners; the men riding in chariots (three or four four-horse chariots were shown in Exekias' sequence of plaques representing a funeral in the mid-sixth century: Technau, 1936, pls 14-19), or dressed in their hoplite armour; the women lamenting and tearing their faces and hair (cf. Herodotus vi 39).[5] Convention required that men should maintain self-control in mourning, whereas women were encouraged to display wild grief: therefore, to restrict female participation in *prothesis* and funeral procession (*ekphora*) to kin and women over sixty markedly reduced both the aural and the visual impact of the procession. In the fourth century and later legal theorists see these limitations on the participation of women as designed to control an unruly element in society: women should not be encouraged to give their emotions free rein (Plutarch *Moralia* 608a ff.), nor given the opportunities for meeting strange men that funerals provided (Lysias i 8; Terence, *Phormio* 91–116). The law of Gambreion controlling funerals, of the third century BC (*SIG*[3] 1219) is to be enforced by the *gynaikonomoi*, who had general responsibility for keeping women in order (cf. Wehrli, 1962). But Solon was probably more concerned with the use of women as a *medium* of display than with the effect on the women themselves. The cortège would stop frequently at street corners for outbreaks of lamentation (Alexiou, 1974). When the dead was cremated, which seems on the whole to be the most honourable kind of funeral (and was more expensive), speeches in honour of the dead were made at the pyre; the mourners filed round it, valuable cloth and other possessions were laid on it with the corpse. Animals might be sacrificed. The mourners remained round the pyre until it had burnt through, then quenched it with wine. In both inhumations and cremations, speeches and sacrifices would be made at the graveside,[6] and friends and kin would heap up the earth over the grave and burn offerings over the 'offering trenches' (*Opferrinnen*) [7] which are found in association with the richest archaic tombs, or (more frequently, later in the sixth century) at 'offering places' nearby. The funeral party would then circle other graves of the same family in the same area, lamenting, celebrating the fame and virtues of the dead and perhaps making further offerings. The size of the mound heaped up over the tomb by the male kin and friends of the dead was intended to be a sign of his power and honour to all future generations: a further symbol might be added on top of it to show what kind of man he was. The funeral would end with a feast in the house of the heir [8] or, in the most elaborate ceremonies, with funerary games and perhaps even musical competitions.

Further commemorative rites were carried out on the ninth and thirtieth days after death. [9] Thereafter, some families may have made further commemorative offerings: this is suggested by the practice attributed to Clytemnestra in Sophocles' *Electra* (277-81) of celebrating a monthly festival of thanksgiving on the anniversary of the death of Agamemnon, and by the provision in Epicurus' will for commemoration of himself and his pupil Metrodorus on the 20th of every month (Diogenes Laertius x 18). But such monthly rites may not have been strongly institutionalised in early times. There is better evidence for annual commemorations at the festival of the Genesia, 'known to all the Greeks' according to Herodotus (iv 26) and celebrated in Attica on 5 Boedromion (September). Jacoby (1944a), following Mommsen (1898, p. 174), suggested that the date of the Genesia was fixed by Solon, families having previously chosen their own anniversary dates; but Herodotus' words do not necessarily imply that individual choice of date was the practice in his day outside Attica, and Genesion is known as the name of a month at Magnesia on the Maeander (Kern, 1900, no. 116), which should imply a fixed festival for the Genesia in that city. However, Jacoby in any case made an important point in stressing that a fixed date for the festival implied that each individual could only attend commemorative rites in a single cemetery. The scope for gratifying powerful relatives or friends by attending their family rituals was limited by duties to one's own immediate ancestors, [10] and only those ancestors who were buried together would be commemorated. The effect would be that those who felt strongly about the duty to honour all their ancestors would take pains to ensure that all members of the family were buried together, and that those who carried out Genesia at the same group of tombs would take on in their own eyes some of the characteristics of a descent group (as in the case of the Bouselidai in [Dem.] xliii). But we shall see that the evidence for large-scale and long-lasting groupings of this kind is rare.

The Athenians had another festival of the dead in the Spring, the Anthesteria; but this was an *oikos* festival in which the dead were supposed to visit the households of the living. It did not involve visits to tombs, and the dead, the *kēres*, do not seem to have been individualised; they appear to be anonymous like the 'souls' of All Souls' night. Some individuals, however, clearly celebrated private anniversaries as well as the Genesia.

Monthly commemorations have already been mentioned. According to Diogenes Laertius (ii 14), Anaxagoras was commemorated by an annual school holiday at Lampsacus in the month in which he died (cf. Aristotle *Rhetoric* 1398b18). Epicurus specified that the annual celebration of his birthday which had begun during his lifetime was to be continued after his death by his friends who were also to commemorate the birthdays of Metrodorus and of Polyaenus of Lampsacus (Diogenes Laertius x 18). The association founded by Antiochus of Commagene to honour himself and his family was to meet monthly on the dates of birth of Antiochus and his father (Waldmann, 1973, pp. 203-4, Wagner and Petzl 1976, Clarysse 1976; cf the similar provision in Dunant and Pouilloux 1958, pp. 93-9, no. 192). The confusion in late sources of *genethlia* (birthday) with *genesia* (commemoration of the dead) seems, *pace* Jacoby 1944a, p. 67, to have had an institutional as well as an etymological basis.

Other occasions on which kin would in any case gather together might also be used for mourning demonstrations, as happened after the battle of Arginoussai at the phratry festival of the Apatouria (Xenophon *Hellenica* i 7.7). Electra in Aeschylus' *Choephoroe* (470 ff.) speaks of bringing offerings to her father's tomb on her wedding day (*choas gamelious*).

IV Public commemoration of the dead: speeches and monuments

Solon's restrictions on funerary ostentation refer only to burial, but 'some time later' (*post aliquanto*, Cicero *de Legibus* ii 64) a further law was passed that no grave monument was to be more elaborate than the work of ten men could accomplish in three days, that tombs were not to be adorned with *opus tectorium* or have 'herms' erected on them, and that the dead were not to be praised except in public funerals by the orator officially appointed for the task. *Opus tectorium*, in the view of Boardman (1955), would refer to the painted plaques hung round built tombs in the sixth century which provided a permanent representation of the funeral ceremony in its various stages: 'herms' seems to be a general term for any standing stone grave marker. Archaeologists agree that there is a change in Attic burial practice corresponding to this law, although they disagree on the exact date within the period c. 510-480 BC to which the change should be assigned (cf. Stupperich, 1977). Stone stelai are not clearly attested archaeologically after this period, until the time of the Peloponnesian war. White-ground lekythoi of the middle years of the fifth century show small grave mounds with stelai on them, but they may represent monuments made of wood. (See below, p. 105).

The reference in Cicero's text to public funerals does not necessarily refer to the recurrent ceremony of burial and commemoration of war dead immortalised by Thucydides' version of Pericles' funeral oration in 431 BC. Evidence for 'public' funerals goes back to the origins of the *polis*. In the seventh century the Corcyreans buried a *proxenos* from Oiantheia in the Corinthian gulf at public expense (*IG* ix 1 867, Meiggs and Lewis, 1969, no. 4). The Athenians gave a public funeral to Pythagoras of Selymbria in the middle of the fifth century, and may have done the same earlier for other benefactors (*IG* i² 1034 = i³ 1154; Peek, 1955 (*GVI*) no. 45).[11] Military commanders had presumably made funerary speeches before cremating war dead on the battle-field from early times: it would be from this custom that the polemarch, the original commander-in-chief of the Athenian army (see Hammond, 1969), derived his responsibility for the annual ceremony for war dead in the Kerameikos. Thus even if Jacoby (1944b) was right in claiming that the ceremony in the Kerameikos described by Thucydides (ii 34) was instituted only in 465 BC,[12] the concept of the public funeral as a tribute paid by the *polis* to those deserving special honour had developed much earlier. The aim of the celebration of public funerals, *and* of the legislation restricting ostentation in private celebrations, was to reserve the right of conferring 'heroic' honours on the dead to the *polis* (the same of course is true of legislation or norms prohibiting burial within the city, except in cases where the city gave special permission). Control over the honours permitted at burial to citizens of different status (kings, soldiers dying in battle, etc.) was still more detailed at Sparta (cf. Herodotus vi 58; Wallace, 1970; Chrestos, 1965; Hartog, 1982). But Athens too seems to have succeeded in imposing this discrimination with remarkable uniformity in the fifth century, and its effects remain visible even when private monuments again become elaborate in the fourth century: this is one case among others where we can trace the gradual demarcation of a threshold between public and private life.

The provision in the law recorded by Cicero that tombs should not involve more than three days' work for ten men must refer to grave-mounds; sculptured monuments are covered by the prohibition of 'herms', and it is scarcely credible that their ostentation could have been thought of in terms of the labour-time involved in making them. The epitaph of the Corcyrean *proxenos* mentioned above, stating that his *kasignētos* Praximenes came from his homeland and laboured with the *demos* to make his monument (*sāma ponēthē*), refers to a mound enclosed by a stone wall.[13] In a sixth-century epitaph from Troezen (*IG* iv 800, Pfohl, 1967, no. 160), Praxiteles' *hetairoi* make his *sāma* and finish it in a single day: the point of the record here is evidently that the size of the mound shows how many *hetairoi* must have taken part in the work.

The use of tomb mounds as 'signs' of the graves of men of honour and renown is already established in the Homeric poems. In the *Odyssey* (xi 75-6) Elpenor, lost at sea, asks Odysseus to bury him by the seashore and heap up a *sēma* 'for future men to know' (*kai essomenoisi pythesthai*), and to fix his oar in the top of the mound (*tymbos*). The *sēma* consists of mound plus oar – the former denoting Elpenor's status, the latter his role at the time of death. In the *Iliad* (xxiii 245-8) the Greeks build a modest *tymbos* for Patroclus, which they are to increase in size when Achilles too has died and has been buried beneath it.

Archaeologically, mounds are difficult to detect unless they are of considerable size or are made with earth brought to the cemetery from outside. Earth was being brought in to the Kerameikos for the construction of large mounds by the second quarter of the seventh century (Kübler, 1959, mound Θ), and the largest mounds in the Kerameikos on the whole belong to this century, with the exception of two huge mounds of about the middle of the sixth century (Hügel G, Kübler 1976; Südhügel, Knigge, 1976).

Homeric mounds were heaped up to honour and perpetuate the memory of individuals or, as in the case of Achilles and Patroclus, a pair of *hetairoi*. The Greeks, of course, die far from home in the Homeric poems: but Hector too has an individual mound, with no mention of burying him by the tombs of his ancestors (*Il.* xxiv 797-801).[14] Likewise, when simple signs of the form of Elpenor's oar are replaced by paintings, inscriptions and sculpture, the monuments commemorate individuals، As in the case with Homer's mounds, piled in foreign lands to give information to strangers of future generations, some of these archaic inscriptions are clearly directed at those who did not know the dead man.

> ['Ό]στις μὴ παρ[ε | τ]ύνχαν', ὅτ᾽ ἐ[χσ] | ἐφερόν με θ[αν] | όντα,
> νῦν μ᾽ ὀ[λω] | φυράσθω. Μν[ῆμ]α δὲ Τηλεφ[άνε] | ος.

Whoever was not present when they buried me,
Let him mourn me now. *Mnema* of Telephanes.

> (*IG* xii 8. 396, Thasos, c. 500 BC; Pfohl, 1967, no. 18)

> [Εἴτ᾽ ἀστό]ς τις ἀνέρ εἴτε χσένος ἄλοθεν ἐλθὸν:
> Τέτιχον οἰκτίρα|ς ἄνδρ᾽ ἀγαθὸν παρίτο:
> ἐν πολέμōι | φθίμενον, νεαρὰν ἥβεν ὀλέσαν | τα:
> Ταῦτ᾽ ἀποδυράμενοι νέσθε ἐπ|ὶ πρᾶγμ᾽ ἀγαθόν.

Whether you are a citizen or a stranger from abroad,
Pity Tettichos, a good man, as you go by;
He lost his fresh youth by death in war.
Mourn for him, and go on your way with good fortune.

> (*IG* i² 976 = i³ 1194 bis, Attica, c. 560-50 BC; Pfohl, no. 55)

> [Πάσα]ς αἰχμέτο, Χσενόκλεες, ἀνδρὸ[ς | ἐπισ]τὰς؛
> σἐμα τὸ σὸν προσιδὸν γν[όι | σετ]αι ἔν[ορέας].

Anyone who has any understanding, will know
when he looks at your *sēma*, Xenocles,
that it belongs to a spearman.

> (*IG* i² 984 = i³ 1200, Athens, c. 550-30 BC; Pfohl, no. 30)

> ῎Ανθρōπε hὸς ⟨σ⟩τείχεις : καθ᾽ ὁδὸ|ν : φρασὼν : ἄλ‹λ›α μενοιōν
> στέθι | καὶ οἴκτιρον : σἐμα Θράσōνος : ἰδόν.

Man, as you go on your way with your mind on other things,
Stand and feel pity, as you look at the monument of Thrason.

> (*IG* i² 971 = i³ 1204, Athens, c. 540 BC; Pfohl, no. 32)

Several epitaphs mention explicitly that the grave is by the roadside, as graves normally were (e.g. *IG* i² 974 = i³ 1197, c. 550 BC, Pfohl no. 27); and the more frequented the road, the better the site. The

Kerameikos cemetery lay just outside the main entrance to the *agora*, through which passed the sacred way leading to Eleusis. But even at Velanideza near the east coast of Attica, which is not on a main route (it lies on the road from Spata, Erchia, to Loutsa, Halai Araphenides), the tomb of Philodemos and Anthemion is proudly said to be by the roadside (*IG* i² 1026 a = i³ 1255, *SEG* x 458; Pfohl, no. 64).

Nevertheless, the use of sculptures representing the dead as tomb-markers - even though by our standards the figures are not 'portraits' - gave the tomb-monument a new sense for those who had known the dead. It could be thought of not only as a *sēma*, a sign bearing information for those who needed it, but also as a *mnēma*, [15] a record or memorial which would preserve for all time the physical appearance of the dead - most commonly as a *kouros*, a young warrior - just as the words inscribed on its base would preserve his name, his virtues and (very often) the names of those responsible for making and setting up the monument. Kleoitos' epitaph says,

Παῖδὸς ἀποφθιμένοιο Κλεοίτο τô Μεν | εσαίχμο:
μνêμ' ἐσορôν οἴκτιρ', ὸς καλὸς ὸν ἔθανε.

Look on the *mnēma* of Kleoitos, the son of Menesaichmos,
and pity him for dying, with such beauty.

(*IG* i² 982 = i³ 1277, Athens, c. 500 BC; Pfohl no. 81)

The thought still seems to be directed to the stranger who would not know, without the statue, what Kleoitos had been like; but the basis for treating the statue as a focus for the mourning memories of his family clearly exists (cf. Ducat, 1976; Vernant, 1977, 1978, 1982). In the epitaph of Learete of Thasos (*IG* xii 8. 398; Pfohl, no. 20, c. 500-490 BC) the process has developed a little further:

⁵Η καλôν τῶ μνῆμα [πα] | τὴρ ἔστησε θανώσ[ηι] |
Λεαρέτηι. Ὠυ γὰρ [ἔτ] | ι ζôσαν ἐσωφσώμ[εθα].

Beautiful is the *mnēma* which her father set up to the dead
Learete; for we shall see her alive no longer.

(Cf. later still, c. 430-20 BC, the tombstone of Mnesagora and Niko-chares, *IG* ii² 12147; Pfohl, no. 117).[16]

Taken by itself, the archaic funeral monument detaches the individual commemorated from his background to present him as an archetypal figure of timeless human significance. This is not to say that the family of the dead are entirely unrepresented. They naturally played a prominent part in the funeral, as discussed above; they may be mentioned in the inscribed epitaph; finally, the individualising memorial may have formed part of a family group, as will be discussed further below. But archaic funerary monuments do not stress family unity[17] in the same way as those of the fourth century which will be considered later in this paper; and we must make an effort to understand this difference.

The majority of archaic funerary monuments in Attica were set up by parents in commemoration of their children, usually children who died as young adults: young men who died in war, adolescent girls who died before marriage (IG i^2 1014 = i^3 1261, Pfohl no. 61 Phrasikleia). Of 20 inscriptions which record the relationship of the commemorator to the dead, 13 are set up by parents to children, 2 by parent and spouse in association, 3 by siblings and only 2 by children to fathers, one specifying that it was 'at the command of our mother'.[18] These monuments are *not*, therefore, the product of a belief that it was a sacred duty for a son to see that his father received proper honours after death. This conclusion is reinforced by analysis of sculptured representations of the dead (Jeffery, 1962); very few represent men or women of middle age.

A few monuments seem to have been set up not by kin but by *hetairoi*. *IG* i^2 920 = i^3 1399 (Pfohl no. 75, c. 500) was apparently set up by an *erōmenos* to his *erastēs*;[19] *SEG* xiv 23, xv 75 (*IG* i^3 1231, Pfohl no. 78, Peek, 1957, p. 66 no. 218; Athens, c. 500 or later) was set up by Dexandrides to two men, Philoitios and Ktesias, one of whom was his brother and the other apparently unrelated.

There are only six monuments which certainly commemorate more than one person. The monument of Philoitios and Ktesias is one, and *IG* i^2 1026a = i^3 1255 (Pfohl no. 64) also commemorates two young men, whose relationship to each other is unknown. It may have been set up over the double house-tomb found under the mound excavated by Stais at Velanideza (see below). Two monuments commemorated a brother and sister: *SEG* x 452a/xvi 26 (*IG* i^3 1265, Pfohl no. 62) for Archias and Phile; *IG* i^2 981 = i^3 1241 (Pfohl no. 33) for an adolescent boy and his younger sister. In addition, the statues of Phrasikleia and of a *kouros* of similar date, which were recently found where they had been buried together in antiquity (Mastrokostas, 1972) presumably belonged to members of the same family; but the monuments were distinct. *IG* i^2 1001 = i^3 1221 was probably set up to two brothers or a father and son, and *IG* i^2 1016 = i^3 1266 (Pfohl no. 58) to 'the children' of Kylon. The relief stele NM 3892 shows two youths: Jeffery (1962, no. 60) suggests that it might belong to *IG* i^2 1023 = i^3 1271 and represent two brothers. There are only two extremely doubtful cases of stelai listing more than two names which *might* be tombstones, but probably are not: Jeffery, 1962, nos 20 (8 names; see, however, Wiseman and Shaw, 1970) and 55 (Pfohl no. 71).

One final inscription will serve to introduce the discussion of evidence for the grouping together of graves belonging to the same family:

Οἴμοι Πεδιάρχο | τô 'Ενπεδίōνος.
Πεδίαρχος ἄρχει τô ‹ν› σ|ēμάτōν.
Woe for Pediarchos, son of Empedion!
Pediarchos begins the *sēmata*.
(*SEG* iii 56, Liopesi, c. 540 BC; *IG* i³ 1267, Pfohl no. 57)

Once again we have an individual singled out for special honour: his monument states a relation to his family but at the same time distinguishes him from them. He is not placed among the tombs of his ancestors; on the contrary, he apparently begins a new set of tombs in which his own will serve as the focus round which that of other family members (especially, in all likelihood, his parents) will be grouped.

V The grouping of tombs belonging to the same family

Evidence for tomb grouping begins, for the purpose of the present research, in the Geometric period.[20] A grave enclosure of the 740s-30s was found in the Kerameikos containing perhaps as many as 13 graves (Kübler, 1954, pp. 17 ff., graves 51–63) enclosed by parallel rectangular borders of stone, with some child burials, not much later than the original inhumations, dug into the low mounds covering these. This orderly planning of the placing of burials did not, however, continue for more than a short time.

Another enclosure of the Geometric period was found in the Agora, adjoining an ancient road (Young, 1939) containing eighteen tombs, two other deposits (nos XII, XV) and two child burials which belong to a later period (late seventh-early sixth century) and may not be deliberately associated with the Geometric group, which extends over a period of about sixty years.[21] Six adult skeletons were studied: two adolescent females, one probably young male, and one female of 50-55 from single burials; in graves XIX–XX an individual of indeterminate sex aged 40-45 was buried first and later a male of 30-35 was buried above. Grave IX was a simultaneous burial of two children in a pithos. Dr Lawrence Angel, who studied the skeletons, suggested that there were grounds for thinking this was a family group; the measurements would have to be seen in relation to those of a larger population in order to assess the weight of his arguments, but the conclusion seems *a priori* probable. Another Geometric 'family lot' (Smithson, 1974) contained nine burials.

It was in the Geometric period also that an enclosure was built round nine Middle Helladic tombs in the West cemetery at Eleusis, six of which had been opened in antiquity and, Mylonas suggests (1975, ii, pp. 153-4, 262-3), may have been identified as the graves of the six warriors killed in the expedition of the Seven against Thebes. Possibly the enclosure of these tombs may have stimulated a few eighth-century Athenian families to honour their own dead in the same way.[22] But the fashion did not spread widely at first. It recurs, as will be seen below, in the classical period.

The essential problem in trying to understand the spatial organisation of archaic cemeteries is the grouping of monuments and mounds; and unfortunately it is extremely difficult to get any clear answer from the evidence so far available. In the Kerameikos, the use of earth brought in from outside to make mounds larger than the small raised area created by the earth removed from the tomb itself begins in the 660s-40s (mound Θ). After c. 640 shortage of space begins to be noticeable and mounds become smaller and steeper; about 610-600 the use of mounds began to be replaced by the construction of built 'house-tombs' of mud brick. But about 580 a new mound (Π) was built *over* those of the seventh century, inaugurating a new series of mounds, mostly smallish, which culminated in the huge Südhügel (c. 540) and Mound G (c. 555-50), the latter conjecturally identified by the excavator as the tomb of Solon (Kübler, 1976: its huge size and disregard of earlier burials, many of which were shovelled into the fill, suggest that it was a monument set up by the state; the date, c. 550, is too early for Pisistratus).[23] Mound G (and the other archaic monuments to be discussed here) lay south-west of the Sacred Way, between it and the 'Weststrasse'; the Südhügel lay south-east of the Weststrasse, behind a pair of public monuments set up (later) to foreign ambassadors who had died at Athens.

Mound G was originally built to cover a single tomb, but twelve or more further shaft graves of comparable richness were dug into its sides not long after the original burial; it seems, therefore, that the kin of the man for whom this heroic monument was erected used it as a family burying ground after his death. The Südhügel covered two shaft graves of which one (Knigge, 1976, no. 2, HW 52) had been destroyed before the excavation. The other (3, HW 87) contained exceptionally rich finds of mainly East Greek origin, of c. 540 BC. No further related

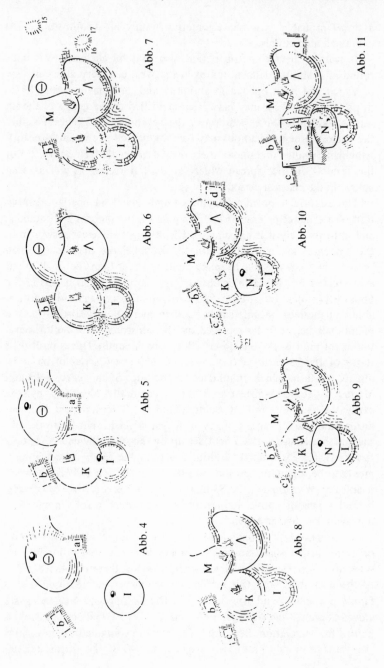

Abb. 4

Abb. 5

Abb. 6

Abb. 7

Abb. 8

Abb. 9

Abb. 10

Abb. 11

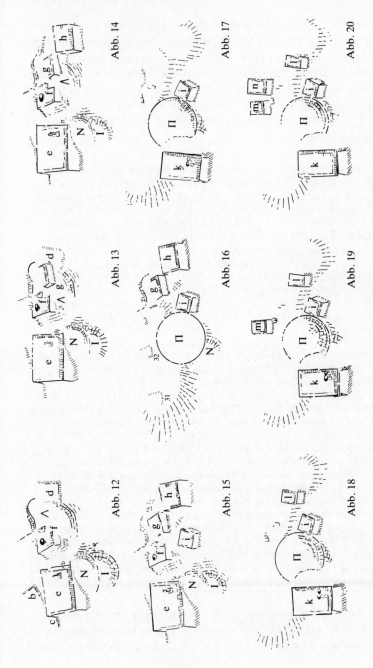

FIGURE 1 *Kerameikos vi. I Abb. 4-20. Development of mounds and built tombs on a single site, c. 650–570 BC* *(De Gruyter, Berlin)*

burials were dug into this mound. Knigge suggests that it was a monument set up by Pisistratus to an honoured foreign guest. (She thinks
that the mound covered grave 2, HW 52, only accidentally).

Like Mound G, the earlier mounds and built tombs in the area
between the Sacred Way and the Weststrasse were erected in the first
place to cover single burials and to honour single individuals. Nevertheless, it is possible that monuments belonging to the same family were
grouped together.

> This is certain in the case of some of the built tombs: q, r and s
> (graves 42, 43, 45) are adjacent and must have been deliberately
> placed as a group (c. 600-580; tomb 44, next to r, may also belong).
> The same is true of built tombs t, u and v (early 590s-70s), built on
> the site of an earlier mound (P, 630 or slightly later) and next to
> mound Σ (c. 580). Tomb 49, adjacent to this group, had a stele
> leaning against built tomb u.
> Mounds Ξ (28, 610-600) and O (29, 590s), with the child burial
> 30 (590s) and the built tombs o (38) with its extension (39) and (?)
> p (41, 570s-60s), and tomb 40 (570s) also seem to constitute a
> group. It is much more doubtful whether they have any connection
> with the earlier mounds E-Z (tombs 6-7, c. 660) which they partially
> covered.
> Kübler (1959, p. 16) suggested that mounds Γ (690 or soon
> after), E and Z (c. 660) belonged to a single family and might also
> be linked to A (c. 710) and Δ (c. 680), since the whole group was
> covered by the large mound H in the 660s or 650s.
> Adjacent to H – perhaps in rivalry? – another large mound Θ
> (665–60; covering B, of c. 710) began a new series of monuments
> (Fig. 1). Two smaller mounds, Λ (635-30) and M (630s-20s) were
> built on to the side of it; built tombs b (c. 650) and d (c. 610) may
> be associated with Θ and Λ, respectively; built tomb f (c. 600), was
> built on to the side of the Θ/Λ/M complex, and built tombs g-h
> (c. 590) seem to be associated with each other and with d. Built
> tomb i (early 580s) may also belong with mound Λ, although the
> lapse of time makes this less certain.
> A further group consists of mound I (650s), the contemporary
> and adjacent mound K, built tomb e on the side of K (c. 600),
> mound N over mound I (c. 610), and perhaps built tomb c, adjacent
> to K, of the same date as N. The remains of I/K/N (together with the
> ruins of built tomb f of c. 610, in the preceding group) were covered
> c. 580 by mound Π, and built tomb k was erected beside it c. 575-70.

In the crowded conditions of the Kerameikos, it is impossible to say,
except in the case of built tombs erected side by side, that these juxta-
positions *must* have been the result of the deliberate grouping of family

tombs. A sixth-century wall surrounding 48 Geometric and Archaic burials within the city (Young, 1951) gives us little more information. It ought to have been possible to learn more from the archaic mounds and tomb enclosures excavated in the Attic countryside; but unfortunately the excavations of the Greek archaeological service here have produced extremely little published evidence on the point under examination.[24]

The most important site is at Vari. Here Oikonomos and Stavropoulos in 1935-8 [25] examined five mounds and two walled tomb enclosures, containing at least six built tombs, with finds running from the late seventh to the middle of the fifth century. One walled enclosure, completely excavated, contained 25 tombs of which 5 were built tombs of stone, one double (21/22,A). The largest of these built tombs (24/B) was placed in the middle of the enclosure and was a cenotaph.[26] Two of the other burials were pot burials of children. Several sculptured monuments were found in the area (none inscribed), and it was thought that at least some of these may have stood on the periphery wall surrounding the grave-group – which would of course markedly have increased the impression of group unity which the visitor would receive. Mound I contained a (single?) burial of c. 620, and later offerings were also thought to be associated with it: the excavators suggested that it might have held the tomb of an official, perhaps a *genarchos*, but no evidence for this assertion was ever supplied (Walter, 1940).[27] Mound III held seven graves of which two were undisturbed and belonged to the end of the sixth century. Mound V contained burials ranging in date from c. 550-450. This excavation does indeed seem to have hit on the remains of the tombs of a part at least of the elite of the deme Anagyrous, but without more precise information on the extent of the cemetery and the dating of the tombs, it is impossible to draw any substantial conclusions from it.

Further excavations in a different area in Vari in 1961-4 (Andreiomenou, 1963, pp. 37-9; Kallipolitis, 1964; 1967, pp. 112-17) uncovered a wall of the late sixth century which appeared to be part of an enclosure surrounding tombs of the sixth-fifth centuries. (There were also late Geometric tombs in the area, but no proof that the builders of the wall were aware of this.) Some of these graves were grouped (Kallipolitis, 1964, *taphika ktismata* A, graves 4-8, late seventh century; B, graves 11-12, same date; C, graves 22-25, late fifth century) but none of the groups was large or marked by an impressive monument.[28]

Two large mounds were examined at Anavyssos in 1911

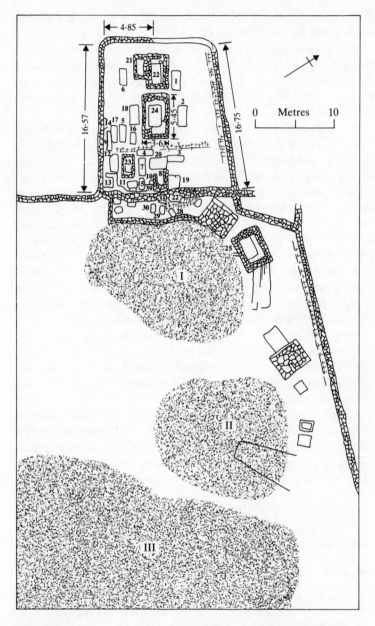

FIGURE 2 *Archaic cemetery at Vari (drawn by Richard Davidson of the Cartographic Unit, University College London, from the plans published in Lemerle, 1937, p. 450 and Walter, 1940, cols 177-8, fig. 34)*

(Kastriotis and Philadelpheus, 1912). The excavation of the northern one was rapidly abandoned, but the southern contained more than twenty-five graves, some of which were Late Geometric in date (Coldstream, 1968: LG Ib-IIb), while others were sixth-century. No full report or plan was ever published.

In 1890, V. Stais excavated mounds at Petreza, Velanideza and Vourva (Stais, 1890a, 1890b; Helbig, 1900). The Petreza mound (middle sixth century: *ABV* 347, Athens 1055), covered only a single tomb, with further burials dug into the mound later. At Vourva the mound covered two built tombs (A-B) and a small stone mound (Γ), all three of which had previously been free-standing, plus a fourth tomb, Δ, with which the mound must have been contemporary. It is dated c. 580 by Kübler (1959, pp. 95 ff.), and tombs A-Γ were not very much earlier. Still within a short span of time, three more burials were made in the side of the mound. If this was a family burial ground, it belonged to a limited group and was not in use for long. The mound at Velanideza was erected over a double built tomb, E/Z, and an inhumation, H, assigned by tomb type to approximately the same period as the Vourva graves, but supplying no definite dating evidence. Later burials were made in the sides of the mound and in the adjacent peribolos in the late sixth century and later – some apparently even in Roman times.

The archaeological evidence on burial in archaic Attica is thus unsatisfactory and difficult to interpret. It seems that there was a gradual escalation in the size of the mounds heaped up over those given 'heroic' burial (although for a time built mud-brick tombs, some hung with painted plaques – a fashion perhaps started because of shortage of room in the Kerameikos – were a popular alternative); and that the large size of some of these mounds encouraged their re-use by members of the same family content with reflected glory instead of an individual monument. Except in the case of the Vourva mound and Mound G in the Kerameikos, where the numbers involved were small and the period limited, the evidence does not allow us to judge how long such secondary burials continued without break.

Few literary references give historical data on burials of the archaic period, but Herodotus (vi 103) records that Kimon Koalemos, who won the four-hourse chariot race at Olympia in three successive festivals and was allegedly assassinated by the sons of the tyrant Pisistratus in 527, shortly after his third victory, was buried 'in front of the city, beyond the road leading through Koilē' (SW of the city, probably beside the Piraeus road) with his horses 'opposite him' (on the other side of the road?).[29] This must have been a sensational funeral, and may indeed have helped to provide motivation for the undated law restricting funerary extravagance quoted by Cicero. The monument was a well-known landmark, and other members of the family were later buried in the same area: possibly Kimon, son of Miltiades, in c. 449 (Plutarch, *Cimon* 19.5; but this may be an erroneous inference from the fact that the area was known as *ta Kimoneia mnēmata*), certainly his sister Elpinike (Plutarch, *Cimon* 4), and perhaps the historian Thucydides (*APF*, p. 233; Marcellin, *Vita Thucydidis* 17, 55). Davies (*APF*, p. 310) suggests that Kimon Koalemos may have lived in this area; but all we can say for certain is that his brother Miltiades held land in Lakiadai to the north-west, and that the family's attachment to the *genos* Philaidai *prima facie* connects them with the Brauron area. In any case, there is no reason to suppose that Kimon I and his horses were placed in a burial ground already appropriated by the family. It was no doubt the ostentation of his monuments which attracted other burials later.

According to Demetrius of Phaleron (*ap.* Plutarch *Aristides* 1, 27; *FGrH* 228 F 43, 45; Wehrli, 1949, F 95-6) Aristides was given a state funeral and buried at Phaleron, where his tomb was pointed out to later visitors, on his own land. But this information may not be reliable; a state burial in a family burial ground on private land seems strange, and Phaleron was not Aristides' deme.

After the Persian wars, archaeological evidence for funerary monuments in Attica almost entirely disappears for about fifty years, with the exception of the representations of tombs on vases. Pictures of visits to the tomb on white-ground lekythoi, from the second quarter of the fifth century onwards, show that small, steep individual mounds, often crowned with stelai, continued to be erected. One lekythos (New York, Met. Mus. 35.11.5, Vouni painter: Kurtz, 1975, pl. 26.2) shows a double mound; two others show a woman sitting between two mounds and touching both (Athens 2026, *ARV*^{2} 761/9, Tymbos painter; Athens 19354, *ARV*^{2} 1168/131 bis, painter of Munich 2335). Three of these classical mounds have been excavated, two outside the Erian Gates (Bruckner and Pernice, 1893, pp. 95-100; Grace, 1969) one in the 'Tauros' cemetery south of the city (Schilardis, 1969b, 1975). One of those outside the Erian Gates (Grace, 1969) covered three burials of the second quarter of the fifth century (A, E-F), and a further burial (B) was dug into the mound about 450 or later. The others covered single burials.

For the fifth century there is a fair amount of scattered evidence for multiple burials in the same grave (a systematic search would no doubt add to this list):

Soteriades, 1940, p. 38: in the classical cemetery at Marathon, grave 12 contained teeth of both an adult and a child.

Schilardis, 1975: in the Tauros cemetery, grave 2 (c. 425-10 BC) contained two adults of undetermined sex.

Hondius, 1921: double tomb of the late fifth century near Hagios Kosmas, containing an adult (?) below and a child above.

Alexandres, 1976, pp. 32-5, cemetery at Achilleás and Iasonos 52, on the Kolonos road: of 29 classical tombs reported, 4 contained two burials (XV, XXII, XXIV, end of the fifth century; I, early fourth century) and 1 contained three bodies (XXVI, last third of the fifth century).

ibid. 144-6, graves at Psaromelingou 6 and Kalogerou Samouel: of 20 fifth-century tombs reported, 2 (XIV, XVI) contained double burials.

Mylonas, 1975: in the West cemetery at Eleusis tomb Z 17, a sarcophagus, contained a man buried about 465-55 BC and a child buried about 430; tomb E 25 contained a woman and child buried simultaneously, about 475-50.

Freytag, 1976, pp. 35-6, 3 siblings (?) buried successively in graves 11-13, c. 430. Cf. Bingen 1967, p. 52 nos 65-7, 3 cremation pyres on the same spot in rapid succession, in the fifth century.

Some of these cases might belong to the period of the plague (on which see Thucydides ii 52), but not all; and many of those who died in the plague will have been cremated, making detection of multiple burials unlikely.

There may conceivably be an allusion to joint burial on the stele of Ampharete, which shows her holding a baby: her epitaph says, 'I hold the child of my daughter, whom I used to hold on my knees when we both saw the light of the sun: now dead, I hold him, dead too'.[30] But the reference may well be to the sculptured representation alone.

From a later period (the end of the fourth century) we have the instructions in Aristotle's will that his wife Pythias, 'according to her own wish', is to be exhumed and reburied with him (Diogenes Laertius v. 16) – a valuable warning that the circumstances underlying multiple burials may be more complex than we might otherwise imagine. (Cf. Euripides, *Alcestis* 365-8.)

Towards the latter part of the fifth century we also find the beginning of the practice of surrounding groups of graves with a stone peribolos, which was to lead to the monumental family tomb-enclosures of the fourth century.[31]

The cemetery at Thorikos seems to have been already laid out in 'terraces' at this period:[32] terrace 18 contained two tombs of c. 450 BC, one of a newborn child (Bingen, 1968, 1969). The series of monumental periboloi along the sacred way from the settlement at Rhamnous to the temple of Nemesis, currently being excavated, is thought to begin in the middle of the fifth century with a circular monument which held bases for three stone vases, probably a loutro-phoros and two lekythoi. (Pottery dated 475-50 was found nearby, but there is no firm dating evidence from within the peribolos.) It is to be hoped that these tombs, when thoroughly studied and pub-lished, will provide valuable information about the development of family tomb precincts in the fifth-fourth centuries. At present only brief reports are available (*Ergon*, 1975, 7-11; 1976, 3-8; 1977, 7-12; Petrakos, 1977, 1978, 1980). Various curved walls in the West cemetery at Eleusis were interpreted as peribolos walls, but few of them were sufficiently preserved to give a clear indication which graves they had enclosed. The best preserved was in section *I*, enclosing 16 fifth-century graves, of which only two belonged to adults (Mylonas, 1975, ii nos *I* 9-15, 17-22, 27-9). This does not look like a family group.

In the area round the city itself, Vierneisel (1964) has published a peribolos of c. 420 BC on the north side of the Sacred Way; it seems to be possible to trace a continuous evolution from mud-brick structures to stone periboloi on this site. The imposing peribolos and complex of monuments commemorating Dexileos and his family, discussed further below, was probably laid out in 394. There were periboloi in the mainly fifth-century cemetery on the site of Royal Stables excavated in the 1920s, but the excavation was never published (Kyparisses, 1925, p. 70; Karouzou, 1947/8). In a cemetery area containing burials of c. 425-390 excavated by Charitonides (1961a) several single graves were enclosed by peribolos walls, and one such wall enclosed a group of five burials, identified by the associated finds as one adult female, one adult of uncertain sex, one young male and an infant. The final burial was unidentifiable.

VI Commemorative monuments of the classical period: stress on family unity

Sculptured monuments begin again at about the time of the beginning of the Peloponnesian war; it has been suggested that this renewal may reflected an upsurge of piety towards the dead after the plague of 429/8, in reaction against the disregard of normal burial practices forced on the city during the emergency (Fuchs, 1961, pp. 241-2; Stupperich, 1977). However, the representations of elaborate tomb-markers on vases shows that the wish to set up such monuments existed well before the plague, even if the practice was rare.[33] The representations on these reliefs of the late fifth century onwards are from the beginning markedly domestic in character. Even when the dead is portrayed as a warrior, very often he is shown taking leave of a family group containing women and small children. The atmosphere of the reliefs is private and non-heroic, and the same is true of classical epitaphs.[34]

In order to understand this change it is necessary to look at the painted vases which (to some extent at least) took the place of sculptured monuments during the Pentecontaetia. (Some were placed inside the tomb, but others, to judge from the representations of tombs on the vases themselves, stood over it on a plinth or stepped mound which was often represented as crowned by a stele.)

It is difficult to be sure how far these vases, in their depiction of tombs, adhere to actual usage, and how far they represent wishful thinking. It seems plausible that one of the reasons for the popularity of representations of tombs, and of the visits of survivors to tend them, was that families which hankered after impressive grave monuments of the types forbidden by law could at least flank the tomb with vases which showed what they would have liked to do. This seems particularly likely in the cases where the vases represent statues on or beside the tomb: the life-size equestrian statue of the huge red-figure loutrophoros, Athens (ex Schliemann) – Berlin 3209 (Plate IIa, c. 440-20; Bakalakis, 1971), and the two miniature Polykleitan athlete figures on the white-ground lekythos, Boston Museum of Fine Arts 01. 8080 (Kurtz, 1975, pl. 31.1, shortly after 450; cf. pl. 36.3, Athens 1938). The tall, narrow shape of the vases used for this purpose, lekythoi and loutrophoroi, would encourage painters to exaggerate the height of mounds and stelai. Nevertheless, a painted representative of a monument was not the same thing as the monument itself. It did not draw the attention of the passer-by in the same way; it would scarcely be noticed except by those who already belonged to the circle of the dead's kin and friends – and it is, I believe, with the substitution of painted vases for monumental sculpture that the radius of those whose attention is claimed by the tomb narrows to this circle.

To some extent, therefore, the tomb-vases are already much closer in spirit to the sculptured monuments of the late fifth and fourth centuries than to those of the period before the Persian wars. This is confirmed by some coincidence in themes: for instance, the white-ground lekythos Berlin (W.) Staat. Mus. 2443 (Plate I*b*, c. 450) shows a seated woman and a nurse holding a child. The latter theme occurs again in the third quarter of the century on B.M. 1007.7-10.10; and a small child is commemorated, embarking in Charon's boat with his go-cart, on New York, Met. Mus. 09. 221. 44, a little later. Very similar scenes and figures can be found on relief stelai.[35]

There are, however, differences between the painted funerary vases and the later sculptured monuments. The vases give a much more central position to the dead, and very often (though not invariably) recognise the fact of death much more openly than the reliefs (Thimme, 1964). They show *prothesis* themes (but not funeral processions); they occasionally show (sometimes in mythical dress) the moment of burial.[36] They convey the sense of a personal relationship between the dead and the mourner (or mourners: but often there is only one) who comes to care for the tomb. One may be reminded of the recurrent theme of offerings to Agamemnon's tomb in the Electra tragedies, and of Antigone's insistence on burying Polynices. At the same time, however, the vases clearly *separate* the dead from the living. In the pictures showing visits to the tomb, there is very seldom any ambiguity about the identity of the dead, when he or she is repre-sented. To some extent at least the lekythos is conceived as a communication addressed *to* the dead rather than a statement *about* him or her: a statement about the grief which this death has caused, a reassurance to the dead that he is not forgotten. It is in keeping with the double function of these vase-paintings, as statements both about the continuing communication between the living and the dead and about the care shown by the living to commemorate the dead, that in some of them it is not clear whether the painter is representing a sculptured monument or a memory-image of the dead (Plates I*a*, c, II*a*).

Relief sculptures, on the contrary, rarely include funerary monu-ments in their figured scenes. The dead is shown as if still alive, and very often as a member of a united family group. (Such representa-tions are rare on vases: Athens 1762, Riezler, 1914, pl. 66, *ARV*[2] 1241, shows the dead boy standing in front of his tomb with his father and mother on either side of it.) It is difficult in many cases to decide which of the persons represented is the one who has died (cf. Clairmont, 1970, pp. 55-71). This ambiguity is partly due to the fact that many relief monuments would stand on the façade of a peribolos intended eventually to contain the tombs of all those depicted in the relief. The tombstone of Dionysios of Oenoe was set up to commemorate 'of those before', his father and uncle (*theios*, FB?), *and* 'those portrayed in the picture' - Dionysios and other living members of his family (*IG* ii² 6971; Clairmont no. 67, beginning of the fourth century). Kirchner thought that many of the stelai which list several members of the same family in a single hand were set up when the first member of the group died (*ad IG* ii² 5235). [37]

However, this concern to provide for future burials (or in some cases to commemorate those of the past) is not the only reason for the stress on family unity in the tomb reliefs of the late fifth and fourth centuries. These representations and inscriptions, and the peribolos frame which surrounded them - which rapidly took on more elaborate architectural forms - gave monumental expression to the images of domestic life which had developed earlier in the more intimate art of vase-painting.[38] (In the fourth century, similarly, New Comedy made a major dramatic genre out of the family intrigues previously presented to the Athenian public in the sketchy narratives of courtroom speeches). The achievements and virtues commemorated in epitaphs are now, in the great majority of cases, those of family life.

A new phenomenon in the inscriptions of this period, in complete contrast to those of the sixth century, is the celebration of longevity.

The well-known relief of Ampharete and her grandson, c. 410 (*IG* ii² 10650), has already been mentioned. *IG* ii² 6288 (Clairmont no. 26) and 11998 (Peek, 1955 (*GVI*) 499) both commemorate grandmothers also, as does *IG* ii² 5673 (set up by the woman's sister, who intends to be buried with her in due course). Lysimache, priestess of Athena Polias for 64 years in the late-fifth-early fourth centuries, died when over 80 (or over 90) and had lived to see four generations (*genē*) of descendants (*IG* ii² 3453; *APF* no. 4549.) A tomb enclosure at Rhamnous held the remains of Euphranor son of Euphron of Rhamnous, who lived to the age of 105, with his two sons, daughter, grandson (SS), a female relative [39] and another woman, probably wife of a son (*Ergon*, 1975, pp. 7-9; Petrakos, 1977, pp. 6-11, with pl. 3; *SEG* xxvi. 302). Another fourth-century monument commemorates a man who lived to be 100 (Davaras, 1967; Clairmont no. 55 bis; *SEG* xxiv 256); *IG* ii² 5452, a man of 90 (Clairmont no. 58); Pantos (1974) publishes the epitaph of a 90-year-old woman, buried by her daughter; *IG* ii² p. 879, 5421a (Clairmont no. 65) commemorates a grandfather; *IG* ii² 13098 (Clairmont no. 72) a man of 70.

Sophrosynē is already a virtue commemorated by stelai of the second

half of the sixth century, but a civic virtue, of men; by the late fifth
century it extends also to women and children, and has begun to take
on some of the tone of the modern Greek *phronimos* (North, 1966,
pp. 13-14, 252-3). The late fifth-century epitaph of Aristylla, daughter
of Ariston and Rhodile (*IG* i² 1058 = i³ 1311, c. 430; Clairmont no.
27, Pfohl no. 113) ends with a direct address to her, σωφρῶν γ' ὦ
θύγατερ' – 'what a good girl you were! Dionysia is praised by her
husband Antiphilos for loving him and *sophrosyne* more than clothes
and jewellery (*IG* ii² 11162, *GVI* 1810; after 350). Another wife is
praised as hard-working and thrifty (*ergatis kai pheidolos*; Nikarete, *IG*
ii² 12254, *GVI* 328, before 350).[40]

Sixth-century grave monuments set up to children by their mourning
parents represent those of their qualities that even a stranger could
admire: beauty, courage, the flowering of youth. Fourth-century
memorials are more intimate. The tombstone of the young boy Philostratos, son of Philoxenos, tells us that he was named after his father's
father and that his parents nicknamed him 'chatterbox' (Neollarion;
IG ii² 12974, Clairmont no. 17, *GVI* 1499, after 350). As in relief
sculptures such as that of Mnesagora and Nikochares, c. 420 (*IG* ii²
12147, Pfohl no. 117, Conze, 1893, no. 887, Stupperich, 1977, no. 158)
and in the funerary lekythoi of the later fifth century (e.g. Athens
1936, Riezler, 1914, pl. 77, *ARV*² 1239; Athens 12771, Riezler pl. 3,
*ARV*² 743), so too in inscriptions there is a new attempt to present
toddlers with the characteristics of their age, instead of portraying them
as miniature adults.[41] Neollarion was a 'comfort and delight'
(*paramythion*) to his parents. The reality of the loss brought to the
family by death is made vivid by detailed information. The epitaph of
Xenokleia (*IG* ii² 12335, *GVI* 1985, c. 360) tells us not only that she
died of grief for the death of her 8-year-old son at sea, but also that she
left two daughters not yet married. Kratista, daughter of Damainetas
and wife of Archemachos, died in childbirth and left her husband with
an orphan child (*IG* ii² 11907, *GVI* 548, after 350).[42] Telemachos, son
of Spoudokrates, of Phlya, is remembered by all his fellow-citizens for
his virtue and sadly missed by his children and wife; he lies buried
beside his mother, maintaining his devotion to her even in death (*IG* ii²
7711, *GVI* 1386, 390-60). A husband addresses his buried wife and is
answered by her, 'Greetings, and kiss my family for me' (*IG* ii² 12067,
Clairmont no. 39, *GVI* 1387).

With the exception of the monuments to the very old, verse epitaphs
and reliefs do not emphasise the continuity of a lineage over time;

Table 1   *Peribolos of Meidon of Myrrhinous (SEG xxiii 161 + 137-8, 155-8, 160, 166; on 137 see further SEG xxv 258)*

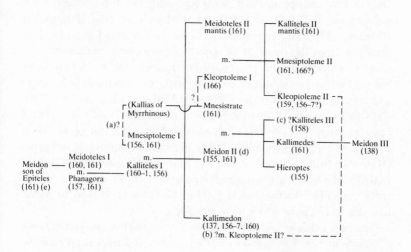

(a)   The linked names Mnesiptoleme, Kleoptoleme, Mnesistrate, suggest that all three women came from the same family. The simplest assumption is that Kallias, father of Mnesistrate (and of Kleoptoleme I?) was the brother of Mnesiptoleme, with two *epikleroi* daughters claimed by their cousins (FZS) as next-of-kin.

(b)   Kallimedon is represented on 137 as a youth, but his epitaph mentions *hymenaia* and he was not commemorated by a loutrophoros, so it appears that he died soon after marrying. He appears on relief lekythoi with

    (i)   Kalliteles (F) and Meidoteles (FF or B): *SEG* xxiii 160
    (ii) Phanagora (FM) and Kleoptoleme: 157
    (iii) Kalliteles (F), Mnesiptoleme (M) and Kleoptoleme: 156

It seems quite possible that he married his niece (BD) Kleoptoleme II, and that it is she rather than her mother who figures on these lekythoi. (If so, the 12-year-old daughter of Meidoteles II and Kleoptoleme I commemorated on no. 166 cannot be she, but may be Mnesiptoleme II). On the other hand, since Kleoptoleme I is not named on no. 161, she presumably outlived all those listed there, and may have played a very active part in organising the peribolos monuments.

(c)   No. 158 represents a small boy with bird and ball, called Kalliteles. I have suggested that he may be a first son of Meidon II (named according to convention after his father's father) who died in childhood; but obviously no certainty on this point is possible.

(d)   Probably the councillor Meidon of Myrrhinous of ? 336/5 BC Charitonides, 1961 b, line 174.

(e)   A funerary stele of Meidon, son of Epiteles of Myrrhinous, was published by N. Kotzias in *Ethnos* 20 July, 1948 (quoted by Charitonidea, 1961b), but dated 'fourth to third centuries BC'; it is not clear whether this can belong to Meidon I or must be attributed to a later descendant not recorded elsewhere.

they portray the intimate relationships of the nuclear family in an idealised, timeless present. Piety to dead ancestors is not their theme. Only a few inscriptions and periboloi contradict this impression. A stele of the first half of the fourth century from near Markopoulo (Etienne, 1975) lists in a single hand the names of a father, son and grandson from the deme of Oē and of four women, presumably the wives of these three and of a fourth male member of the family, who has set up this monument to commemorate his ancestors and his wife, and intends that his own name shall be added to it when he dies. *IG* ii^2 6218 lists members of three generations of a single family in the same hand, and may have been set up by the daughter in the third generation.

An even more remarkable stele was found in a peribolos at Myrrhinous (Merenda), listing 11 members of the same family, spanning six generations.[43] The peribolos contained monuments to 17 members of the family in all (see further below p. 117 and Table 1). It must be noted that this was a family of religious specialists.

The only other group of comparable size is attested, less precisely, in a literary source. The speaker of [Dem.] xliii, who takes great pains to present himself as a member of an *oikos* of impeccable solidarity and piety towards the dead (Thompson, 1976), claims that the descendants of Bouselos, his great-great-grandfather (MFFF, also MMPaFF), shared a common burial ground ([Dem.] xliii 79). According to the information given in Isaeus xi and [Dem.] xliii, this burial place might have contained at the time of the latter speech up to 22 members of the family (not counting those who died before producing offspring) spanning four generations. Probably the number was smaller, but the speaker's boasts of family solidarity are to some extent supported by the range of kin who agreed to come and act as his witnesses on genealogical matters (cf. *APF*, Table 1, no. 2921).[44] This solidarity, and the genealogical knowledge which went with it, had no doubt been encouraged by the lawsuits over the estate of Hagnias with which the two speeches are connected: the estate was large and all those who considered they might have a claim to it kept a close and watchful eye on each other. It was also fostered by intermarriage (five cases of cousin marriage in the group, Thompson, 1967) as was also the case, I have suggested, in the family of Meidon of Myrrhinous. There is also, however, some sign of interest in traditional religion among the descendants of Bouselos. One of his grandsons (SS) had held the office of *basileus*, making him for a year the head of the Athenian state in all religious matters, and the fact was remembered with pride ([Dem.] xliii 42-3).

But both archaeological and epigraphic evidence suggest that groups of this size were unusual. Many periboloi enclosed only two or three graves, or at most half a dozen.[45] The fourth-century mound of Eukoline in the Kerameikos held only four or five (Schlorb-Vierneisel, 1966, pp. 77-8). Inscriptions tell the same story. A count of the family relationships attested on c. 600 fourth-century tombstones shows that only a small proportion commemorated more than one to four individuals. It is true that some memorials to individuals or small groups may have stood originally in family enclosures holding the graves of a wider family circle;[46] few were found *in situ*, so there is no means of telling how many. But the classical cemeteries so far excavated show that large monumental periboloi were the exception rather than the rule.

A count of c. 600 fourth-century funerary inscriptions of Athenian citizens, giving deme affiliations, from *IG* ii^2, gave the following results. The majority of tombstones were set up to single individuals,[47] 234 to men and 102 to women. 88 tombstones commemorate a husband and wife together (contrast the complete absence of memorials of this category in sixth-century Attica). Husband and wife with a child or children account for 50 definite cases, and 15 more stones are probably to be so interpreted. 34 stones commemorate a father with a child or children (plus 15 doubtful cases); 7 stones (plus 5 doubtful cases) a mother with a child or children. Twelve stones (plus 4 doubtful cases) commemorate pairs of siblings.[48] Thirty-seven inscriptions record larger groups which will be analysed further below; these include stones found too recently to have been included in the *IG* sample. These inscriptions, the only ones which group together persons who were not at some stage in their lives members of the same nuclear family, thus represent well under 5 per cent of the total of fourth-century Attic grave monuments.

Apart from the joint burials of siblings already recorded, six inscriptions commemorate a set of siblings together with one or more spouses: two brothers and the wife of one on *IG* ii^2 5970 (different hands) and 6551 (in the latter case with an epigram for the wife, and the name of a second woman, perhaps daughter of the married couple, added later); a brother and sister with the brother's wife on *IG* ii^2 6476 (one hand); a brother and sister with (presumably) the spouses of both *IG* ii^2 6216 (one hand); probably a brother and sister with the sister's husband on *IG* ii^2 5479 and

5712 (Agora 81, different hands). Further relatives of the sibling
pair commemorated on ii^2 5479 (found at Sepolia near the
Academy) were buried on Salamis (*APF* no. 4719). *IG* ii^2 5753
commemorates two brothers and a sister with (probably) the spouses
of one brother and the sister; the names of two other women were
added later (Peek, 1942, no. 365). These cases are interesting
because they show one partner in a marriage being separated in
burial from his or her family of origin in order that the other partner
can maintain both the close bond of siblingship and the marriage tie.
Of course it is more common for a woman to be buried with the
family of her husband than for a man to be buried with the kin of
his wife, but the latter situation does occur.[49]

Other stones group together the offspring of siblings: cousins,
or uncles and aunts with nephews and nieces. *IG* ii^2 5768 [50] commemorates Stratonides, son of Eudoros, of Aphidna with Eudemos,
son of Euphanes, of Aphidna, who died as a child – perhaps a
brother's son who died while under his uncle's guardianship. *IG* ii^2
5676-8, found in a group in the Kerameikos, commemorated
Olympiodorus, son of Olympichos, of Anaphlystos with his wife and
son (Olympichos II) and his brother's son (Olympichos III, son of
Nautes). Olympiodoros had two brothers, apparently buried elsewhere, and probably a second son (*APF* no. 13905). *IG* ii^2 6006
commemorates Kallistratos, son of Kallistratides, of Rhamnous with
his wife and son and Kallistrate, daughter of Menedemos of
Rhamnous – probably Kallistratos' brother's daughter. *IG* ii^2 6346
(one hand) was set up for the brothers Antisthenes and Androkles
II, sons of Androkles I, of Kephale, with Phanostrate, wife of
either Androkles I or Androkles II, and Antisthenes, son of
Alkisthenes, of Kephale who must have been a first cousin (FBS) of
his homonym. *IG* ii^2 5533, with 5541 and 5579, all found at
Trachones, were set up for Aristion, son of Peithias, of Halimous,
his wife and (probably) his mother; on ii^2 5533 the name of his
cousin Aristion, son of Perichares, of Halimous was added later. *IG*
ii^2 5954 again commemorates two homonymous cousins (FBS),
Philonides, son of Aischylides, and Philonides, son of Philokrates,
both of Gargettos, plus a third man   ]on, son of Architekton,
of Thorikos. *IG* ii^2 7319 commemorates Sotairos, son of Sokrates,
of Prospalta and Sotairos, son of Deinon, of Piraeus: one is probably
mother's brother's son to the other, named after his maternal grandfather.[51] *IG* ii^2 5501-4, all found at Brauron, commemorate
Mnesarchos, son of Mnesippos I of Halai Araphenides (5502) with
his two sons, Mnesippos II (5504) and Mnesarchides (5501), plus
Mnesippos III, son of Mnesagoras (the latter presumably a brother of
Mnesarchos), with his wife (5503), and Mnesippos IV, son of
Charitaios of Halai, who is commemorated together with
Mnesarchides (5501) and was perhaps his father's sister's son.[52]
IG ii^2 6097, from Liopesi, commemorates Apolexis, son of Euaion

of Erchia (also named on *IG* ii² 6109), with his son Eualkides and with Eualkos, son of Eualkos, of Erchia, who was probably the nephew (BS) of either Euaion or Apolexis. Delias, daughter of Nikias of Kydathenaion (*APF* no. 10807), also named, was presumably the wife of one of these men. Eualkides' son Phrasisthenes was buried with (presumably) his wife, Aristokrateia, at Spata (*IG* ii² 6135). [53]

Table 2 *Peribolos of Hierokles of Rhamnous*

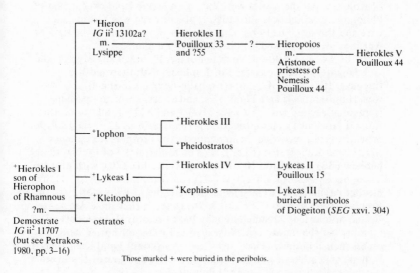

Those marked + were buried in the peribolos.

Of the seventeen three-generation groupings I have been able to find,[54] three record a single line of descent with only one person or one married couple in each generation: *IG* ii² 10650, Ampharete and her grandson (DS), with a gap in the intervening generation; *Ergon* 1975, pp. 9-11 (cf. also 1976, p. 3; Petrakos, 1977, pp. 15-25 *SEG* xxvi 300); Diogeiton and his wife (?) Habro, their son Lysimachos with his wife (?) Choronike, and the latter's son Lysistratos. A number of other persons, including Lykias, son of Kephisios, of the family set out above in Table 2, were later buried in the same peribolos; their relation to the foregoing group is unknown. *IG* ii² 6929, from Piraeus, has the names (in a single hand) of Epigenes, son of Diaitos, of Xypete, his son Nikippos, and Nikippos' daughter Praxo. *IG* ii² 5943, 10607 and 12865, all found at Tatoi, and dated in the first half of the fourth century, commemorate Phanias of Dekeleia with his wife Philoumene I (12865), their son Nikodemos with his son Phanodemos and (in a later hand) his wife, daughter of Aeschines of ? Phegous (5983), a second son, Anenkletos, who died unmarried (5980) and a daughter, Philoumene II, who may have died in child-birth since she is represented with her mother and an infant (10607).

Four stones, or groups of stones, record a sibling group with their parents and spouses and the children of one sibling. *IG* ii² 7717-18 (Piraeus, before 360) commemorate a brother and sister, Antimachos and Pausilla, with their father Antibios of Phrearrhioi, Glyke, daughter of Aischines of Erchia (presumably wife of Antibios)[55] Antimachos' son Theodoros, and Philoumene, daughter of Batrachos, of Kolonos. All the names were cut by the same hand except that of Philoumene, which was added later; possibly she was Theodoros' wife and the stone had originally been set up, perhaps at the time of Antibios' death, when Theodoros was still unmarried.

IG ii² 6417 (c. 390-65) commemorates Philiskos and Myrto, son and daughter of Hippokrates I of Kephisia, with their mother Eupaleia, Heragoras of Samos (probably Myrto's husband), his two sons Hippokrates II and Thrasyllos, and another woman, perhaps Heragoras' second wife.[56] *IG* ii² 6100-1 and 6120-1, all found near Liopesi (ancient Paiania), together perhaps with 6122-3, the findspot of which is not recorded, commemorate the brothers Kalliphanes (6123) and Kallistratos (6122), sons of Kallikrates I of Erchia, their nephew (BS) Kallikrates II, son of Antikrates I (6120), with his son Theophilos (6120); Kallikrates' elder son Antikrates II (6100-1), his mother Archestrate (6100-1) and Aristaichme, daughter of Lysis of Erchia (6100). Davies (*APF* no. 9576) suggests that since Antikrates II died unmarried, Aristaichme may have been his fiancée. Several members of the family otherwise attested were not buried here, unless their monuments have been lost: Antikrates I and Kallisthenes, fathers of Kallikrates II and Kallikrates III; Kallikrates II's brother Aristaios; Kallistratos I's son (?) Polykleides.

IG ii² 6218 (after 350) commemorates Demochares, Hedyle and Nikostrate, children of Attabos, of Thorikos, with Charmides and Sosigenes, sons of Euthippos, of Thorikos, Paramythos, son of Stephanos, of Aphidna, and Paramythos' daughter Myrte. Since the relatively uncommon name Paramythos is attested later on in Thorikos, Kirchner suggests that Myrte was Demochares' wife. Probably one of the sons of Euthippos was married to one of Demochares' sisters. All names were incised by a single hand: Kirchner comments, 'Ex ratione, qua nomina recensentur, *sc.* eo ordine, quo singuli huius familiae cognati et agnati e vita abierunt, colligitur hoc monumentum post maiorum discessum ab uno ex posteris animo pio dicatum esse.'

IG ii² 5374, 5376, 5378 and 5379 commemorate Pamphilos and Archippe, children of Meixiades, of Aigilia (5374), Archippe with her husband Prokleides, son of Sostratos, of Aigilia and their son Prokles (5376; the name of Prokleides, son of Pamphilos, apparently named after his mother's brother, was added later), Prokleides' parents Sostratos and Praxagora (5378) and Sostratos again, with Prokleides (5379). Pamphilos and his son have been drawn into the circle of Archippe's affines: the earlier age of marriage of women made this probably a not uncommon occurrence.[57]

Three groups of monuments record a set of siblings with the descendants of one of them. *IG* ii^2 6212 (c. 350) commemorates Demetria and Demophilos, children of Demetrios of Thorai, with Demophilos' son Demetrios II, Demetrios II's son Boulis, and Protonoe, probably his mother. The order in which the names were engraved is problematic.

IG ii^2 6217, 6226-7 and 6230, found together in the Kerameikos in the tomb enclosure dominated by the monument of the cavalry-man Dexileos of Thorikos (d. 394) commemorate Dexileos (6217), his brother Lysias (6227), his sister Melitta with her husband (6230) and Lysias' son Lysanias II with his wife and son (6226). Another brother, Lysistratos, with a son Lysanias III, are known to have existed but were apparently buried elsewhere. Presumably it was Lysias who was responsible for the funerary enclosure – which did not contain the remains of Dexileos, interred in the public grave of those who fell at Corinth (*IG* ii^2 5222; Tod, 1948, no. 104, cf. 105; Vermeule, 1970). ii^2 7257 and 7263, found together in the Kera-meikos, commemorate Euphrosyne and Eubios, children of Phainippos of Potamos, with Eubios' sons Bion and Archias, Archias' wife Dexikleia, daughter of Philon of Oion, and their son Archikles. 7263 has the names of Euphrosyne, Eubios and Bion in one hand, with those of Archias and Dexikleia added later; 7257 commemo-rates Bion, who died unmarried, with his nephew Archikles (BS). Archias (I), son of Eubios (II) (*IG* ii^2 488.5), crowned in 304/3, was presumably the son of a brother of Archikles named Eubios after his paternal grandfather but not commemorated in this group.

Four more three-generation groupings remain to be considered. The centenarian Euphranor of Rhamnous, mentioned above, was buried with two sons and a daughter, a grandson (SS), a female relative and another woman whose relation to the group is unclear (*Ergon*, 1975, pp. 7-9; Petrakos, 1977, pp. 6-11; see n. 39). In the largest peribolos so far excavated at Rhamnous Hierokles I, son of Hierophon, of Rhamnous was buried with his sons Hieron, Iophon, Lykeas I and Kleitophon, another son] ostratos,[58] Iophon's two sons Hierokles III and Pheidostratos, and Lykeas' two sons Hierokles IV and Kephisios. Lykeas III, probably a grandson of Lykeas I, was buried not in his own family's peribolos but in that of Diogeiton. Lysippe, wife of Hieron, was buried with her husband (*IG* ii^2 13102a), and so probably was Demostra[te], wife of Hierokles (*IG* ii^2 11707) (see Table 2).

A stele from Koropi (Kotzias, 1948, no. 2) commemorates Philokedes I, son of Amoibichos I; his sons Amoibichos II and Aresias; Amoibichos III, son of Gorgythos, probably a cousin (FBS) of Amoibichos II; Philokedes II, son of Amoibichos II; Diopeithes, son of Amoibichos II or III; and two women, probably spouses.

IG ii² 7528 and 7501 were set up at Ambelokipi, inscribed by the same hand, to commemorate Timotheos, son of Agasikles of Sphettos and his father (or son?) Agasikles, son of Timotheos. At a later date the names of Timesios, son of Timotheos, Archedike, daughter of Chairileos, of Aithalidai (Timotheos' wife?), and Lykiskos, son of Diodotos, of Epikephisia (son of a sister or daughter of Timotheos?) were added to Timotheos' stele (7528).

IG ii² 6008, from the Kerameikos, commemorates Koroibos I, son of Kleidemides I, of Melite, his son Kleidemides II, Kleidemides II's son Koroibos II, and Euthydemos, son of Sosikles I, of Eitea, with his son Sosikles II. Each name is inscribed in a different hand. If Euthydemos and Sosikles II are related to the descendants of Kleidemides I, Euthydemos probably married a sister of Kleidemides II. The wife of Koroibos I was Hegeso, daughter of Proxenos, also commemorated in the Kerameikos, by a very well-known relief of the late fifth century (*IG* ii² 1079, N.M.A. 3624, Conze (1893-1922), no. 68; cf. *APF* no. 12267, VI*c*). Kleidemos, son of Kleidemides (probably Kleidemides II), died unmarried and was commemorated by a loutrophoros also found in the Kerameikos and presumably originally sited in the same family plot (*IG* ii² 6859). But Aristomache, daughter of a Kleidemides of Melite, very likely either Kleidemides I or Kleidemides II, who married Philochoros, son of Demonikos, of Melite, was buried with her husband at Liopesi (*IG* ii² 6832).

In four cases four-generation groupings are recorded. One comes from a literary source: Plutarch (*Moralia* 838b-c; cf. *APF* no. 7716) tells us that Isocrates was buried in Kynosarges with his father and mother, his mother's sister Nako and her son Sokrates, his brother Theodoros, his wife Plathane, his adopted son Aphareus, and Aphareus' two sons (see Tuplin, 1980). This was of course an exceptional case; Isocrates was a famous man, his monument (a pillar 30 cubits high with a 7-cubit siren on top, according to Plutarch) was conspicuous; there were good reasons for his kin to wish to share in his lustre. However, it should be noted that Isocrates had two further brothers and a sister, who were evidently buried elsewhere.

A stele found recently near Markopoulo (Etienne, 1975) commemorates the son, grandson (SS) and great grandson (SSS) of Themyllos of Oe (Themyllos II, Antiphanes and Themon), with their wives and Archestrate, daughter of Meletos of Angele. All the names are inscribed by the same hand, and it seems likely that the stone was set up by a son (or brother?) of Themon to mark the graves of his ancestors and his wife (Archestrate).

IG ii² 5432-3, 5408 and 5450 were found together in Piraeus (see Table 3 and *APF* no. 8065). 5450 commemorates Philon I, son of Kallippos I, of Aixone with his wife Phanagora, with

Alkimache, daughter of Kallimachos of Anagyrous, whose relationship to them is unclear, and with Philon's daughter Philostrate. 5433
commemorates Philon I's sons Kallippos II and Philostratos, with
Kallippos II's sons Philon II and Proxenos. (Kallippos II was also
commemorated alone on 5432.) 5408 names Hedyline, daughter of
Philon (I or II), with Aristagora, perhaps her mother. Philon I was
probably also the father of the Philokrates son of Philon of Aixone
who was buried at Vari (*IG* ii^2 5448).

IG ii^2 6746, 6719, 6722-3, 7400 and (?) 5434, all from the
Kerameikos, marked the graves of a family into which Hipparete,
granddaughter (SD) of the notorious Alcibiades, married (Table 4;
APF no. 600, p. 21). 7400 names Hipparete with her husband
Phanokles of Leukonoe and Kritolea daughter of Phanokles of
Kettos, probably his mother. 6746 names Phanokles alone. 6719 and
6723 commemorate the sons of Phanokles and Hipparete, Alkibiades
and Aristion; 6722 commemorates a son of Aristion, probably the
Phanokles commemorated on 5434 with his wife Kleo daughter of
Kleon of Aixone.

Finally, a very impressive group of monuments, already mentioned (cf. Table 1), commemorated Meidon I, son of Epiteles, of
Myrrhinous and five generations of descendants: his son Meidoteles I
with his wife Phanagora, their son Kalliteles I and his wife
Mnesiptoleme I; three sons of Kalliteles I, Meidoteles II, Meidon II
with his wife Mnesistrate, and Kallimedon; three children of
Meidoteles II, Kalliteles II who followed his father in the profession
of *mantis* (seer), and his sisters Mnesiptoleme II and Kleoptoleme II;
two sons of Meidon II, Kallimedes and Hieroptes; and finally, in the
last generation, Kallimedes' son Meidon III (who died unmarried).
A single stele lists the names of Meidon I, Meidoteles I, Phanagora,
Kalliteles I, Mnesiptoleme I, Meidon II, Mnesistrate, Meidoteles II,
Kalliteles II (with a commemorative epigram), Kallimedes and
Mnesiptoleme II. It may have been set up by Kalliteles I.[59]

The monuments in the peribolos of Meidon certainly constitute a
remarkable testimony of family piety and continuity. But it is clear
that the family was an unusual one. Two of its members were religious
specialists, while a third bore the rare name Hieroptes (Sacrificer; cf.
Curtius, 1894, p. 524). There was probably a good deal of intermarriage
within the group. They represent very well the ideal pattern which
Athenian speakers had in mind when trying to present themselves to a
jury as models of familial piety – but they do not represent the typical
Athenian family. Still less do they testify to an unbroken tradition of
patrilineal tomb groupings stretching back into the mists of time. They
represent, instead, fourth-century traditionalism – a very different
phenomenon, which was neither widespread nor long-lived.[60]

Table 3 *Peribolos of Philon of Aixone (IG ii² 5408, 5432-3, 5450; APF 8065)*

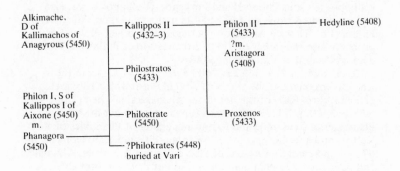

Table 4 *Peribolos of Phanokles and Hipparete (IG ii² 6719, 6722-3, 6746, 7400 and ? 5434; APF 600)*

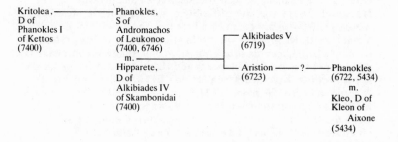

VII Post-classical commemoration

Only a very brief indication can be given here of the forms taken by familial piety in the post-classical age. But it is important to note a few key points. In the first place, the commissioning of elaborate sculptured tomb-monuments came to an abrupt end not long after the erection of the latest monument in the peribolos of Meidon; this type of ostentation was forbidden by the sumptuary legislation of Demetrius of Phaleron.

Demetrius was a philosopher and his legislation on tomb-monuments, besides following in the footsteps of Solon, followed a philosophical tradition of lack of concern with the practical aspects of burial which went back at least to Socrates (cf. also Plato *Laws* 958c-960b). Nevertheless, the philosophers were by no means opposed to all forms of commemoration. Much of our evidence for regular commemorative meetings by the family and friends of the deceased comes from Diogenes Laertius' collection of philosophers' wills, as has been indicated above.

This brings me to my second point: the ideal of perpetual commemoration elaborated in the fourth-century ideology of the pious *oikos* could well be felt to demand something more than the artistic representation of family solidarity. There is, indeed, an implicit contradiction in the use of a tomb-monument, which communicates its message to the world at large, to make statements about the unity of the domestic family group and its continuing concern for the dead.

The deceased might well no longer feel content with a monument which by recording his deeds and virtues assured him of a place in the memory of the community; he might want to continue to have a place in the smaller society of his own family and friends, which was coming to mean more to most Greeks than the *polis* as a whole. Hence the commemorative meetings of philosophers – and hence the practice which grows up from the late fourth century onwards of leaving capital to endow a fund which would pay for periodic commemorations in perpetuity. Like the familial monuments of fourth-century Athens, these foundations are a new development and not a continuation of traditional practices. The founders of such institutions, as Kamps (1937) pointed out, were not concerned with ensuring the continuity of a family line, 'perpetuating the *oikos*', but with securing perpetual ritual attention for themselves personally. No religious beliefs of the kind postulated by Fustel restricted participation in such rites to agnates.

Poseidonios of Halicarnassos (*SIG*[3] 1044, Sokolowski, 1955, no. 72, third century BC), endowing an association for the worship of Apollo, the Mother of the Gods, Zeus Patrōios, the Fates, the Agathos Daimon of himself and his wife and the Agathē Tychē of his father and mother, specifically states that the husbands of female descendants may be eligible to hold office. Epikteta of Thera (*IG* xii 3.330, Dareste, Haussoullier and Reinach, 1898, ii 1. pp. 77ff., c. 200 BC) endows a perpetual cult to herself, her husband Phoenix and their two sons; the association responsible includes not only their descendants, male and female, but also her *kyrios* Hyperides, son of Thrasyleon, with his two sisters, her father

Grinnos, his adopted son Antisthenes, and Antisthenes' family of
origin (who were probably kin to Grinnos and Epikteta).[61] It is only
a small step further – a natural step for the philosophers, for whom
friends to a considerable extent took the place of kin – when
Epicurus in 270 BC (Diogenes Laertius x 16 ff.) makes his heirs
Amynomachos of Bate and Timocrates of Potamos responsible for
commemorative sacrifices to Epicurus' parents and brothers and rites
in memory of Epicurus himself, Metrodorus and Polyaenus.[62]

It might seem, so far, that the history of the commemoration of the
dead in Athens is one of a progressive narrowing of the circle involved,
from the outward-looking monuments of the archaic age, addressed to
the community as a whole and to the passing stranger, to the intimate
groups of kin and friends provided for by the foundations of the
Hellenistic period. But the foundation technique was soon used also to
provide funds for larger groups.[63] Even among the philosophers, Lykon
(third century BC: Diogenes Laertius v 69 ff.) left an olive grove in
Aegina to be used to supply oil annually for anointing the *neoi* in his
memory. Such bequests became common practice among the class who
liked to be hailed as 'benefactors' of their *polis*, the scope of participation in the commemorative distributions limited only by the funds
available to pay for it. The very rich were never content for long with
purely private forms of commemoration.

VIII Conclusion

There are certainly many more fourth-century family tomb plots to be
discovered in Athens and the Attic countryside – like those currently
being excavated at Rhamnous – but it is unlikely that new discoveries
will radically change the picture which emerges from the evidence
available now. Really large, extensive groupings were unusual. Several
tomb enclosures were designed to hold no more than two or three
graves. Groupings of six to ten are not uncommon in excavated
enclosures or on inscriptions; larger groups are unusual. In some cases
we can see special circumstances which may have encouraged a family
to keep together: litigation in the case of the Bouselidai, the religious
interests of the 'Meidonidai' (to coin a name), pride in descent from the
famous Alcibiades, perhaps, in the case of Hipparete's family, the
longevity of Euphranor of Rhamnous. More excavation in the Attic
countryside may reveal further cases of continuity over several generations among the local squirearchy. But limits to this continuity were set

by the disruption of life in the country during the Peloponnesian war, the gap in tomb markers between the sumptuary laws of c. 510-480 and the revival of stone monuments during the last third of the fifth century – which not only deprives the historian of evidence for continuity but also made it more difficult for the Athenians themselves to keep track of their family tombs – and the mobility, both spatial and social, of Athenian society. The very concept of a 'squirearchy' can only be used with the greatest caution. A family wealthy enough to put up an elaborate series of grave monuments in the local deme was very likely also to have some of its male or female members living in the city, who might also be buried there. Every Athenian was asked before taking office (Kahrstedt, 1936, p. 59; *Athenaion Politieia* 55. 2-3) where 'his tombs' (*ēria*) were, but it is by no means certain that he had to locate the tombs of all the ancestors whose names he had to state (father and grandfathers); the location of the tomb of a single lineal ancestor (F or FF) may have been enough. It is conceivable that in the period of Cleisthenes' reforms landowning aristocrats who had been registered in city demes took a pride in making public their ancestral links with a particular rural area in this way; but by the fourth century everyone had ancestral tombs just as everyone had an altar of Zeus Herkeios.

This is one of the most significant factors in the history of the commemoration of the dead in Attica. Commemoration in the archaic period was sharply stratified: mounds and sculptured monuments, like ostentatious funerals, loudly proclaimed that the dead belonged to the elite. Paying visits to the tombs of famous ancestors was not a pious duty, but a way of reminding contemporaries of the glory of one's own family. It was the state funerals for war dead which first brought the honours of heroic burial within the range of every Athenian citizen, and I would suggest that it was this significant change which stimulated the development in the late fifth and fourth centuries of monuments commemorating the domestic virtues of the ordinary citizen. Far from being gradually destroyed by the growth of the state, as Fustel thought, the idea of a visible tomb for every man and the 'continuity' of all *oikoi* may have been generated by it.

Fustel's idea of a traditional practice of commemorative cult at family tombs, as the basis of a group solidarity which was gradually sapped by the growth of the state, bears little relation to the complex picture which is now beginning to emerge. At all periods there is a dialectical interaction between the expression of the feelings of the bereaved, the socially accepted channels and the material resources available for this expression, the standards of ostentation felt appropriate by different classes, and the other functions which such ostentation accumulated. Emphasis shifts, from period to period and from one class or occupational group to another, between the funeral ceremony, the monument and the commemorative feast, [64] and between the opposing poles of intimate remembrance and permanent commemoration – the private and public faces of death.

Notes

1   Ariès (1977), ch. 11. Discussions of this problem in Germany were already current in 1730, cf. Graeven, 1730; Saurmann, 1737. Luther himself had expressed a preference for burial outside the city; the differences between Protestant and Catholic views (not unrelated to conflicts over the sharing of cemeteries, cf. Ariès (1977), pp. 310 ff.) need further study.

2   Iconographic evidence is discussed by Kurtz and Boardman, 1971; Ahlberg, 1971; Boardman, 1955; Zschietzschmann, 1928.

3   The text is one letter too long with the negative, one letter too short without it. Roux, 1967, p. 172, n. 26, defends the latter reading; but in the archaic period, the men might have stayed behind to make the mound?

4   The text is not certain.

5   Both men and women mourners cut their hair and wear black; in Euripides' *Alcestis* 422-31 even the horses are to have their manes cut as a sign of mourning!

6   [Plato] *Minos* 315c reports that the Athenians in olden times used to sacrifice before the *ekphora*, and perhaps regards this as being the normal Greek practice. The law of Iulis permits *prosphagia*, but these, according to Euripides *Alcestis* 845, took place at the tomb (*LSJ* s.v. *prosphagma*). Cf. Garland, 1981.

7   Kübler (1959, p. 87) suggests that all present lined up along the offering trench for this rite, since the length of the trenches seems to co-vary with the richness of the burial. Offering trenches were used only once and then covered over (ibid., p. 88); they did not serve repeatedly for periodic commemorative rites. Note that in the archaic peribolos at Vari (Fig. 2) most of the offering trenches run alongside the peribolos walls.

8   There seems to be some variation in the timing of the feast. In *Iliad* xxiii 29-34, it is held before Patroklos' cremation, in xxiv 801-3 *after* the cremation of Hector.

9   At some time the right to participate in the thirtieth-day ceremony may have been restricted to members of the jurally recognised kindred: Harpokration *s.v. triakas*, Pollux 1.66, Hesychios *s.v. 'atriakastos', 'exō triakados'*. The exact date of celebration varied from city to city; the Labyadai celebrated on the tenth rather than the ninth day.

10 According to Demosthenes xxiv 107, one could be sued for *kakōsis goneōn* if one failed to pay the customary honours to parents, grandparents and great-grandparents (perhaps only on the father's side). Cf. Xenophon *Memorabilia* ii 2.13 on *kosmēsis taphōn*. Plato *Laws* 717e prescribes annual commemoration. But I find it hard to believe that those Athenians whose

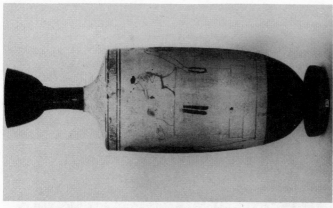

PLATE I (a) Berlin 3372, Woman painter (Antikenmuseum StMPK, Berlin) (b) Berlin F2443, Achilles painter (Antikenmuseum StMPK, Berlin) (c) Athens 1815, Sabouroff painter (National Museum, Athens)

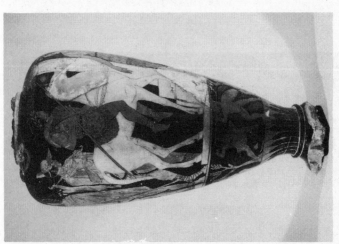

PLATE II *(a) Berlin 3209, giant loutrophoros (Antikenmuseum StMPK, Berlin) (b) Cabinet des Médailles 373, Achilles painter: Euphorbos and Oedipus (Bibliothèque Nationale, Paris)*

ancestors' tombs were scattered (almost certainly the majority: see below) would visit all of them. (Neglected tombs whose 'owners' were unknown: [Dem.] Iv 14-15.) In Euripides *Troades* 1180-4 Hecuba says that Astyanax used to promise to bring all his friends to honour her tomb with prayers and gifts; such visits from non-kin were forbidden by Solon's law.

Harvey (1955, p. 169); cf. Nilsson, 1911, p. 633) suggests that some of Simonides' and Pindar's dirges (*thrēnoi*) may have been written for commemorative rites. (Pindar *fr.*137B Schröder, Σ Pi. Py. vii. 17, comes from a *thrēnos* for the Alcmaeonid Hippokrates: *APF* 9688, III). Plutarch *Kimon* 4 tells us that Archelaos wrote a consolatory elegy for Kimon after the death of his wife Isodike. The fragments of such poetry which survive are philosophical in character, and this may have influenced the suggestion that the poems were sung at commemorative gatherings rather than at funerals. But the character of the fragments is largely determined by the philosophical interests of the later writers who quote them, and may be somewhat misleading.

11   Cf. also *IG* ii^2 5224 (Tod, 1948, p. 84; Peek, *GVI*, no. 47), public burial of two Corcyrean envoys, c. 375. (Reinscribed? cf. Knigge, 1972);*IG* ii^2 5220 = i^3 1178 (cf. Knigge, 1972; Lewis, D. M., 1979, pp. 243-4).

12   See however Gomme, 1956, pp. 94-101; Bradeen, 1969. The question of the commemoration of war dead buried overseas is likely to have presented itself at least from the time of the Battle of Mycale (479), if not already raised by Miltiades' unfortunate expedition to Paros in 489.

13   *Kasignētos* is the epic term for brother; the normal Oiantheian term was *adelphos* (Buck, 1955, no. 93).

14   On the *sēma* of Hector's ancestor Ilos, eponym of the city, see Price, 1973.

15   On the uses of *sēma* and *mnēma* see Eichler, 1914; on the terminology of funerary monuments in general, Guarducci, 1974, pp. 142-6. Vase as *sāma*, ibid., 126.

16   Μνῆμα Μνησαγόρας καὶ Νικοχάρος τόδε κεῖται·
     αὐτὼ δὲ οὐ πάρα δεῖξαι · ἀφέλετο δαίμονος αἶσα,
     πατρὶ φίλωι καὶ μητρὶ λιπόντε ἀμφοίμ μέγα πένθος,
     ὀνέκα ἀποφθιμένω βήτην δόμον ''Αιδος ἔσω.

'Here lies the *mnema* of Mnesagora and Nikochares,
but *them* it is impossible to see. Fate took them away
both leaving great grief to their dear father and mother,
because they died and went to the house of Hades.'
Cf. also, from the beginning of the fourth century (Amandry, 1949, pp. 526-7),

Πᾶσι θανεῖν ‹ε‚ἵμαρται›, ὅσοι ζώσιν·σὺ δὲ πένθος
οἶ|κτρὸν ἔχε ‹ι›ν ἔλιπες, Παυσιμάχη, προγόνοις
μητρ ‹ί‚ | τε Φαινίππηι καὶ πατρὶ Παυσανίαι.
σὴ ‹ς‚ δ'ἀρετὴ ‹ς‚ μνη|μεῖον ὁρᾶν τόδε τοῖς παριῶσιν
σωφροσύνη ‹ς‚ τε.

'Death must come to all, but you, Pausimache,
have left pitiable grief to your parents,
your mother Phainippe and your father Pausanias,
and (have left) this *mnēmeion* of your virtue and *sophrosynē*
for passers-by to see' (relief of young girl looking at herself in a mirror).

17   Boardman, 1978, no. 229, a three-sided relief on a capital of c. 550 BC from Lamptrai is unique in showing the horseman for whom it was set up flanked by mourners, a man on one side and two women on the other.

18 Tomb set up by:
    Father to son: *IG* i² 983 (*IG* i³ 1214, Pfohl, 1967, no. 42); *IG* i² 985 (i³ 1220, Pfohl 44); *IG* i² 986 (i³ 1211, Pfohl 37); *IG* i² 987 (i³ 1215, Pfohl 80); *IG* i² 1016 (i³ 1266, Pfohl 58, two children); *IG* i² 1025 (i³ 1257, Pfohl 65); *SEG* xv 69 (Pfohl 25); *SEG* xxii 74 (*IG* i³ 1218, Pfohl 46); *SEG* xxv 60 (*IG* i³ 1263). Total: 9.
    Father (and mother?) to son and daughter: *IG* i² 981 (i³ 1241, Pfohl 33; cf. Daux, 1975).
    Mother to son: *SEG* x 439 (*IG* i³ 1206, Pfohl 34).
    Father or mother to daughter: *IG* i² 1012 (i³ 1251, Pfohl 59).
    Wife/mother to husband and son: *SEG* xxii 68 (*IG* i³ 1213, Pfohl 29).
    Husband and mother to wife/daughter: *SEG* xxv 59 (*IG* i³ 1229).
    Brother to brother: *SEG* xxi 192 (Pfohl 78), set up to Philoitios and Ktesias by the brother of one of them (Peek, 1957, p. 66 no. 218); ? *IG* i² 1023 (i³ 1271, Pfohl 74; possibly set up by two brothers to a third person).
    Sister to brother: *IG* i² 975 (i³ 1210, Pfohl 40).
    Children to father: *SEG* xv 66 ('at our mother's orders'; Pfohl 52); *SEG* xxii 77 (*IG* i³ 1225, Pfohl 45).
    Tomb shared by:
    Father and son: *IG* i² 983? (i³ 1214; *SEG* x 435, Pfohl 42, Friedländer, 1948, no. 69).
    SEG xxii 68 (*IG* i³ 1213, Pfohl 29).
    ? *IG* i² 1001 (i³ 1221; possibly two brothers, or the same man on both sides of the stele).
    Brother and sister: *IG* i² 981 (i³ 1241, Pfohl 33); ? *IG* i² 1014 (i³ 1261, Pfohl 61, Phrasikleia); *SEG* x 452a, xvi 26 (*IG* i³ 1265, Pfohl 62).
    Siblings: *IG* i² 1016 (i³ 1266, Pfohl 58).
    Mother and child?: Boardman, 1978, no. 237, NM 4472, c. 530, from Anavyssos.
    Two males, relation unknown: *SEG* xxi 192 (Pfohl 78); *IG* i² 1026a (i³ 1255, Pfohl 64).
    The number of inscriptions recording relationships is less than a third of the total. The proportion of males to females commemorated, both in inscriptions and in sculptures, is c. 6.5:1.
19 Friedländer, 1948, no. 59; this, however, is not the interpretation of Dover (1978, p. 124). *IG* i² 1022 (Pfohl 73) was set up by Peisianax (Davies, *APF* 9688, VIII) to Damasistratos son of Epikles, who was probably not his father or brother. *SEG* xv 74 (*IG* i³ 1205, Pfohl 38) was set up by Terpo for Melissa; if the restoration is right, the expression *sēma tod' e[cheuen]* is rather surprising for a woman.
20 For a possible tomb-enclosure of Proto-Geometric date at Nea Ionia see Smithson, 1961; for Geometric enclosures similar to the Kerameikos 'Plattenbau', Walter, 1940, p. 182.
21 Coldstream (1968) assigns the finds from grave XVI to MG II (c. 800-760) and those from grave V to a class of Subgeometric ware contemporary with early Proto-Attic (c. 700).
22 On the relation between epic, hero-cult and contemporary burials see Andronikos, 1968; Bérard, 1970; Price, 1973; Coldstream, 1976. Snodgrass, 1982, puts forward a new version of Fustel de Coulanges' views on the relation between tomb-cult – this time in the form of hero-worship – and landed property. I remain sceptical.
23 Knigge (1976, pp. 10-11, n. 26) attributes G to the Alcmaeonidae.
24 It would also be desirable to make a comparative study of the grouping of

tumuli on other Greek sites. Cf. especially Boehlau and Schefold, 1940; and Hammond, 1977, for the geographical distribution and possible origins of tumulus burial.

25 Fig. 2; Karo, 1936, cols 123-5; Riemann, 1937, cols 121-4; Walter, 1940, cols 175-8; Lemerle, 1937, pp. 450-1. Cf. also Stais, 1891.

26 If this is the meaning of the report that the tomb was empty.

27 Bourriot (1976) examines possible evidence for *genos* tombs in Attica, with negative results.

28 Kallipolitis, 1964, refers to a 'low mound' covering the whole site, but it is not clear whether he regards this as intentional and monumental.

29 Cf. burial of two horses in the Kerameikos, c. 400 BC, Freytag, 1976, p. 33 no. 15 (VEck 9); further references in Andronikos, 1968.

30 *IG* ii^2 10650, Pfohl no. 104, Clairmont no. 23, c. 410 BC. Clairmont thinks that the stele was bought ready-made, on the grounds that the woman looks too young to be a grandmother; but an Athenian woman could be a grandmother by 30.

31 Garland, 1981, contains a catalogue of classical periboloi in Attica. The connection between periboloi fronting on roads and larger enclosures such as that at Vari, and also the relation between the development of private periboloi and the architectural history of state graves, remain to be clarified. The practice of marking graves with stone *horoi* also beings in the fifth century (Karouzou, 1947/8); a collection of these would be useful.

32 Thorikos terrace 3 has burials from the late sixth century, but all seven burials were of children. The use of terraces continued in the fourth century, but most contained only a few graves.

33 We really do not know what was meant by the prohibition of 'herms' in the law on funerary monuments quoted by Cicero, nor whether the Athenians regarded this law as still in force after the Persian wars.

34 Contrast the public or semi-public monument erected to Pythion, probably in 446 BC, *IG* i^2 1085+ (*IG* i^3 1353, Meiggs and Lewis, 1969, no. 51, Pfohl no. 91; erected by the three tribes whose names appear at the end of the inscription?). In the sixth century, the family is represented in pictures of *prothesis* and *ekphora*, which often include children (cf. especially the Louvre plaque MNB 905, Sappho Painter, c. 500, in which each member of the family is labelled with a kin term); some of these, painted on plaques or vases intended to stand over the tomb, were intended as permanent monuments. But they are statements about the performance of funeral rites rather than statements about the identity of the dead. There are in fact two different cultural changes taking place during the period under study: a shift of emphasis from funeral rites to commemorative monuments, and a change in the conceptions of identity embodied in the latter.

35 See Karouzou, 1947/8; Zapheiropoulos, 1958.

36 Toledo Museum of Art 69.369, Akrisios, Perseus and Danae (Kurtz, 1975, pl. 37.2, shortly before 450); B.M. D. 58, Thanatos Painter, Hypnos and Thanatos burying a warrior (Kurtz, 1975, pl. 32.4, 450-425). One lekythos shows the dead man inside the tomb (B.M. D. 35, Kurtz, 1975, pl. 23.1, 475-50). A BF loutrophoros-amphora (NM 450, Kurtz and Boardman, 1971, pl. 36) and a BF bail-amphora (Lausanne, coll. Gillet; Kurtz and Boardman, 1971, pls 37-8), both by the Sappho Painter, show actual funeral rites.

37 This being so, it is of some importance, when stelai of this kind are found, that the excavators of the associated periboloi should check whether the number and sex of the burials corresponds to the names on the stone, if this is possible.

38 Cf. Metzger, 1951, on domestic themes in the vase-painting of the second half of the fifth century.

39 Presumably Habrylla was the wife of Euphron, after whom she is listed, and Phainarete daughter of Kleophon the wife of Euthyphron. She was probably also a relative of the family, to judge from her name.

40 Cf. the more general praise of a wife in *IG* ii^2 6551, and the stones set up to nurses: *SEG* xxi 1075; Möbius, 1966, pp. 156-7; Karouzou, 1957; Alexandres, 1976, p. 68.

41 Cf. Ariès, 1960; Stone, 1977. The change in the visual representation of children in the fifth century is illustrated in pls IIb, Ib.

42 On representations of childbirth set up over the tombs of women who died in this way see Möbius, 1966, p. 155, Asgari and Firatli, 1978, no. 1.

43 See Table I; my reconstruction differs slightly from that of Mastrokostas (1966). R. Garland, who kindly examined the stone for me, thinks that there are five or six different hands: Hand I, lines 1-4 (Meidon I, Meidoteles I, Phanagora); Hand II, lines 5-9 (Kalliteles I and Mnesiptoleme); Hand III, lines 10-19 (Meidon II, Mnesistrate, Meidoteles II); Hand IV, lines 20-25 (Kalliteles II and Kallimedes); Hand V, Mnesiptolome II; Hand VI?, the epigram for Kalliteles II. The stone might well have been erected initially, therefore, by Kalliteles I.

44 See Humphreys, 1983.

45 In the courth century peribolos at St John Rente south of the city (Kallipolitis and Petrakos, 1965, pp. 46-50) there were seven marble sarcophagi, one clay larnax, two child burials in larnakes, and a third in an additional compartment attached to the side of the peribolos (the skeletons were 'excellently preserved', but do not seem to have been studied). All finds were fourth century except six coins of types usually attributed to the early third century. A peribolos at Glyphada (Liakouras, 1976, pp. 159-60) held seven sarcophagi and one pit burial. A round funerary monument of c. 380 (Amandry 1949, pp. 525-6) had two burials, a father and son. A 'burial terrace' of the second/third quarter of the fourth century (Alexandres, 1969) had six graves, one a child's, statues of three women and a girl, and a lekythos with a relief of two men. Thorikos terrace 4 held three graves (Bingen, 1968, pp. 74-7). See further below on inscriptions.

46 Of the ten tomb-monuments found in the peribolos of Meidon's descendants (Table I), five commemorated (and represented) single individuals.

47 The count was made on fourth-century tombstones in *IG* ii^2 which included demotics. If stones without demotics had been included, the proportion of monuments to single individuals would have been still higher; the proportion of women would probably also have risen.

   Tombstones of women, in all but 17 cases, find a place among those with demotics through the identification of the woman by reference to a male guardian. Husband and father are both named in 12 cases, father alone in 16 cases, husband alone in 8 cases. On 49 stones the relationship is expressed solely by the genitive case; I am not sure whether this could be used for the husband as well as for the father. Where not identified by reference to a male, women's stones have the demotic with a *-then* ending; e.g. *IG* ii^2 6285, 6897; cf. Linders, 1972, pp. 7-8 n. 5; Bradeen, 1974, no. 117.

48 | | | |
    |---|---|---|
    | Husband and wife with son(s) and daughter(s) | 11 + | ?2 |
    | Husband and wife with son(s) alone | 24 + | ?5 |
    | Husband and wife with daughter(s) alone | 15 + | ?8 |
    | Father and son(s) | 30 + | ?13 |
    | Mother and son | 2 + | ?1 |

Father and daughter	4 + ?2
Mother and daughter?	5 + ?4
Brother and brother	7 + ?3
Brother and sister	5 + ?1

49 Further cases of men and women buried with the kin of their spouses will be found in the larger groups analysed below.

50 The stele is re-used, which is unusual.

51 The relief shows a woman with the two men; did one marry the sister of the other? Note also the stele republished by A. Liakouras (1976, p. 153) of two men from different demes: perhaps they too were linked by marriage.

52 See *APF* 10242. A homonymous grandson of Mnesippos IV is commemorated on *IG* ii² 5505 (third century), but its provenance is not known. Kirchner makes Mnesippos V a patrilateral parallel cousin (FBS) of Mnesarchides, but in view of the striking consistency of the names of the rest of the family, it is perhaps more likely that Charitaios was a fellow-demesman who married into the family.

53 Another inscription which perhaps belongs in this category is *IG* ii² 5752, commemorating Thoutimos III son of Aristogeiton II of Aphidna (*APF* 12267) with his wife Theosebeia and with Thoutimos IV and Androkles II, sons of Androkles I of Poros, who must have married a sister of Aristogeiton II or Thoutimos III, or a daughter of the latter. A metic tomb-stone belonging to this category may also be cited: B.M. 1107, c. 410 BC (Pfohl 107, *GVI* 218; see Wilamowitz, 1930) was set up by a woman from Parion in the Sea of Marmora to her two sons, her brother and her daughter. Wilamowitz suggested that the two latter names might have been added later, but Susan Walker of the B.M. kindly informs me that the stone does not support this view.

54 One of these, Agora 519, belongs to a metic family. The stele commemorates Adrastos, son of Aristion, of Kios, Theano and Poa, daughters of Euaristos of Kios (one of them probably Adrastos' wife; the names of the fathers suggest that this might have been a marriage between previously related families), Adrastos' children Philothea, Kallis and Hermogenes, Damon of Mylasa with his sister Aristonike, Nanous and Boidas, sons of Dios, of Heraklea, and Plangon, daughter of Lakleides of Aegina. It is possible that Damon and either Nanous or Boidas were the husbands of Philothea and Kallis, and Plangon the wife of Hermogenes – but no certainty is possible, and the study of groupings of metic tombstones would be a task in itself.

55 She is named after Antibios and before his children.

56 The name of Hippokrates II, son of Heragoras, shows that his mother was a daughter of Hippokrates I. Either Heragoras first married Myrto, or the second woman (whose name is lost), identified as Heragoras' wife, was Myrto's sister. Heragoras will have acquired Athenian citizenship when it was granted to the Samians in 405 BC, and was assigned (*IG* ii² 1 1.34) to his future father-in-law's deme. His second son, Thrasyllos, was presumably named after the general, no doubt a popular figure among the Samians.

57 *IG* ii² 5376 and 5379 were found together in the Kerameikos; 5378 came from the 'Theseion', and 5374 has only the provenance 'Athens', so it is not certain that all four monuments originally stood together.

58 The reconstruction of the family tree in Petrakos' latest report (1980, pp. 3-16) differs somewhat from that suggested in earlier notices.

59 See n. 43 above, and Table I, with notes. Note that with the addition of the epigram and loutrophoros honouring Kalliteles II the stele took on more of the look of a monument to a single individual.

60   It may have helped to generate the antiquarian interest in famous graves
      attested by the early third-century monograph of Diodorus the periegete
      on Attic graves (Jacoby, *FGH* no. 372).

61   Hyperides' relationship to Epikteta is unclear. The inscription names
      about twenty-five initial members; the association is to be maintained in
      future by the agnatic descendants of all those named, plus the descendants
      of *epiklēroi* (brotherless daughters) and of a number of specially named
      women among the current members. The foundation of Pythion of Cos,
      second century BC (Fraser, 1953; Sokolowski, *LS* [1969], no. 171) is
      patrilineal.

62   Epicurus was childless, but Polyainos had a son and Metrodorus a son and
      a daughter, both apparently minors at the time when the will was made.
      There seems to be no concern to transfer responsibility for the cult to them
      and their eventual descendants.

63   See Laum, 1914; Fraser, 1953; Fraser, 1977, pp. 62-8; Schmitt-Pantel,
      1982.

64   For a discussion of the relations between funeral ceremony, monument and
      commemoration in the period when the modern tomb-cult began, see below,
      ch. 6. The tension between the demands of private mourning and public
      commemoration is clearly shown in the reform proposals of Amaury Duval
      (1801), who proposes a double *prothesis* ritual, the first to be held at home
      and restricted to the family, the second to take place in one of the
      communal 'temples' to be set up for this purpose. It is further noteworthy
      that no distinction of rank or status is to be made among the biers laid out in
      the 'temple' (cf. Athenian funerals of war dead); but the rich may use their
      wealth later, in providing music for the funeral cortège and elaborate com-
      memorative monuments.

6 Fustel de Coulanges, *The Ancient City*

Part I

In the 1860s and 1870s scholars working in different countries and in different fields produced radically new interpretations of ancient societies. H. S. Maine and J. J. Bachofen perhaps opened the series in 1861 with, respectively, *Ancient Law* and *Das Mutterrecht*. Numa D. Fustel de Coulanges followed up with *La Cité antique* in 1864, J. F. McLennan with *Primitive Marriage* in 1865. Bachofen's *Die Sage von Tanaquil* was published in 1870, E. B. Tylor's *Primitive Culture* in 1871, and L. H. Morgan's *Ancient Society* in 1877. To these we must add two books by W. Robertson Smith, *Kinship and Marriage in Early Arabia* and *The Religion of the Semites*, which successively appeared in 1885 and 1889. All these authors were of course aware of the recent achievements of comparative philology and mythology. They accepted the existence of an Indo-European civilisation unconnected with Semitic civilisation, but only Maine and Robertson Smith worked out their own models of ancient social life within the framework of these great prehistoric units characterised by common language and common political and religious institutions. The others - even Fustel de Coulanges, who gladly used the Indians for comparison with Greeks and Romans - elaborated evolutionary schemes that were essentially unrelated to the notions of Aryans and Semites. Each of the scholars mentioned seems to have worked independently of the others, although (for instance) Morgan quotes Fustel and was on friendly personal terms with McLennan; the only clear exception is Robertson Smith's avowed debt to McLennan on totemism.

Fustel de Coulanges was born in 1830 and educated at the École Normale Supérieure of Paris, where one of his teachers was J. D. Guigniaut, who translated and vulgarised F. Creuzer's ideas about ancient religion. Fustel started with a history of the island of Chios (1856), notable for its sweep from the origins to the nineteenth century. He obtained his doctorate in 1858 with two theses, one on

Polybius (*Polybe, ou la Grèce conquise*) and one on the cult of Vesta
(*Quid Vestae cultus in institutis veterum privatis publicisque valuerit*),
in which some of the interests and theories of the *Cité antique* are
anticipated. *The Ancient City - La Cité antique* - was written at
Strasbourg, where Fustel became a professor. It was very much the
work of a scholar who lived on the borders of German culture and
had a poor opinion of it. Fustel was acquainted with what G. B.
Niebuhr and A. Schwegler and young Theodor Mommsen had written
about early Roman history. He was probably also well informed about
the books of K. O. Müller, A. Boeckh, F. G. Welcker, and G. F.
Schoemann on Greek mythology, religion and institutions. Furthermore, he was necessarily dependent on German scholars for his notions
about Indo-Europeans (or Aryans) because they had done most of the
spadework in this field. But he intentionally disregarded modern
authorities in his *Ancient City* and, though he involved French and
English writers in his provocative silence, there is no doubt that they
were not his main target. In a posthumous fragment by him one reads:
'I would rather be mistaken in the manner of Livy than that of
Niebuhr.' In 1864 Fustel was still mainly a classical scholar with an
extraordinary familiarity with classical texts. His knowledge of other
Aryan groups was as yet superficial and in the case of Indian civilisation
always remained so. The main attraction of the Aryan idea for him was
that it freed him from having to include the Semites - and therefore the
Jews and the dangerous Bible - in his discourse.

After publishing *The Ancient City* Fustel became increasingly
involved in the question of whether medieval French institutions were
mainly German or Celtic or Roman in origin. He embraced the Roman
thesis. As his main work on the subject, the *Histoire des institutions
politiques de l'Ancienne France*, began to appear after the great crisis
of the Franco-Prussian War of 1870-71 (more precisely in 1875), it
became symptomatic of the revulsion against Germany that then pre-
vailed in France. After 1871 Fustel did indeed stand up as the leader
of the new nationalistic historiography. But he is not responsible for
the extravagant notions about the Gauls produced by his pupil C.
Jullian and even less for the use Ch. Maurras and other extreme rightists
of the Action Française made of him. Moreover, the main outlines of
his ideas about the origins of French civilisation were expressed by
Fustel before the war, early in 1870, in lectures he had been invited
to deliver in the presence of the Empress Eugénie as soon as he had left
the University of Strasbourg to become a teacher at the École Normale.

Though it would be wrong to play down the emotional impact of the events of 1870-71 on the later development of Fustel (who died prematurely in 1889), his transition from classical interests to a concern with problems of French history should be dated about 1865.

There are, however, traits that remained constant in his activity. One of these, which we have already noticed, is his distrust of German scholarship. This goes together with a certain uncritical attitude towards his sources, because source criticism had been perfected by the schools of Niebuhr and Pertz (the latter in the context of the *Monumenta Germaniae*). The reader of *The Ancient City* must be on guard at every step about what Fustel states as given in his sources. For instance the notion – essential for the validity of Fustel's theories and presented by him as a fact – that the Greeks and Latins buried their dead in family tombs within their own estates is simply not supported by the evidence he produces (or by any evidence discovered subsequently). Secondly, throughout his career Fustel was involved in a polemic against socialist and generally egalitarian ideas. He defended the institution of private property against French and German socialists by making private property one of the original institutions of mankind (and, as we shall soon see, connecting it with the cult of the dead). He maintained with equal firmness that the revolutionaries of 1789 had deceived their followers by presenting the ancient republics of Athens, Sparta, and Rome (more especially Sparta) as models of liberty. In agreement with B. Constant and indeed with a whole line of anti-Jacobin thinkers, Fustel believed that there was no respect for individual liberty in ancient Greece and Rome (not even in Athens). Individual liberty was to him the product of Christianity, which in its turn he considered unthinkable without the universality of the Roman Empire. Here is the root of Fustel's ambiguity about ancient values. On the one hand he admires, and feels nostalgia for, the ancestral traditions that ensured private property and family solidarity in the days of old. On the other hand he feels that without Christianity there would be no respect for the individual or even separation between state and religion; therefore, though a confessed unbeliever, he chooses to remain within the Catholic Church and avoids discussing the Bible.

Fustel's ambiguous attitude towards his historical materials and the values inherent in them goes beyond the subjects of private property and individual freedom and seems to pervade his whole historical outlook in *The Ancient City*. Paradoxically, this gives the volume both its superficial appearance of compact argument and its ultimate reality of self-contradictory historical construction. We are introduced to a simple world where people claiming to have the same ancestors live together on privately owned ground sanctified by the tombs of the ancestors themselves and by the hearth in which the spirits of the ancestors are supposed to live perennially as gods: 'the religion of the dead is the oldest in man'. Keeping the fire alive means keeping the ancestors alive. Because the dead expect to be kept alive by their descendants, celibacy is a crime. The tomb establishes an indissoluble union between the land and the extended family living on it (let us call it the *gens*, in Roman terminology). Thus the dead are at the root of both religion and property. The father is the priest of the family cult and also king over his family; land is inalienable; daughters do not inherit because they marry outside the family and join the ancestor cult of their husbands. But the sons are not all on an equal footing. The first-born inherits the priestly and sovereign rights of the father. If the evidence about primitive Rome does not show any trace of the right of primogeniture (unlike that about India and, according to Fustel, Greece), we must postulate its existence. Indians, Greeks, and Romans (and the other Aryans) must have passed through this stage, in which the extended family ruled by the eldest living member was the only political and religious corporation.

But how could this coherent society disintegrate and give place to cities in which different families without common ancestors lived together, in which religion was no longer limited to the household, and in which property rights in land became alienable? Fustel admires such a society just because it appears immutable. The internal contradictions revealed by Marxist analysis did not yet exist for him. For an explanation he relies on what I have called his ambiguity and would now call more precisely his dualistic attitude towards historical developments. He has one or two trump cards up his sleeve. Somewhere, somehow, another religion developed that had nothing to do with ancestors. It was the cult of natural phenomena, the worship of sun, moon, stars, etc. Besides, Fustel unexpectedly adds, it was not quite true that everyone lived happily inside the family structure so far outlined. Somewhere, somehow, the original family had been complicated by the admission of clients who in exchange for help had agreed to worship the ancestors of their patrons and had been admitted into the extended family in a subordinate position. Furthermore, somewhere, somehow, there existed families unable either to create a religion of their own or to accept the religion of others. These unfortunate families remained outside the original civilisation of the Aryan *gentes* in a near-beastly condition. The religion of natural phenomena and the existence of clients inside the *gentes* and of plebeians outside them were the driving factors in the dissolution of the old order.

When the original *gentes* recognised the narrowness of their ancestral groups, the common cult of physical objects like the sun helped them to combine in the greater unit we call the city. In the city each family group preserved its own ancestral cult, but shared these 'physical' gods (for instance, Jupiter) with other families. In addition, certain features of family worship were extended to the city; hence, the common hearth for the city personified in Rome by the goddess Vesta. At first the cities preserved the monarchic government each family had had in isolation. But it was soon recognised that a confederation of families, as the city was, would be better governed by a council made of family heads, that is, by an aristocracy. The transition from monarchy to aristocracy in the young cities did not represent a revolution, but rather a revival of a traditional institution, and therefore involved no bloodshed. The real revolutions came from clients and plebeians. As soon as the city had been founded by the association of various families, the combined strength of their clients began to exercise pressure on the ruling class. In their turn the outsiders or plebeians tried to penetrate into the city and obtain recognition in it. Clients and plebeians were natural allies. The changes, or real 'revolutions', in the social and economic structure of the ancient cities – the abolition of clientship, the parification of patricians and plebeians, the liberalisation of land tenure and of inheritance rules – are all deduced by Fustel from the unstable position of the *gentes* within the cities, where the clients became ungovernable and the outsiders claimed political rights. Shrewdly enough, Fustel saw the point of real weakness in the patricians, that is, the need they had of the military co-operation of clients and plebeians in war.

It is superfluous to go into the details of the various revolutions. Even in explaining the last revolution of the ancient world – the substitution of a universal empire for the city states – Fustel produces a historical factor he had not mentioned before. He had previously presented Rome as an ordinary city beset by all the problems characteristic of the other ancient cities. Now, suddenly, Rome becomes an exceptional city. We are told that from its very beginnings Rome collected different nationalities, even different cities, within its own territory. Consequently, Rome was prepared to transcend the limitations of the ordinary city-state and to pave the way for a universal state and a universal church. Fustel explains all the transformations of ancient society, before and after the creation of the city, by introducing new elements whose presence he cannot properly account for. We must conclude that the earthly paradise of the *gentes* worshipping their ancestors on the land they had inherited from them cannot have existed, because the very notion of this paradise is incompatible with the existence of the hostile forces that allegedly destroyed it.

                                                                    A. M.

Bibliographical Note

The preceding pages try to carry the analysis of the *Cité antique* beyond the point I had reached in my paper of 1970. The reader is referred to this essay (Momigliano, 1970) for further information and bibliography. Three important contributions have since appeared: Carbonell, 1976; Grossi, 1977; and Finley, 1977. For the development of the discussion on the difference between ancient and modern liberty there is now a good book by L. Guerci (1979). The old biography of Fustel by his pupil, P. Guiraud (1896), is still indispensable. Jane Herrick's *The Historical Thought of Fustel de Coulanges* (1954) is a useful general introduction. The penetrating little book by T. O. Beidelman, *W. Robertson Smith and the Sociological Study of Religion* (1974) is very relevant.

Part II

Fustel's conception of the earthly paradise of primitive society was very much the product of his own times. His model of the evolution of society is vitiated at the outset by two basic inconsistencies: although he stresses the importance and cohesion of the *gens* as a *group*, he is trying to use its primordial role in human history to defend the primordial character of *individual* private property, which he derives from the burial of *individuals* on their own land by their heirs.

Tombs, in antiquity, were usually placed beside roads, and although land used for burial became private property and might in various ways be safeguarded from abuse or alienation, I know of no evidence that it was regarded as particularly desirable to be buried in land that formed part of a larger family holding. On the contrary, the most desirable sites were those on main roads leading out of the city, where the tomb would be most in the public eye. Exceptionally, those who merited heroic honours might be buried inside the city, perhaps even in the public square (Bérard, 1970). Fustel's thesis, therefore, is not an obvious or even a natural inference from the ancient sources. In fact, many antiquarian writers had discussed the funeral rites and tombs of the ancients before him, without laying any particular stress on the relation of burial to private estates or the religious duties of the heir. The features of ancient practice selected for attention varied, predictably, with the writer's interests and culture. In the sixteenth and early seventeenth centuries it was the magnificence of the funerals of great men, attended by crowds of supporters and hangers-on, that attracted the most attention. Toward the end of the seventeenth century other interests begin to appear: for example, embalming is discussed in detail and recommended to contemporaries by the doctor Thomas Greenhill in *Nekrokedeia; or, The art of embalming, wherein is shewn the right of burial, the funeral ceremonies, and the several ways of preserving dead bodies in most nations of the world* . . . (1705) – it was used particularly by doctors in preserving bodies for dissection. Protestants, from about 1730 onward, concerned themselves especially with the ancient prohibition of burial inside cities and with demonstrating that burial in and beside churches was not a practice going back to the earliest days of Christianity; such discussions belong to the contemporary campaign against burial in churches and city churchyards as an unhygienic practice. Protestants were prominent in this campaign, no doubt, partly because in many cases the new religion had had to set up its own new burial grounds on sites unhallowed by tradition. But even those who resisted the proposals for change were defending a complex of ritual and material commemorative practices without singling out for particular attention either the right of sons to be buried with their fathers or the obligation of the son to protect and venerate his father's mortal remains. According to Philippe Ariès, whose researches in *L'Homme devant la mort* (1977) provide the essential basis for this reassessment of Fustel's views, the removal of more than 20,000 corpses from the cemetery of Les Innocents in Paris in 1785-87 did not give rise to any public concern for the rights of those disinterred; wealthy as well as poor Parisians were buried in Les Innocents, yet the relatives of the dead showed no interest in visiting them in the new 'catacombs' to which they were transported.

It seems that one can analytically distinguish three separate elements in the commemoration of the dead: the regular celebration of

commemorative rites in church, the setting up of a monument pro-
claiming the status and virtues of the dead where it could be seen by
contemporaries and by posterity, and continued contact with the
physical remains in the tomb. While the custom of burying the dead in
churches or their associated churchyards persisted, the third of these
elements could be taken for granted as a logical consequence of the
others, without being singled out for special attention. The new
practice of burying the dead in surburban cemeteries remote from the
parish churches of the city dissolved the unity of these three elements
and produced an abundant crop of pamphlets and reform proposals,
studied by Ariès, in which a variety of new combinations are suggested;
it is in this context that the theme of burial in private property emerges.

The change in cemetery location had come at the time of the profound general upheaval of society in the French Revolution; the tombs
of the upper classes, notably the royal tombs of St Denis, had suffered
in the violence directed against the symbols of wealth and status. This
thorough shaking up of customary behaviour and ideas allowed new
configurations of sentiment, anxiety, and ambition to emerge, and the
essay competition organised by the Institut de France in 1801 on the
subject of the proper ritual to be performed at funerals and the
organisation of cemeteries gave full scope for their expression. There
are several points to note in Ariès's report of these proposals. The
organisation of cemeteries seems to receive far more attention than
that of funerary rites, except in so far as the latter take on a commemorative character through a focus on speeches praising the achievements of the dead. It seems to be taken for granted that the funerary
monument will be transferred, with the physical remains of the dead,
from the church or its associated graveyard to the suburban cemetery.
This in itself implies that the cemetery is thought of as a place that will
be regularly visited. The idea that the dead should be buried at home is
less prominent, but occurs several times in different contexts. Pierre
Giraud, who in 1796 had already submitted a cemetery project to the
Department of the Seine, proposed to vitrify the remains of the dead
by a special cremation process and use the resulting material to make
two portrait medallions, one of which was to remain on display in the
cemetery while the other would become a family heirloom. He had
directed in his will that his heirs 'should use me as an example by
arranging with a soapmaker or surgeon to have my bones separated
from the rest of my corpse, should burn my flesh and bodily liquids,
and should collect the ashes of these, with my skeleton, in the tomb

which I have constructed for this very purpose in my garden, until such time as my descendants can convert my bones into glass' (Ariès, 1977, pp. 506-9). The tomb in the garden for Giraud himself is in part merely a way of facilitating exhumation, but his portrait medallions are themselves a form of home burial, which can also be seen as a development of the fashion of using part of the body (the hair) as a memento of the dead, in eighteenth and nineteenth century mourning pictures (ibid., pp. 454-5).

The desire to retain some part of the loved dead at home had been growing in strength for some time, and in rare cases mummification had been used to preserve the whole corpse in the house or in a mausoleum on private property (ibid., p. 379). But now burial on private land seemed to offer advantages of a less private character as well. J. Girard, in his competition essay, frankly rejects the traditional church rituals of commemoration and is equally hostile to the 'materialism' of the ostentatious tomb-monument. The essential relation for him is that between the survivors and the physical remains of the dead; and the best place for the latter is on the dead man's own land. Attachment to the land will be increased by the presence on it of ancestral tombs; patriotism will be solidly grounded in a chain of loyalties spreading outward from the tomb to property, locality, province, and nation; land will be less frequently alienated, and society will be more stable (ibid., pp. 503-4). Here we have not only the recommendation of burial in private property, which can also be amply documented from many other sources of the period, but the precise tie between such burials and attachment to land-ownership that was to become central to Fustel's argument sixty years later - although, by the time *The Ancient City* was written, the practice of private burial was on the decline, largely because the frequency with which land changed hands made burial in the public cemetery seem a better guarantee of the continued respect and cult of the tomb.

Fustel's concern with the extended family also reflects contemporary ideas. Frédéric Le Play's monumental study, *Les Ouvriers européens*, published in 1855, related three main structural types - patriarchal extended family, stem family, and nuclear family - to ecological and occupational variables. In *La Réforme sociale en France*, published, like *The Ancient City*, in 1864, Le Play recommended laws on inheritance that would strengthen the stem family, in which a single heir has control over the whole parental estate (with obligations to maintain siblings if they continue to live and work with him), as a remedy against the subdivision of land-holdings. Fustel failed to distinguish clearly between extended and stem families – indeed, part of the ambiguity of his argument lies here. His view of the gradual growth of the *gens* implied an expanding extended family. But his emphasis on primogeniture points to the stem family as his preferred model.

The main achievement for which Fustel will be remembered, at least among anthropologists, is not his inconsistent picture of the earliest stages of human evolution but his account of the *gens* as a fully developed institution and his awareness of the evolutionary problems it raised. Together with Sir Henry Maine, he introduced into evolutionary theory a body of material that was already familiar to classicists, but one that was also capable of illuminating the new discoveries anthropologists were to make in Australia, Africa, and North America. It was Fustel's insistence on the *rules* governing agnation and the composition and activities of the *gens* that was to prove important, rather than his attempt to find a plausible psychological origin for these rules in the cult of the dead. Both Fustel and Maine clearly emphasised that kinship was a cultural rather than a natural phenomenon: cultural rules determined who was and who was not a kinsman in different societies; kinship could be created or destroyed by social rites. The *gens* was not a casual agglomeration of families: Fustel specifies that it had a name, rules of recruitment, its own religious cults, a common tomb (*sic*), its leader, its assemblies, and its own body of regulations governing members' behaviour (*The Ancient City*, pp. 94-7). These two key ideas of kinship as a set of social rules and the descent group as a corporation, together with the general notion of a stage of social evolution in which kinship forms the basis of the structure of social relationships, provided the foundation for the social anthropology of kinship systems. Fustel's views on the decisive role of religion in social evolution also had their influence in sociology and social anthropology, particularly in stimulating Durkheim, Lévy-Bruhl, and later Evans-Pritchard to ask why religious obligations and beliefs should be so much more imperative and unquestioned in simple societies than in complex ones. Durkheim 'stood Fustel on his head' by arguing that it was not religious beliefs that shaped social structure, but social experience that gave religious beliefs their force.

Among classicists, Fustel currently holds a much less prominent position in the gallery of famous ancestors. This is partly because it has never been universally accepted that the Roman *gens*, or Greek *genos*, was an institution common in early times to all strata of society. For Rome, those who believed that the division between patricians and plebeians went back to the earliest settlement of the city tended also to believe that the organisation in *gentes* was confined to the patricians. The belief that patricians and plebeians were in origin two separate groups with distinct ethnic origins, culture, and institutions was particularly prevalent in the later nineteenth century, as historians of early Rome grappled with new data on the interrelations of the Italic languages and with the evidence for population movements produced by archaeology; while those who rejected the 'ethnic' model tended to concentrate on trying to reconstruct the immediate bases for the class conflict that broke out in the fifth century B.C., rather than dwell on a possible earlier stage of greater homogeneity. More recently, the growing acceptance of the view that the distinction between patricians and plebeians hardened into a fundamental social cleavage only after the expulsion of the kings implicitly favours the view that the *gens* could have been an institution common to both groups; but the latest discussion of the origins of the plebs (J.-C. Richard, 1978) devotes only a few pages to the *gens*. Students of Roman law, too, are increasingly feeling discouraged by paucity of evidence from attempts to reconstruct a 'gentile' stage of society. Alan Watson (1975) has only this to say: 'It may well be that at an earlier stage the *gens* was a political unit, but if so its importance was gone before the XII tables. There is no evidence that in historical times a *gens* had any formal organisation or a leader.' (Franciosi, 1978, is confused and very imperfectly acquainted with modern anthropological theory.) The most useful contribution to the problem from this quarter has been J. M. Crook's suggestion that the Roman doctrine of *patria potestas* and agnation, on which Fustel and Maine based such a large part of their theories, should be recognised as an anomaly among Indo-European institutions and regarded as a product of Roman interest in precise legal formulation, rather than as a Indo-European 'survival' (Crook, 1967).

It may be worth pointing out here that the problem of distinguishing a kernel of genuinely early institutions from the archaic-looking products of later legal thought was one that already preoccupied Maine, especially in the very important *Dissertations on Early Law and Custom* (1883), in which he revised his earlier views in relation to subsequent research on Indian law and on the structure of Indian and Slavonic extended families. Modern research seems to confirm the point that Maine already recognised here, that extended and nuclear families, rather than representing successive evolutionary forms, should be seen as stages in a single cyclical process of growth and dispersal. Neither the joint Hindu family nor the south Slav *zadruga* supply evidence for a stage of evolution in which nuclear family units were unknown. (Cf. Sontheimer, 1977; Byrnes, 1976.) However, the importance of ancestor-worship remains much greater in Indian studies of the history of the family than in recent accounts of Greece and Rome. But it should also be noted that the major twentieth-century attempt to trace Roman institutions back to their Indo-European origins through comparison with Indian and other sources, that of Georges Dumézil, takes a totally different line from Fustel's and regards the three original Roman tribes as quite possibly in origin occupational castes (most recently, Dumézil, 1969).

The situation with regard to ancient Greece is somewhat different. Fustel's main follower here, G. Glotz (1904, 1928) accentuated Fustel's tendency to confuse two meanings of *genos*, which may denote either a corporate, named group holding rights to priestly office or the bilateral network of kin on whom a particular individual can call for support. The latter group, of course, is different for each individual and does not give rise to any permanent corporate descent group, and the evidence for 'solidarity' and combined action cited by Fustel and Glotz belongs to the *genos* in the latter and not the former sense. The view that the *genos* as a formalised corporate descent group is confined to the aristocracy has, on the whole, been the majority opinion throughout the history of the question, and is reiterated by the latest specialist studies (Bourriot, 1976; cf. also Momigliano and Humphreys, 1974; Humphreys, 1982).

Furthermore, study of family burials in ancient Attica lends little support to Fustel's thesis. It is true that collective burials in chamber tombs are common in Bronze Age Greece, but no continuity can be demonstrated between these tombs and the burials of the historical period. The most prominent funerary monuments in archaic Attica (seventh-sixth century BC) were set up by parents for children, not by pious sons for their fathers; tombs that can be interpreted as family groupings are unusual in this period and almost unknown in the preceding Dark Ages; and tomb-groupings that ostentatiously proclaim family unity are a phenomenon of the fourth century BC and later, rather than of early times – although they always remain in a minority (cf. ch. 5).

Yet, however much of Fustel's argument we may reject, the task he proposed retains its attraction, despite its difficulty. There is no reason to reject *a priori* the idea that something may be learnt by comparing the kinship systems of the different Indo-European societies. The task becomes steadily more difficult to attempt, because of the need to combine familiarity with the original sources in each culture and the historical circumstances that produced them, command of modern anthropological theory, and a critical awarenesss of the way in which research and theory may be influenced by the interests and problems of the researchers' own culture. What we have tried to show here is that the weaknesses in Fustel's argument are intimately connected with the vitality of his reactions to the beliefs and problems of his own society; yet it is also this vitality, as well as the validity of his structural insights, that gives his work its enduring value.

S. C. H.

7 Death and time

My grandfather's clock was too tall for the shelf
So it stood ninety years on the floor
It was taller by far than the old man himself
Though it weighed not a penny-weight more,
It was bought on the morn of the day that he was born,
And was always his treasure and pride;
But it stopped short, never to go again,
When the old man died.

I want to look at the relation between death and time from three different angles, which are relatively independent, although not totally unconnected:

1 What is the 'right time' to die?
2 What is the temporal structure of death as a *rite de passage* by which a person is transformed from being one of the living to being one of the dead?
3 What kind of time, or timelessness, characterises the world of the dead?

I am asking these questions on a comparative basis, but can only draw on limited material, mostly from ancient Greece and modern western societies, in suggesting the range of possible answers.

The good death

First, then, what is the right time to die? The question, obviously, is not one to be answered merely from demographic statistics. The cultural model of a good death is not necessarily the kind of death which is statistically most frequent, although demographic patterns certainly have to be taken into account. The *kalos thanatos*, good death, for archaic Greeks was that of a young warrior in battle, but this need not imply that death in battle was commoner than the death of the elderly – still less that it was commoner than the death of infants. In Victorian novels, the good death is that of a virtuous and preferably innocent person; hence the impressive death-bed scenes in Victorian fiction are often those of children or young women.[1] It is *after* the 'demographic transition', when such deaths are becoming less frequent, that they acquire especial cultural significance.

The ideal of the 'good death' is related, obviously, to conceptions of virtue, but also to conceptions of the overall shape of man's existence – life plus after-life. When Croesus asked Solon whom he considered the most blessed of men, he refused to grant the title to anyone still living: a life could only be judged when completed by its death (Herodotus i. 30-32). The first place went to Tellos of Athens who died in battle and received the honour of public burial on the battle-field, when he had already produced sons and grandsons, the second place to Cleobis and Biton, two Argive youths who died in the sanctuary of Hera after displaying heroic strength and exemplary piety by hauling their mother six miles in an ox-cart to a religious festival. They were commemorated by statues at Delphi; to have a permanent monument, tomb-mound or statue, was an important element in the 'good death'.

Tellos was a grandfather – to leave sons behind to inherit was important. But Tyrtaios states firmly that it is shameful for old men to die in battle rather than young ones (fragment 10, West, 1972), and he is making an aesthetic point as well as a moral one. The hero who died well had to look well in death; and in the archaic period old age seems to have been seen as a kind of decay which was more to be dreaded than death. Mimnermus refers to Tithonus' everlasting old age as a fate worse than death (fragment 4, West) and speaks of the brevity of youth in terms later used for the brevity of life as a whole (fragment 1, West); for him old age is more or less equivalent to death, and the fates offer man a choice between the two, of which death, he implies, is preferable (fragment 2, West). The same motif of choice appears in the *Iliad*, where Achilles has a choice between a heroic death at Troy and eternal glory (*kleos aphthiton*) or old age without fame (*Iliad* ix 410-16). Just as the good Christian death is one which transports the dead to heaven before he or she has become too much contaminated by the world, so the good Greek death is one which translates the dead into heroic immortality (embodied in sculpture or verse) while he is at the height of his strength and beauty.

Such conceptions – depending in the one instance on the concept of the hero's death and in the other on a marked devaluation of this life in comparison with the next – may be rare. But it seems likely that many cultures have some idea of the 'right' shape for a satisfactory life, and make judgments that some deaths are untimely while other people have lived too long. Apart from the intrinsic interest of such ideas about the shape of a living career,[2] they also have a bearing on my next topic, the temporal structure of the process of becoming one of the dead, which begins with the decision that someone is dying.

Becoming dead

The process of dying, in its widest sense, stretches from the decision that a person is 'dying' (as opposed to being temporarily unconscious, or seriously ill, but with chances of recovery) to the complete cessation of all social actions directed towards their remains, tomb, monument or other relics representing them. Besides the beginning and end of this process, I shall pay particular attention to the transition from dying to being dead, the rituals surrounding removal of the corpse from the immediate proximity of the living (burial or other forms of disposal), and the transformation of the decaying cadaver into a stable material representation of the dead (mummy, skeleton, ashes, tomb, monument, ancestral tablet, etc.).

In this process we can analytically distinguish at least four separate levels of transformation and reorganisation which do not necessarily harmonise with one another. Social relationships have to be reorganised, and rights over property and persons reallocated to fill the gap left by the deceased. Mourners have to adjust psychologically to their bereavement. The process of bodily decay has to be dealt with. And, in the beliefs of most peoples, some insubstantial part of the deceased leaves the body and starts on a new career. All these processes 'take time' and demand different kinds of attention from the bereaved. All of them, needless to say, may be influenced by the social status of the deceased.

Dying

David Sudnow (1967) has pointed out the problematic nature of the decision that someone is to be classified as dying, and has shown that in the modern hospital the decision may be markedly affected by the age, social status and perceived moral character of the patient. More strenuous efforts in treatment are likely to be made with young or well-to-do patients than with the old, the poor, alcoholics or addicts.

In the county hospital where Sudnow did his research, to be classed as dying meant a decrease in attention from hospital staff, and often from kin as well. In other circumstances, however, a sick person may claim to be dying in order to attract greater attention; it would be interesting to have information on the situations in which such claims can be effectively made. (In our culture, of course, they are associated with rich persons who have competing heirs.) How long can the process of dying (real or feigned) be prolonged? Bourdieu (1977, p. 166) was told by an old Kabyle woman that in the old days 'death came slowly, it could take a night and a day or two nights and a day. Death "always struck them through their speech": first they became dumb. Everyone had time to see them one last time; the relatives were given time to assemble and prepare the burial.' This remark makes several valuable points. The rituals of dying and of burial have their appropriate *dramatis personae* who have to be brought together; the time required to collect together kin widely scattered (or to transport the corpse back to its kin) appears to have been one of the main motives for the development in the USA, first of airtight coffins with lids partially made of glass and then of embalming (Habenstein and Lamers, 1962; ice was also extensively used). The fact that among the Kabyle silence is a sign of approaching death shows one way in which the status of dying person may be claimed and the status of living social actor renounced.[3] There are presumably many other ways in which this is done. The dying Jew, at the end, turns to the wall, away from the living, to pray. The ancient Greek summoned kin and trustees to hear his last will and testament (even if the will had been written, it should preferably be confirmed by being read aloud at the death-bed) and gave instructions for the payment of all his debts and for his burial (see ch. 5 for references). The death of Socrates as reported by Plato in the *Crito*, regarded as a voluntary suicide rather than a public execution, became the model for philosophical displays of calmness in the face of death, professions of faith concerning the after-life and a new version of the heroic death under the Roman Empire, that of the secular martyr for freedom (Tacitus *Annals* xvi. 34-5, cf. xi. 3; Pliny *Letters* iii. 16; Wirszubski, 1950, p. 142). The Christian rites of dying, as practised in earlier centuries (Ariès, 1975, 1977), combine reconciliation to make a peaceful conclusion to all social relationships, confession and absolution from all wordly sin, and a profession of faith in the after-life which may be influenced by the tradition of the Christian martyrs. In nineteenth-century fiction one often meets the idea that the dead have a vision of the after-life in their last moments – frequently in the form of a vision of dead kin waiting to greet them 'on the other side'.

The ethnography of dying is extremely poor, no doubt because ethnographers have been inhibited by their own taboos from studying it; yet it is clear that in many societies dying is far from being a private matter, that the re-arrangement of rights and roles occasioned by death may well begin during the process of dying, and that the rituals carried out and the roles in them of kin of different statuses or of specialists can provide important insights into cultural values.

Death

It is common in English to speak of 'the moment of death': death is thought of as an easily recognisable natural event which happens suddenly and rapidly. Cases in which the brain ceases to function while the heart and other organs do not, so that social death precedes 'natural' death, are extremely disturbing and have provoked attempts to legalise the acceleration of organic death in order to close the gap – either by legalising euthanasia or by redefining 'death' in terms of brain functioning. But this conception of a critical moment which marks the transition between a period of 'dying' and the subsequent stage in which the dead person is 'laid out' for final rites before being removed from the social context of the living does not necessarily exist in all cultures. W. H. R. Rivers (1926) asserted that on Eddystone Island the words usually translated 'living' (*toa*) and 'dead' (*mate*) in fact formulated a different opposition, between a person who was in a lively and healthy state and one who was seriously ill, old and weak, or dead. Consequently the decision to classify a person as *mate* could set preparations for burial in train immediately, and the burial was not necessarily delayed until all movement and vocalisation had ceased. Something of a similar kind occurs both in the 'ritual murder' of divine kings (Huntington and Metcalf, 1979) and in the discreet measures to avoid prolonging the process of dying practised in modern hospitals (Sudnow, 1967). Even the suicides of Roman senators who preferred death to exile from political life can be seen as a way of harmonising social and physical death; the whole subject of the ways in which the dying can exercise control over the timing of their own death, and the conditions in which they might wish either to accelerate or to delay it, requires study.

Assuming the more common situation in which an event called
'death' must be recognised before the body becomes a corpse, there are
still at least three important processes which may take place either
during the process of dying or after death: the farewell greetings from
kin and friends, the redistribution of roles and property rights and, in
societies where this is a normal part of dealing with all deaths, the
determination of the cause of death. All of these are of more interest
to the living than to the dead - but may well be of interest to the
moribund. In our society the rights of the dead to have their wishes
carried out (and, if necessary, their deaths investigated and avenged)
are protected by a specialised legal apparatus. Without this, the dying
person may have to mobilise public opinion to support his authority:
preparations for death, in relation to the transfer of property, may be
made well in advance - or, conversely, the culture may attribute a
charismatic authority to the words of a dying man which is difficult to
overrule (cf. Strathern, 1981 and Moore, 1981).

There are, in any case, some temporal constraints on the duration of
the early stages of 'becoming dead', both social and technical. The
start of the process is difficult to predict, and it therefore has to run its
course in competition with other activities already planned, and this
may generate pressures to curtail it; and secondly, once organic death
has occurred, the decay of the cadaver has to be taken into account.
The ideal funerals of the *Iliad*, in which the gods magically embalm the
bodies of Patroclus, Hector and Achilles to preserve them untouched
for nine and even, in Achilles' case, seventeen days of ritual lamentation
before their cremation, well illustrate the operation of these conflicting
pressures in Greek thought: for society to suspend its operations for as
long a period as possible added to the honour of the dead, yet physical
decay profaned it. In the sumptuary legislation of Solon at Athens
c. 590 BC on funerals, and in the funerary regulations of other Greek
cities, the period during which the dead were exposed for ceremonial
'viewing' was limited by law. Even in the *Iliad*, another form of cultural
control over the length of the 'viewing' period is hinted at in Achilles'
dream that Patroclus comes to him and asks for speedy burial so that
his soul may depart for Hades. The *Iliad* is also interesting for its
combination of (supernaturally accomplished) embalming and cremation: it seems more usual for these two processes to be regarded as
alternative means of avoiding the problems of physical decay, either by
indefinitely postponing or by forestalling it. At present, it seems,
Americans embalm but rarely cremate; the British cremate but rarely

embalm. Herodotus' report that Egyptian embalmers were suspected of practising necrophily with young and beautiful female bodies (ii. 89) perhaps suggests that the Greeks subconsciously felt preservation by mummification to be almost too much of a good thing.[4]

The period immediately preceding and following death is that which faces the bereaved with the most conflicting demands. On the one hand they are expected to share in some sense in the journey of the dead away from society; on the other hand they are involved in an intense social activity of reaffirming relationships, mobilising resources for the entertainment of guests or the destruction of wealth, legitimating an altered social order. Contact with the corpse is often considered polluting, and the mourners, whether for this reason or others, are often required to segregate themselves from normal social intercourse. Granet (1922) says of Chinese mourning, 'De même que la mort retranche le défunt de la vie familiale, le deuil supprime, dans le courant des jours, les rapports entre parents. Chacun, strictement isolé, est contraint à la vie la plus ralentie qui soit, et, dans ce néant, ne doit point avoir plus de sentiments actifs que le mort lui-même.' It is perhaps not surprising, in view of these conflicting demands, that many societies assign to women the roles which involve the closest contact with the corpse and the most marked detachment from the rhythms of everyday life, while leaving men to deal with the more public aspects of the funeral. But the situation here is far from simple. The less intense participation of women in public social life, which functionally justifies associating them with the dead rather than the living when a division of labour along these lines is required, may often itself be ideologically justified by ascribing to women qualities for the manifestation of which death offers exceptional opportunities. In ancient Greece, the opposition between men and women is associated with the distinction between emotional control and unrestrained emotional displays (Just, 1975); emotion was not only non-social, it was anti-social, and its uninhibited release in funerals was dangerous and disturbing: funerary laws restricted the public participation of women in funerary processions to close kin and those over the age of sixty. Even so, a funeral was one of the few occasions (the others being also ritual) on which a young man could see an unrelated girl and fall in love with her (Lysias i. 8; Terence, *Phormio*, 91-116). Maurice Bloch (in press) suggests other reasons why women may be given a prominent role in death rituals.

One would expect *a priori* – the expectation seems to be more or less borne out by the ethnographic data I have been able to consult, but the subject requires further discussion – that societies in which power is personal and labile will show a more intense interaction between the living on the occasion of death (as in Andrew Strathern's Melanesian material, Strathern, 1981) whereas those in which it is solidly anchored in corporate groups may focus their attention more on the care of the dead. This is a point which needs further research.

Burial and reburial, monuments, commemoration

Robert Hertz' famous 'Contribution à une étude sur la représentation collective de la mort' (1907) presents us with a model of primary and secondary disposal of the remains of the dead in which the process of decay of the corpse, the mourning regulations imposed on the bereaved and the supposed experiences of the spirit of the dead move in parallel: when decay is finished and secondary burial accomplished, mourning comes to an end and the spirit of the dead is definitively established in its new existence. There is no reason to expect, however, that in all societies the correspondence will be as neat as it is in this model (cf. Huntington and Metcalf, 1979). Seen in a wider context, both the collection of bones for secondary burial after the flesh has decayed and the belief that at death a spiritual part of the person leaves the body to become established in some new form of existence form part of the tendency to try to transform what was a living person and is now a decaying cadaver into something permanent and stable – mummy, monument or memory, ash, ancestor or angel. Broadly speaking, there seem to be three main ways of accomplishing this. The deceased may become identified with some stable material object, usually a part of, receptacle for, or representation of, his or her own body; or he or she may be reincorporated into society as an ancestor or by reincarnation; or he or she may start a new life in the world of the dead. These alternatives are not by any means mutually exclusive; they frequently coexist in a somewhat loose and apparently inconsistent articulation (cf. Cunha, 1981).

I shall not spend time here on discussion of primary and secondary burial, of which good accounts are available (Hertz, 1907; Huntington and Metcalf, 1979; Bloch, 1971), except to remark that secondary rituals obviously increase the room for manoeuvre in those aspects of funerary rites which are concerned with renewing, reorganising and re-legitimising relations between the living. There is a great deal of variation in the interval between primary and secondary disposal both within and between societies (Miles, 1965). Even when the time of secondary burial is supposed to be related to the duration of the decaying of the corpse, this process can take very different lengths of time within a single society, depending on differences in soil (Ariès, 1977), and widely divergent culturally standardised intervals are cited: the Balinese permit secondary disposal (cremation) after 42 days (Huntington and Metcalf, 1979, pp. 85-6), while the Chinese village studied by Emily Ahern (1973) allowed six to seven years for the corpse to become clean.

As I have already said, allowing the bones of the dead to become separated from the flesh which once encased them is only one of a number of ways of representing the separation of a part of the person which is capable of achieving immortality from the parts which are subject to destruction by time. In ancient Greece, what it was important to preserve was the memory of the deeds of the dead, embodied either in immortal words or in stone (cf. Svenbro, 1976; Vernant, 1978). The inscribed slab, relief sculpture or statue which stood over a Greek tomb was the product of the convergence of two different ideas: the *sema* or sign which indicated the burial place of a hero - which might be simply an earth mound, but might also have some object fixed in it to signify the status of the deceased in life, as Elpenor in the *Odyssey* asks to have his oar set up over his grave - and the *kolossos*, a stone substitute for the deceased, either aniconic or anthropomorphic, which symbolised the fixity of the dead: it could be used to pin down troublesome ghosts (Vernant, 1962, 1976, 1977, 1978) and, as the use of anthropomorphic statues developed, was also used to create a perpetual relationship between a deity and the worshipper whose statue was dedicated in his or her shrine (cf. Ducat, 1976). Vernant's work on the category of the 'double' in Greek thought, as represented by the *kolossos*, has been strikingly confirmed recently by D. Lanza's discussion of Aristotle's views on death (1980): Aristotle states roundly that a corpse is no more a human being than a statue or painting is: both lack the characteristics of a functioning living organism which are essential to the concept of man, and are therefore called 'man' only by homonomy.[5] The memorial statue, like the corpse, both is and is not the deceased. Through the inscriptions engraved on its base, it has a voice: it hails the passerby, explains whose monument it is, and asks for a tribute of mourning (cf. ch. 5):

Man, as you go on your way thinking of other things, .

stand and pity, seeing the *sema* of Thrason.

$$(IG \text{ i}^2 \text{ } 971 = \text{i}^3 \text{ } 1204)$$

Sema of Phrasikleia. I shall be called maiden for ever,
For the gods allotted me this name in place of marriage.

$$(\text{i}^2 \text{ } 1014 = \text{i}^3 \text{ } 1261)$$

It is particularly clear in the case of the second inscription that Phrasikleia is fixed eternally in the form of a beautiful maiden through the setting up of the monument (cf. Vernant, 1978).

Maurice Freedman (1958, p. 84) made a distinction between ancestor-worship and memorialism which seems to me more appropriate to the ancient Greek data than for the contrast between domestic 'remembrance' of the deceased who were personally known and structurally significant ancestor-worship to which it was originally applied. What the Greeks hoped to achieve for the dead was perpetual remembrance, by strangers as well as kin. The dead did not become ancestors (they had no effect on the lives of their descendants and were not reincorporated into society to serve as focal points in the genealogical definition of social relationships): they became *monuments.*

I have discussed elsewhere (ch. 5) the individualising character of archaic Attic funerary sculpture and inscriptions. Family solidarity was apparently manifested before Solon's legislation at funerals, when the participants, after interring the newly dead, would make a round of other graves - presumably of members of the same family - making offerings, probably, lamenting and praising their occupants. But the fact that Solon forbade this practice shows that he considered it one of the ways in which the living flaunted their prestige in a provocative and factious manner, rather than a pious obligation to the dead. The evidence for the grouping of tombs in a single enclosure or under a single mound, in the archaic period, is far from clear; but if family solidarity *was* manifested in this way, it was not made explicit in inscriptions or sculpture. It is significant that the majority of monuments were set up by parents to children, especially to youths who died a hero's death in battle.

There is a hiatus in the inscriptional and sculptural evidence from c. 500 to 430 BC - funerary monuments being forbidden by law - and in the late fifth and the fourth centuries the situation is different. Funerary reliefs often show a family group of two or more persons (see Clairmont, 1970), inscribed *stelai* may carry a number of names, and funerary enclosures group the tombs of members of the same family.

Nevertheless, large groupings are rare. The largest yet found is an enclosure which contained monuments to 17 members of a single family, spread over six generations; one stone listed 11 of these together. It is not irrelevant that two of the men were professional diviners (*manteis*). Out of a sample of c. 600 tomb inscriptions of c. 430-317 BC surveyed, only 37 grouped together persons who were neither spouses, parent and child, or siblings (ch. 5). The aim of the grouping of kin on tombstones and in tomb enclosures seems to be to perpetuate eternally a closeness which existed in life and was to be renewed in the grave, rather than to make a statement about family continuity.

The texts on which Fustel de Coulanges based his belief that the Greek son had a sacred duty to make offerings regularly at his father's tomb, and that to be deprived of such offerings was the worst of fates, occur in fourth-century law-court speeches dealing with situations which arise out of adoptions. The speakers of course appeal to feelings which seem 'natural' to their audience – the desire to see one's identity perpetuated in an heir, the desire to 'keep property in the family', the lack of proper feeling of an heir whose first act was to grub up and sell for firewood the olive trees which had been the pride of the estate ([Demosthenes] xliii. 69). From the time of Homer and Hesiod, it had been considered a tragedy for a man to leave no sons, so that his estate was divided among his kindred (*chērôstai*). The customs of adopting a young kinsman, if one had no children, or of passing the estate to a daughter's son through uxorilocal marriage to her next-of-kin if there were daughters only, had developed as ways of avoiding this fate. But it must be remembered that the man with more than one son had to divide his estate equally between them: the continuity of the stem family which Fustel had in mind (cf. ch. 6) was lost if there was more than one heir, and there is little sign that it was important for most Athenians to be able to point to a continuous succession of generations in the tomb. This is confirmed by the form of the endowments for funerary cult set up in the late fourth century and later; although the fund set up to provide income for the cult is sometimes vested in a family group to which future descendants are to be recruited in perpetuity, the cult is to be offered only to the nuclear family of the founder, who become more or less assimilated to divinities. Their descendants are to officiate, not to share in the cult when their turn comes to die. And there was no feeling that the cult had to be restricted to descendants. Those who could afford it would leave property to endow a commemorative festival for the whole city, administered by its magistrates (Schmitt-Pantel, 1982).

The medieval Christian who arranged to be buried in or close to a church, and donated property to pay for perpetual masses for his soul, used the same mechanism of the funerary endowment (already employed by Hittite and Egyptian kings), but with a different end in view. Whereas the pagan looked for continuity of existence in men's thoughts, and in his tomb or statue as a focus for these, the Christian was concerned about the fate of his soul in a future existence.

The Christian theory that the actions of the living can affect the fate of the souls of the dead in the separate world into which they have passed is, as far as my knowledge goes, uncommon. It is much more usual, where behaviour oriented towards the dead continues after the definitive disposal of the corpse, for it to be based on the belief or hope that the dead have a continued interest in the affairs of the living. Chinese ancestors are informed of all important events in the family (Ahern, 1973); less benign ancestral spirits may have to be placated regularly, and especially when things go wrong (Freedman, 1967). They are reincorporated into the time which governs events among the living; and they may also be subject to the effects of time in that they move further away from the living as newly dead ancestors are interposed between themselves and their living descendants.[6] This is not true for the Malagasy Merina, who mix up all their ancestors together in the tomb (Bloch, 1971), but it is likely to be true for those systems in which a single genealogical map structures the relationships of both the living and the dead.

It would be interesting to collect comparative material on the representation of ancestors. The Romans kept masks of their ancestors at home and their descendants wore them, with the insignia of the highest honours achieved by each in his lifetime, at family funerals (Polybius vi. 53 ff.). The West African Kadara have masks in which they impersonate ancestral spirits to frighten women and children. In the latter case, however, the 'spirits' have a non-human appearance, and it seems possible that there might be an inverse relation between the reincorporation of the dead into society as ancestors – a different kind of being from people – and their figured representation as portraits of the dead.

Monuments, as Panofsky (1964) has pointed out, can be classed as either prospective or retrospective. Prospective monuments represent the dead in his or her future existence: Egyptian tomb-sculptures, late medieval skeletons and depictions of bodily decay, nineteenth-century angels. Retrospective monuments try to recreate the living as an anchor for memory – whether this is the eternal memory that the Greeks considered the deserts of the hero, or the personal memory of the mourners on which the nineteenth-century European and American tomb-cult centred, and which now has new resources of technology to draw on. Sculptured tomb-monuments are now rare (see, however, Jean-Didier Urbain, 1979), but other means of preserving memories of the dead have developed. A study of the use of photographs by mourners is badly needed;[7] and a Boston undertaker recently advertised a tomb which would incorporate film and tape-recordings of the deceased, along with 'a 20-foot scroll containing his writings' (specially aimed at academics? *Boston Globe* Feb. 1974, cited by Vermeule, 1979, p. 211). The custom of dispersing the ashes of the cremated dead in some place chosen by the family, rather than depositing them in a crematorium – which has sometimes been taken to show the end of all concern for the physical remains of the dead – can be a way of strengthening the association of the dead with personal memories of places significant in their lifetime. (I have heard a woman say that she wanted to be cremated because her son had been cremated.) Embalming seems to be another way of providing an acceptable memory-image of the dead to cancel out the sight of them after death; embalmers make efforts to recreate the appearance of the living person, and use photographs to help them in their work. (Cf. the anticipations of modern practice quoted by Ariès, 1977, p. 501.) If the custom of making commemorative visits to the tomb is on the decrease in western civilisation, as it is said to be, then – discounting the obvious effects of increased spatial mobility – one of the probable reasons seems to me to be the reluctance to associate commemorative thought with anything as clearly linked to the idea of death as a tomb or cemetery. The attempt to avoid or deny the existence of death by no means implies a lack of concern with the memory of the dead.

Formal mourning is also increasingly rejected as being a reminder of death which interferes with the process of turning the dead into 'memories' – the only form in which they can continue to exist in this society which no longer believes in an after-life. Formal mourning was a way of signalling the assumption of a role which required correlative behaviour from others in the process of re-structuring social roles made necessary by death. In modern society this process is fragmented: those whose death is felt to be significant to a community wider than that of their personal intimates are commemorated by memorial services at which their career is summed up and given a place in the history of the community, by biographies which perform a similar function, perhaps by memorial funds which go to endow a facility for the community to be personally associated with the name of the deceased. Here we are not so far from the ancient Greek funerary foundation. But in other cases the process of personal psychological adjustment to grief, rather than the readjustment of a wider society, is considered now to be the most significant of the processes set in motion by death. Grief is seen as a kind of illness (Marris, 1974) and the tempo of recovery from illnesses is governed by the patient's own estimate of his or her capacities or, in serious cases, that of an expert therapist. Furthermore, significant points in the period of grief may be marked by psychic phenomena which occur at unpredictable times – particularly poignant feelings of loss, hallucinations or dreams of the dead which may be either distressing or consoling (Marris, 1974; Gorer, 1965). The modern literature on mourning gives a distinct impression that its time-structure is not fully subject to control by the living – hence, partly, the sociological nostalgia for *les deuils d'antan*.

Hence, too, perhaps, the popularity of spiritualist techniques for producing and controlling the renewed contact with the dead which the bereaved in one way or another seek. It would be useful to have material on the contents of these conversations with the dead: whether the bereaved want references to the shared past or assurances of a shared future, what form these take and what general theories of the nature of life and after-life underlie them. It would also be useful to have comparative material on contacts with the dead through dreams, visions or spirit mediumship in other societies (cf. Cunha, 1981).

The world of the dead

It will be clear by now that it is difficult in most cultures to locate the dead unambiguously in one place. They are simultaneously in the remains of their bodies, in their commemorative monuments and in some other place to which their spirits go. What I want to ask, in this section of the paper, is how the absence of the dead from the social time to which they belonged while living is represented in the temporal structure of the world of the dead.

For a start, the cessation of time may be reflected in the monument itself, not merely in the sense that any inorganic representation conveys a sense of immobility, but through the representation of the deceased as dead or sleeping. The idea that the dead are asleep occurs in ancient Egypt (Morenz, 1973) and is hinted at in early Greek thought by the idea that Death and Sleep are twin brothers, children of Night, and by Homer's reference to profound sleep as 'sleep like death' (*Odyssey* xiii, 79; Vermeule, 1979, pp. 145-54). The boon granted by Hera to Cleobis and Biton was to fall asleep in her sanctuary at Argos and never re-awaken; the idea that it is best not to be aware of one's own death is not prominent in antiquity, but recurs in Aristotle (Lanza, 1980). I know no Greek representations of the dead as sleeping, but the Etruscan dead are normally shown in a recumbent position on their monuments - usually reclining on one elbow as at a banquet, a motif which also occurs in Greece, but sometimes asleep (Panofsky, 1964). References to the sleep of the dead occur in literary sources of the Hellenistic and Roman Republican periods (Callimachus, Lucretius, Catullus . . . references are collected in Lattimore, 1942, and Ogle, 1933); they are commoner in Latin than in Greek. Christians took over the motif and gave it a new sense; whereas for pagan philosophers sleep implied freedom from the cares of life, for Christians it was a peaceful way of waiting for the Resurrection (Ferrua, 1962; Stuiber, 1957).

The timelessness of the existence of the dead is also symbolised in Greek mythical thought by their lack of memory - they drink of the waters of Lethe, oblivion (Detienne, 1967; Vernant, 1959, 1960). Their existence has no history in it; they do not produce. In the islands of the Blest harvests occur three times a year (an indication of perpetual spontaneous abundance rather than of the presence of a plant cycle, even here) and agricultural labour is absent, as in the Golden Age. The torments of Hades consist of never-ending repetitive torture or toil: Ixion revolves on a wheel, Tantalus gazes on food and drink he cannot reach, Sisyphus rolls uphill a stone which perpetually rolls down again, the Danaids try to fill a leaking vessel with water, Oknos plaits a rope which is eaten by a donkey as fast as it is produced.[8] The association of work with time is confirmed by Hesiod's myth of the five races of men: the Gold and Silver races neither work nor grow old, nor do they die; the Bronze race and the Heroes grow to maturity, fight and die before they grow old; only in the Iron race do men work and age. It is also confirmed by Hesiod's view of work, in the *Works and Days*, as historical in the sense that it produces irreversible effects: if you work you will be able to buy another man's *kleros*, if you fail to work you may have to sell your own.

Other cultures have different views. In the Egyptian after-life men have to work, unless they have been provided with *ushabti*-figures to take their place when they are called on to do so. In Eddystone Island, according to Rivers (1926), it is believed that the dead go to another island where they lead a life which seems an exact copy of that of the living: they farm, fish, fight and even die. Sexual activity is by no means uncommon among the dead, but what they never seem able to do (cf. Cunha, 1981) is procreate.

Other theories may contrast the time-structure of the world of the living with another kind of time, natural rather than social. Plato in his later works said that the dead shared in the unchanging movements of the stars in the existence 'outside time' which they led between successive incarnations (Burkert, 1972, pp. 365-7). For the Egyptians, the daily reincarnation of the sun was a guarantee of the reawakening of the dead in the afterworld (Morenz, 1973). The movements of sidereal bodies seem both temporal and eternal.

A similar conception of an eternal, cyclical 'natural' time is shown in Wordsworth's

> Rolled round in earth's diurnal course
> With rocks, and stones, and trees.

But the history of the idea of the relation between Death and Nature, from the Romantics onward, is far from simple and does not seem to have been adequately studied (Van Tieghem, 1921, is the only useful reference I have so far found). It is a long way from Wordsworth's lines written on a girl he perhaps anyway saw as a part of nature rather than society (he says nothing like this in epitaphs on friends) to the frankness of

> The daisies in the dell
> Will give out a better smell,
> Because poor Judd is underneath the ground.
>
> *(Oklahoma)*

With the shift in attitudes which turns thinking about death from an unpleasant but salutary moral exercise – the more unpleasant, the more salutary – to a comfortable and comforting kind of melancholy, a natural setting becomes the appropriate one in which to do it (van Tieghem, 1921; Ariès, 1977; French, 1974). Plants provide a vivid though unclear metaphor for the triumph of life over death. (The analogy is unsatisfactory if pursued to its logical conclusion; in ancient

Greece, to compare human life to that of the leaves on the trees was a bitter thought, not a consoling one.) The romantic lover may identify the scent of the roses growing on the grave with the breath of the beloved (Desbordes-Valmore, 'L'Elégie', 1822: Bertrand, 1973, p. 68). In the nineteenth century, especially its second half, flowers replace black drapery in the decor of burial rites (Habenstein and Lamers, 1962). But I do not know how this vaguely formulated association between the dead and the self-renewing life of plants developed into the association between death and fertility which we find in nineteenth-century anthropology, and into the conception of the dead as potential manure which seems now quite common.[9] (Huntington and Metcalf, 1979, pp. 89-92, say that the Mambai of Timor believe that the bodies of the dead help to renew the black earth which feeds plants, which in their turn feed humans; they point out, following M. J. Adams, 1977, that a study of the place of the rotting process and rotting substances in the material culture of different societies could provide insights into their attitudes to corpses.) I suspect that the association between death and fertility in anthropological writings may be an instance of the projection onto 'savages' of a train of thought which was already implicit in the anthropologists' own culture but would have been unacceptable if openly voiced. If this is so, we should regard it with particular caution.

In a loose kind of way, the myth of Persephone seems to provide a link in ancient Greek culture between the cycle of plant death and rebirth and the fate of the dead. Some of the mystery religions may have exploited this suggestion, but we know too little of their cosmologies to be at all certain of this – and the more closely one looks at the evidence, the more problematic the whole situation becomes. In the earliest version we have of the Persephone myth, the probably seventh-century *Hymn to Demeter* from Eleusis, one of the main centres for mystery cult and perhaps the earliest (Richardson, 1974), what the story does is to explain why plants die and agriculture is necessary. Hades snatches Persephone away to the underworld; Demeter, heartbroken, puts a stop to the life of plants which have hitherto grown spontaneously, and this threatens the life of men who depend on plants and thus, indirectly, the supply of sacrifices to the Gods. Zeus is thus motivated to intervene: Persephone is restored to the world of the living for eight months of the year; this division of her time between the living and the dead inaugurates the annual cycle of plant life, and Demeter teaches men the secrets of agriculture. The presupposition of the whole story is that the realm of Hades is already constituted as the land of the dead from which no one returns except by divine intervention, and it seems to be assumed also that men are already mortal before the story begins.

Greek mystery religions, and even the Pythagorean doctrine of reincarnation, seem to be more closely connected to another side of Greek ideas about the after-life which reverses the common idea that death is forgetfulness, Lethe, to assert that the privileged dead can attain *A-lēthe-ia*, non-*Lēthē*, a memory which is knowledge of past, present and future, or of unchanging truth (Vernant, 1959, 1960; Detienne, 1967). Here the timelessness of death is linked to the timeless existence of the gods – who may have a temporal past (Gernet, 1932 suggested that they acquired biographies, by association, from heroes), but are not expected to have a temporal future, although they may be able to foresee the future of men. In this they resemble the dead. To associate the gods with atemporality implies a negative judgment on time: an existence in time is imperfect, incomplete, overshadowed by coming decay. In this line of thought, life may be equated with death and death with life: for Plato, the body is a tomb, *sōma* equals *sēma* (Courcelle, 1966). The true Pythagorean sage can remember all his previous incarnations, but the ordinary man forgets these, and the timeless periods of existence between them, each time he enters a new body. Reincarnation here – as perhaps elsewhere, except where it is restricted within a single descent group so that the reincarnated spirit is assured of the same social status in its next existence – is predominantly negative in its implications, a form of punishment or at best a stage in a slow process of purification. For Greek philosophers, truth and reality are timeless and unchanging. Similarly, in Christian thought, Purgatory is a protraction of the time-bound existence of the living which prepares them for the timeless bliss of Heaven.

Some questions in place of a conclusion

The number of possible oppositions between time and timelessness, decay and permanence, memory and oblivion, movement and stillness, activity and its suspension, incompleteness and completion, is very great, and the possibilities of manipulating these oppositions in fresh combinations increase with developments in material culture and social complexity (the 'memory' attained by the Greek initiate in the after-life could not exist without the *lēthē* of the non-initiate with which it is contrasted). What are the implications of this perspective on death for future research, both anthropological and archaeological? What questions does it suggest, to which we could, but at present do not, know the answers?

(1) One area which is obviously under-researched is dying. Far too many ethnographic reports treat the constatation that someone is dying or dead as non-problematic and begin their analysis of funerary institutions with the announcement of death. The recognition of approaching death, the management of 'false alarms' and the rites of dying and their duration all need study.

(2) More attention should be paid to the differential treatment of the dead at different ages, to ideas about the age at which the 'good death' occurs and their implications for conceptions of the shape of life, to the forms of memorial and after-life considered appropriate for young and old, those with children and the childless.

(3) We have far too little precise information, archaeological, historical or ethnographic, about the length of time for which commemorative rituals continue and ancestors are still individually honoured. Both historians and anthropologists have been too often inclined to accept normative statements about the perenneity of tomb-cults and ancestor-worship, without going into precise details. The demographic probability of the direct line of descent dying out within a limited number of generations, at least in a society such as that of ancient Greece where marriage was monogamous and no value was placed on having a large number of children, should also be considered (Goody, 1973).

(4) I have suggested at various points in the paper that death presents problems of time-management: restructuring of relationships within the family and with outsiders, the psychological adjustment of the bereaved, the preparation of the material equipment and the summoning of the personnel needed for funeral rites, the process of decay undergone by the corpse and the experiences ascribed to the spirit of the dead do not necessarily all harmonise easily on a temporal scale. The unpredictability of death raises interesting questions about the difference between societies in which funerals are the most important form of ritual and those in which a fixed calendar of rites to honour the gods has a more central position. (Secondary burials are sometimes assigned a place in a fixed calendar, as are commemorative rites.) Lavish exchange or destruction of wealth at funerals raises

questions about the institutions through which it is mobilised and about the relations between the alliance structures involved in funerals, marriages, vendettas and other reciprocal ceremonial exchanges. (Here again, as pointed out by Miles, 1965, secondary burials allow more time for mobilisation and more latitude in fixing a date).

(5) I have also suggested that the temporal structure of the after-life - where the dead live in a world of their own and are not reincorporated as ancestors - would repay more systematic study. Since the activities of the dead are usually only a selection from those carried out by the living, it is interesting to see which of the activities of the living are considered too closely associated with the processes of growth, reproduction and decay which characterise life to be carried over into the world of the dead (cf. Cunha, 1981).

In general, the study of the position of death in social and cultural systems has been far too narrowly conceived. It needs to be expanded to take in all the ways in which people may prepare for death - from constructing their own tombs to conferring property rights on their heirs *inter vivos* - and all the ways in which memory of the dead may be preserved. Funerals and cemeteries are not the only occasions and places in which death can be studied.

Notes

1 Beth in L. M. Alcott's *Good Wives*; Humphrey in Florence Montgomery's *Misunderstood*; Theodore, a mentally retarded teenager, in C. M. Yonge's *The Pillars of the House*. Despite Luke 15.7, the deaths of repentant sinners occupy a much less central position.

2 It should not be forgotten that there are careers ending in particular types of death which are exemplary for their badness as well as those which are exemplary for their heroism. The oldness and ugliness of the typical English witch is an obvious example.

3 This association between loss of speech and the onset of death is also made, as Helen King pointed out to me, in the Hippocratic corpus, in *Epidemics* iii. 5-6 and iii. 17. 13-15; cf. *Epidemics* iii. 1.2, *On the Sacred Disease* 10.

4 The theme of necrophily occurs also in the story of Periander of Corinth (Herodotus v. 92), in the myth of Achilles' love for the dead Penthesilea and in Admetus' promise to the dying Alcestis that he will sleep with a statue and with dreams of her (Euripides, *Alcestis* 348-356; cf. Aeschylus, *Agamemnon* 414ff. with the comments of Vernant, 1976). A graffito of the Roman imperial period from Egypt, in which a Greek boy claims that his ashes smell better than Egyptian mummies, preserves echoes of the cultural rivalry between cremators and mummifiers: Perdrizet, 1934.

5 In fact Aristotle (*Meteorologica* 389b 31ff., *De generatione animalium* 734b 25ff., *De partibus animalium* 640b 35ff., *De anima* 412b 10ff.) does not directly refer to statues but to 'flesh made of stone or wood', 'a hand

made of bronze or wood', 'a painted doctor' (evidently a common philosophical example), 'a wooden or painted eye'. It may be significant that he is more reluctant to say that a statue is not a man than to say that a corpse is not a man.

6 Ancestors who have achieved special fame in life keep their prominence for the living longer than the undistinguished (Freedman, 1958, p. 84). In any society in which prestige counts for something, alongside status in a kinship system, it may continue to affect status after death as well as in life.

7 Note the examples of tomb monuments incorporating photographs, sometimes in combination with sculpture, illustrated by Urbain (1979) and Rahtz (1981).

8 See Keuls, 1974, for the argument that these 'sinners' are undergoing purification through toil rather than eternal punishment. The more fortunate Greek dead play draughts (Pindar frr. 129, 130; cf. Herodotus ii. 122), another non-productive activity. I owe these references to Robert Garland. .

9 'Lorsque je serai de retour dans ma patrie, je veux, dans le petit champ que me laissera mon père, creuser moi-même le lieu de ma sépulture . . . . Comme ce lieu sera cher [à nos enfants] s'ils ont nos goûts, s'ils ont mon âme, souvent ils baiseront après ma mort les arbres voisins: c'est sous leur écorce qu'aura filtré la matière qui composait mon corps' (Amaury Duval, 1801, quoted by Ariès, 1977, p. 504). But the essays for the Institut competition of 1801 were in some respects ahead of the thought of their time, and others had different ideas for making use of the physical remains of the dead: Pierre Giraud proposed to vitrify them and turn them into commemorative plaques (Ariès, 1977, pp. 506-9). The idea that the dead turn into earth, which was already common in antiquity (Sassi, 1981) does not necessarily imply that they feed plants. In Scott's *Old Mortality*, ch. 1 (1816), the idea that the body turns into plant food is viewed as 'degrading and disgusting'.

8   Comparative perspectives on death

In coming together as a group of archaeologists, physical and social anthropologists and historians to discuss research on death, we faced problems of comparison on two levels: comparison of the perspectives of different disciplines, and comparison of the practices and cultures of different societies. During our discussions it was, on the whole, the differences in research perspective and data which appeared most salient, and I shall begin with some brief remarks on these. But in retrospect, considering the papers in their final form, it appears to me that we missed many opportunities of reflecting on the differences between our own cultures and those of the other societies and periods discussed; and in the second part of this discussion paper I shall suggest some themes which it might have been interesting to pursue in more depth.

The disciplines represented were limited, and the focus was emphatically on death as a social phenomenon. Even in the papers by physical anthropologists we were never very far from the social frame of reference. Animal and plant death was mentioned (with the exception of Berry's genetic studies and Molleson's introduction distinguishing human from animal death) only where certain animals or plants acquire a particular social or cultural significance which in some respects assimilates them to persons: leopards and cattle among the Dowayo (Barley), pigs for the 'Aré'Aré (de Coppet, cf. also Strathern), a pet lamb in the Romano-British rural cemetery at Owslebury (Molleson), cedar trees in ancient Mesopotamia (Cassin). At the same time, however, this inclusion of selected animals and plants indicates that death was not being defined in religious terms as the separation of the human spirit from the body. The first paper in the seminar, by Theya Molleson, began by distinguishing human responses to death from those of animals in terms of *ceremonial behaviour*; and what seems to me to characterise our approach to the archaeology and anthropology of death, in contradistinction from the traditional approaches inherited from the nineteenth century, is that we focused on this ceremonial behaviour and the discourses associated with it, and tried to derive from them the functions they serve and the assumptions they presuppose, rather than trying to explain them by reference to some preconceived schema of beliefs concerning the after-life. With this shift, some of the themes traditionally prominent in the comparative study of death – the place of death in different religions and, more specifically, concepts of the soul and their implications for the conceptualisation of the personality, or the association of different fates in the after-life with moral conduct during life – have come to be neglected. The only paper in our seminar which focussed on eschatology (Cunha) looked at it from the point of view of the structural relationship between the society of the living and the world of the dead, in order to consider the social functions of and social constraints on eschatological speculations. We were looking at death as the removal of a social person from society, and in dealing with what happens after death most of us unreflectingly adopted the perspective which Vernant has explicitly shown to be that of Greek epic poetry: it is the fate of socially significant aspects of the person (status, exploits, personal relationships) which matters. We did not invite a psychologist to join our discussions. Perhaps we should have.

Almost all those taking part in the seminar were used to working in more than one of the disciplinary frameworks represented, or collaborating across disciplinary boundaries. The archaeologists had close links with physical anthropology and history; the historians with archaeology, social anthropology and, in Macfarlane's case, demography, both social and physical anthropologists were concerned with historical developments over time, and Bloch produced a paper which explicitly addressed from a social anthropologist's viewpoint the archaeologist's problem of trying to interpret material culture with inadequate information on culture and social structure.

Nevertheless, it takes more than inter-personal contact and goodwill to solve the problems of interdisciplinary research. For example, in excavation the physical anthropologist's needs are very different from those of the archaeologist oriented to the study of material culture, and they are unlikely to be satisfied at all adequately while most excavations are directed principally towards the recovery and dating of artefacts, as is still the case in too many areas. The physical anthropologist needs more graves dug than the student of pottery sequences, and is concerned with a far longer time-scale; evolutionary changes will rarely show up in the time-span covered by most excavations on a single site and where, as at Armelagos' Wadi Halfa or Jacobsen's Franchthi, a single site does produce material covering several millennia, the sample of graves excavated is usually too small to provide a secure statistical basis for conclusions. (Carlson, 1974, 1976 studied 240 crania from deposits stretching from c. 3400 BC to c. 1100 AD; his 1977 article compares these with 12 Mesolithic crania.) The same problem of sample size is faced by archaeologists who wish to use cemetery data as a basis for reconstructing stratification patterns, as was emphasised by Hodson and Orton. Again, social anthropologists raise questions about the spatial positioning of the dead in relation to the living (Cunha, 1981; cf. Ucko, 1969; Leach, 1977) which archaeologists could only begin to consider if they had far more complete data on the relations between settlements and cemetery sites than are usually available. The archaeologist's conception of an adequate sample and definition of the 'site' as the unit of research are called into question by the perspectives of other disciplines.

Historians also have problems in adjusting their focus to that of the demographers, as Macfarlane's paper indicated. It would seem reasonable, *prima facie*, to expect the 'demographic transition' which dramatically reduced infant and child mortality to have some effect on attitudes to the death of young children, as Lawrence Stone (1977) and others have argued. But the view that before this change parents refrained from directing too much emotion towards young children assumes a relation between emotion and expectations of stability in relationships which will not be accepted without question by a social historian or social anthropologist. It assumes, indeed, that the individual is free to manage his or her psychological economy in a way which will minimise the risks of severe trauma. Even common-sense or common experience might suggest that there is something wrong about this view. The meaning and intensity of emotional relationships is surely affected by the value placed on them by the actor's culture (which will not necessarily place a high value on the avoidance of all kinds of risk); and reactions to child death therefore have to be related to the status of children in the culture (which may involve considering the significance of future, as well as past, time: cf. Strathern's paper, on the Wiru), and to the meaning attached to intrafamilial relationships in general (a shift to a much greater expression of concern over child deaths took place in Athens in the late fifth to fourth century BC with no demographic change behind it, cf. ch. 5 above; note that the more or less contemporary Herodotus, i. 136-7, ascribes to the Persians the attitude which modern historians ascribe to the pre-bourgeois family). Again, one would expect severe epidemics to affect attitudes to death, and we do indeed have some striking accounts in historical sources of changes in attitudes *during* plagues (Thucydides; Lebrun, 1971; cf. Vanstiphout, 1980). But it is difficult to identify long-term results of such experiences with any confidence. (Note Rahtz's suggestion of a possible connection between the fourteenth-century plagues and the prominence of macabre themes in representations of death.)

Such interdisciplinary confrontations tend to leave archaeologists, in particular, feeling somewhat beleaguered: asked to expand their framework of reference in both space and time to impracticable dimensions, and at the same time warned – as Maurice Bloch warned them – that if they try to interpret material culture without any data on ideology or any other source of information on social structure they are liable to jump to the wrong conclusions. Peter Ucko, one of the founders of the interdisciplinary seminar series of which our seminar formed part, already gave the same warning in a brilliant article (1969) which made several essential points: that a single cemetery site may well not contain a representative sample of the population using it from the point of view of sex, age, social status, cause of death or physical condition at the time of dying; that there is variation in the treatment of the dead within all cultures as well as between cultures; that burial practices are not necessarily stable or closely correlated with other aspects of social structure or beliefs (cf. Cunha's remarks on the instability of eschatology); that it is in the highest degree unlikely that any two societies will resemble each other sufficiently for an archaeologist or historian to be able to make direct inferences from ethnographic data to fill gaps in our knowledge of past societies.

Ucko nevertheless claimed that familiarity with ethnographic data was of the utmost value to the archaeologist or historian because it served to 'widen the horizons of the interpreter'; and I turn now to consider the contribution which the perspectives on different societies represented in our seminar might make to such a widening of horizons. It is a commonplace of social anthropology that experience of other cultures is particularly valuable in relation to phenomena in which we have a deep emotional involvement and which our own culture (and others: Bloch, in press) tends to dignify by classing them as 'natural'; and I shall try now not only to point out some of the more significant differences and resemblances between cultures which emerge from the papers discussed here, but also to analyse the papers themselves as a discourse on death which can tell us something about the culture which produced them.

By way of preamble, it is worth remarking that the ideas current in different societies about the way other people dispose of their dead are in themselves an interesting topic for research. Ancient Greek ethnographers situate Greek funerary practices in the centre of a spectrum which ranges from the utter neglect practised by Persian magi who expose corpses to be mauled by dogs and vultures (Herodotus i. 14) to the over-incorporation of the dead into the world of the living practised on the one hand by the Egyptians (image of a corpse at symposia, Herodotus ii. 78; necrophily, ibid. 89) and, at the other end of the evolutionary scale (cf. Rossellini and Said, 1978), by Indian tribes who eat their dead associates (*hoi malista homileontes* is the term used), the endophagy being sexual as well as social (ibid. iii. 99). (Herodotus seems inclined to oppose the magi who expose corpses to ordinary Persians who cover them with wax - a practice analogous to Egyptian mummification, belonging to the 'civilised' end of the evolutionary continuum - but is not sure of the facts: his hellenised Persian informants may well have been inclined to reticence.) The works of early European travellers, missionaries and anthropologists provide ample material for similar studies. The remark of R. Taggia quoted by Cunha, in which he unhesitatingly recognises among the Krahó the desire to pass eternity in the company of their own kin which played such an important part in nineteen-century European burial practices, is typical of the sympathetic form of ethnocentric distortion: the 'others' are assumed to share 'our' feelings. But the converse attitude of eagerness to swallow any story which heightened the contrast between the practices of 'savages' and 'civilised peoples' was equally common, especially of course in the form of stories about cannibalism. The effects of these western attitudes on colonial administration also require study (cf. Strathern).

We may now be able to see more clearly the motes in the eyes of earlier researchers and the biases in the legacy they have left to us; but how far can we go towards detecting the beams which distort our own vision? What were the significant areas of concentration and neglect in our seminar discussions?

Many of the contributors seemed to share a feeling that death confronts human beings with an awareness of their own transience, to which they react with attempts to salvage out of this disturbing experience some residue to which permanence can be attributed. Tombs, and especially tomb-monuments, are one of the main ways of doing this in western culture, and this is one reason why so much research into death is concerned with tombs. Funerals are thought of as ephemeral phenomena and therefore receive less attention; but Strathern's and de Coppet's papers on Melanesia revealed a different perspective in which funerary exchanges lead on to further exchanges and thus constitute a basis for the incorporation of the dead into a processual, rather than static, permanence. Tomb-monuments in western culture – and in the Indian hero-stones discussed by Romila Thapar – individualise those they commemorate; and most contributions betrayed traces of the Greek attitude sharply delineated by Vernant, in which life is associated with individuality, and death threatens to put an end to differentiation unless the dead person is rescued from the finality of death by preservation of the memory of him or her as an individual. Western culture does its best to hold off the idea of death as indifferentiation. Archaeologists try to use grave-goods and skeletal data to reconstruct as many of the individual features of the dead as possible; even the physical anthropologists' current concern with the survival of genes (which, viewed in comparative perspective as an ideology of death – and what alternatives does our culture now offer? – seems distinctly bizarre) may be seen as related to interest in the transmission of individualising features from generation to generation (in contrast to an earlier focus on the stability of racial types). Other cultures seem particularly striking to us when they reverse this perspective: the Merina who crunch up the bones of the dead all together in order to make the tomb into an ideal representation of group unity (Bloch); the Krahó who think that the images of the dead lack the individualising ties created by affinity and become steadily less differentiated until they end as stocks and stones (Cunha). It was striking that the Greek model of the commemoration of heroic individuality turned up both in India (Thapar) and in Melanesia (Strathern: commemoration of prominent men in exchange cycles). Only de Coppet's paper seemed to escape entirely from the tendency to discuss the fate of the dead in terms of the survival or non-survival of residues of the individual – a significant exception in view of the constant emphasis of de Coppet's teacher Louis Dumont on the distortions which the influence of individualism is likely to introduce in the study of non-modern civilisations (cf. e.g. Dumont, 1975).

Another feature of the majority of the papers in the seminar which seems diagnostic of our own culture is that death was treated as something which happens to others. Only Vernant looked at death from the point of view of the man who confronts it. Martyrdom was barely mentioned. We seemed to be reluctant even to look at the possibility that there might be a wide variety of attitudes towards the prospect of one's own death – with the suffering, or release from suffering, which it may bring – and that these need research.

Besides revealing such aspects of our attitudes to death, the seminar papers and the discussions which took place implicitly demarcated antitheses in our ways of perceiving and classifying the world which underlay our difficulties in communicating between the different disciplinary sub-cultures represented: the oppositions between 'nature' and 'culture' and between 'things', 'persons', and the shared beliefs and interactions which make up society. We failed to develop any general comparative discussion about views on the causes of death, for example, and this was surely due at least in part to a feeling of incompatibility between the explanations of death put forward by scientific medicine and beliefs such as those of the 'Aré'Aré, who divide deaths into those caused by human killers and those caused by ancestral spirits. But we ought to have been alerted by Berry's remark that human biologists do not know what causes aging and death to the realisation that the concept of 'natural death' – if by this one means a death resulting from the operation of normal processes rather than from their breakdown – has as precarious a status in western medicine as it has in those cultures which ascribe all deaths to witchcraft, but nevertheless show less concern to find the witch in the case of the deaths of the very old. Medical explanations of death, though couched in a 'natural' idiom, still seek to apportion blame (to one organ rather than another); and they can easily be combined with moral judgments. Nowadays we are all warned of the mortal dangers of smoking, drinking, over-eating and taking too little exercise; in Victorian novels young ladies died of a 'decline' brought on by falling in love with an unsuitable man, or of infectious diseases caught by showing too much zeal in visiting the poor.

Reluctance to integrate 'natural' and 'social' factors in the study of society is also responsible for noticeable omissions and distortions in many social anthropologists' and social historians' studies of social structure. Because they look for normal and typical patterns of social relationships and have tended, at least until very recently, to regard early death as abnormal and 'accidental' even in those societies where it is statistically frequent, there is a marked bias towards the description of social structure as if each actor lived to a ripe age. Orphans, widows (see, however, Pitt-Rivers, 1977) and widowers, second marriages and step-relationships, the childless, are seldom mentioned (as are the disabled and the chronically sick). Most of the categories listed here are, of course, commoner in monogamous situations; but even in 'polygynous societies' not every man can afford several wives, and variations in family size can still be very significant. Sally Falk Moore pointed out in her paper that the implications of an inheritance rule which favours eldest and youngest sons and leaves their intermediate siblings to seek new land for themselves may be radically affected by demographic change. If, as Bourdieu recommends (1977), we should move from the construction of normative models of social structure to the study of the manifestation in actors' strategies of dispositions shaped by social experience, then the incidence of death is a situational factor which will have to be given serious consideration. If historians must learn to think in terms of the aggregate effects of demographic patterns - as they have recently been doing (Macfarlane) - social anthropologists need to integrate the time dimension and an awareness of the significance of particular historical events (such as a death) into their analysis of even short-term situations.

Between social anthropologists, or historians, and archaeologists the conceptual barrier is based on the antithesis between 'things' and the meaning people attach to them. It is all too easy for social anthropologists to produce examples of burial forms or artefact patterns of which the archaeologist would never guess the meaning without help from ethnographic or written sources; and it is attractive to some archaeologists, in response, to look for a solution in stressing the materiality of their data, in associating themselves with 'science' rather than with history, in seeking ways of 'making the facts speak for themselves'. In so far as archaeological studies in the past have too often relied on unquestioned and ethnocentric assumptions about the relation between beliefs and behaviour, rather than studying the material record thoroughly, and with a full awareness of the possible range of variations which it might reveal, this movement is of course fully justified; but it still conceals unscrutinised assumptions about the place of 'things' in culture which need discussion. The question of the relations between persons and things is one of the areas where the attitudes of western culture are most often taken for granted. Strathern and de Coppet had difficulty in finding a language in which to express the Melanesian view that both things and persons are manifestations of sets of social relationships, or that 'it is the person who is the prime form of movable property' (Strathern). By contrast, we can see that western archaeologists make a more direct connection between persons and things: they see things as *belonging to* persons, as property and above all as symbols of personal status and (for certain categories of objects thought to have had emotional significance to the dead) as residues of personal life-histories. It is because children in Western society do not own property, except for toys, and have no achieved status, that the discovery of children with rich grave-goods becomes problematic. To take the use of things to symbolise status as something to be demonstrated for each culture, rather than as a quasi-universal phenomenon, would immediately indicate a further direction for research which oddly enough seems to have been little exploited by archaeologists concerned with the social significance of grave-goods: it becomes obvious that iconographic evidence for the differentiation of social statuses by dress, possessions and other uses of material objects should be sought and compared with the assemblages found in tombs of the same culture. Such a perspective would also show clearly the value, emphasised by Rahtz, of studying the material culture of societies and periods for which written sources (or ethnographic data) are also available.

The fact that archaeologists tend to pay particular attention to signs of social stratification or ranking in their attempts to deduce social status from grave-goods or from the forms of tombs and monuments (sex, age and other criteria of status differentiation have been less thoroughly researched and are often integrated into models of social stratification) no doubt reflects the preoccupations of modern society. (We had hoped to include in the seminar an archaeological paper on kin groupings in tombs, but unfortunately it was not ready in time.) It is important to be aware of other potential bases for differential treatment of the dead. Archaic Greeks and medieval Indians (Thapar) paid greater attention to those whose manner of death conferred a retrospective glory on their lives; heroes often belonged to an upper stratum of society, a warrior group, but not everyone in this stratum became a hero. Implicitly, it is far too often assumed that the expenditure of wealth and effort on the burial and commemoration of the dead comes from the estate or the kin of the dead person, and that these resources are directly correlated with his or her status in society. But this need not be the case. Where funerals are celebrated or monuments are set up by groups based on some criterion which cuts across lines of economic stratification (as, for example, in the commemoration of saints and martyrs by a religious congregation) this assumption breaks down.

It is an obvious ethnocentric mistake to assume that the behaviour evoked by death is to be seen solely as a reaction to the disruptions of social and emotional equilibrium caused by a particular decease. Death provides occasions and materials for a symbolic discourse on life – through the different treatments accorded to those whose lives have ended in different ways and at different stages of development, through theories about what happens in the after-life, through the symbols used in funerary rites or eschatology to express the contrast between life and death. From this point of view one of the obvious lacunae in our seminar was the absence of any systematic consideration of conceptions of sexuality and procreation in relation to conceptions of death, although the subject was touched on in the papers of Barley and Cassin.

Even in the small sample of cultures represented, the recurrence of the same symbols appeared noteworthy: an association of water in general, or moving water in particular, with life and of dryness, solidity and stillness with death; an association of differentiation with life, as already noted above, and of lack of differentiation with death. Does this recurrence suggest the existence of a set of 'natural symbols' particularly apt for the contrast between life and death, which might provide a lead in interpreting the symbolism found in archaeological data? Unfortunately, closer examination of the examples cited here seems discouraging. The association between water or wetness and life seems obvious enough. But while the Dowayo (Barley) associate wetness with nature and fertility and (relative) dryness with culture and with death (and regard flowing water as 'drier' than still water), the situation for the Krahó (Cunha) is much more complex. Moving water is associated with life and 'ripening', the latter association being connected with the fact that the fruits of the *buriti* palm have to be soaked in water for several days to make them edible (Cunha, 1973); still water is associated with death and changelessness. Yet for the Timbira in general dryness is associated with life and culture, wetness with nature and death (ibid.). Finally, for the Merina (Bloch), water from special sources blown by an elder or a king carries the blessing of life and fertility. In the first case we seem to be dealing with a theory which asserts a 'natural' causal connection between fluids and fertility (with explicit reference to rain and bodily fluids), in the second case with an analogical relation between the pairs moving water/still water and life/death, and also with an analogy drawn from the use of water in the cultural processing of food, and in the third case with water as a fluid medium which can absorb and transmit intangible forces derived from contact with spirits, ancestors, elders or kings. Are we justified in saying that 'the same' symbol is present in all three cases? But again, is it justifiable to try to distinguish between causal theories, analogy or metaphor and what we might be inclined to call magical operations? Do the differences in the underlying models matter, except from our parochial viewpoint?

Again, the idea that the dead – or at least some of them – lose their individuality is present in Merina, Krahó, Dowayo and ancient Greek thought; but its implications are very different in each case. For Greek aristocrats the thought of the anonymity and lack of individuality of the unremembered dead was terrifying; for the Krahó the solidarity of the kin group among the *mekarō* (the 'images' of the dead) is ambiguous, both ideal and unrealisable, negatively marked by the fact that the dead progress on through further stages of loss of personal identity until they become stocks and stones; for the Merina the union of skeletons crushed together in family tombs provides an ideal repre- sentation of the society of the living as it is supposed to be, only kings being allowed to retain their individuality; for the Dowayo the lack of differentiation of the dead seems to be related to their association with a generic control over fertility which benefits groups rather than individuals. More detailed ethnography would be needed in order to work such comparisons out more fully, and there are certainly problems here on which it would be interesting to collect more comparative data. But it is clear that the comparison will have to deal not with discrete 'symbols' or even symbolic oppositions, but with complex combinations of social experience, practical observation, speculation and metaphor for which the notion of 'natural symbols' may provide a heuristically fruitful starting point, but not a ready-made blueprint. (It may be noted here that death itself provides 'natural symbols' used in other *rites de passage* and elsewhere, in ways which need to be studied.)

While the possibility of comparative generalisation was not explicitly ruled out by any of the seminar participants, there was a tendency to be content with the more modest aim of formulating research schedules for collecting data on which such generalisations might eventually be based (cf. especially the papers by Jacobsen and Cullen, Rahtz,

Macfarlane and Humphreys). However, a consensus also seemed to emerge from several papers that if fruitful generalisations are to be produced, comparative studies must be based on a more historical approach than has been common in anthropological studies until recently. There is convergence here between Berry's demand for more historical studies of the genetic patterns found in particular localities, Sally Falk Moore's insistence that inheritance laws change their significance according to the demographic and economic context in which they are operated, Romila Thapar's demonstration that the functions of a single type of grave monument and the status and structure of the groups concerned with erecting and tending it can change over time, Maurice Bloch's hope that a wide-ranging study of changes in material culture over time could tell archaeologists more about the relations between material culture and social structure than analyses concentrated within a limited period, and Manuela da Cunha's search for a theory of 'speech forms' rather than of 'grammar', i.e. an analysis of symbolic communication which shows its relation to the context in which it is produced. Bourdieu's focus on 'strategy' rather than 'rules' (1977) leads in the same direction: to a view that even within a single society and period situations do not reproduce themselves exactly. It is because death both emphasises the impermanence and unrepeatability of social experience and calls forth attempts to preserve or re-create some aspects of it in permanent form that it offers a particularly stimulating focus for reflections on the paradoxical mixture of the transient and the permanent which constitutes society.

Bibliography

ADAMS, M. J. (1977), 'Style in southeast Asian materials processing: some implications for ritual and art', in H. Lechtman and R. Merrill, eds, *Material culture: Studies, organization and dynamics of technology*, West Publishing Co., St Paul, pp. 21-52.

ADKINS, A. W. H. (1960), *Merit and Responsibility*, Clarendon Press, Oxford.

ADORNO, THEODOR W., *et al.* (1950), *The Authoritarian Personality*, Harper, New York.

AHERN, EMILY (1973), *The Cult of the Dead in a Chinese Village*, Stanford University Press.

AHLBERG, GUDRUN (1971), *Prothesis and Ekphora in Greek Geometric Art*, Åstrom, Göteborg.

ALEXANDRĒS, OLGA (1969), 'Peribolos oikogeneiakōn taphōn para tēn hodon pros Akademeian', *Athens Annals of Archaeology*, 2, pp. 257-61.

ALEXANDRĒS, OLGA (1972), '3e Ephoreia klassikōn archaiotētōn Athēnōn', *Archaiologikon Deltion*, 25, 1970, pp. 40-91.

ALEXANDRĒS, OLGA (1976), '3e Ephoreia klassikōn archaiotētōn Athēnōn'. *Archaiologikon Deltion*, 27, 1972, pp. 22-146.

ALEXIOU, MARGARET (1974), *The Ritual Lament in Greek Tradition*, Cambridge University Press.

AMANDRY, P. (1949), 'Chronique des fouilles et découvertes archéologiques en Grèce en 1948', *Bulletin de correspondance hellénique*, 73, pp. 516-36.

ANDREIOMENOU, ANGELIKE K. (1963), 'Anaskaphai eis Athēnas kai Attikēn', *Archaiologikon Deltion*, 17, 1961-2, B, pp. 36-43.

ANDRONIKOS, M. (1968), *Totenkult* (Archaeologia Homerica III W), Vandenhoeck & Ruprecht, Göttingen.

ARENDT, HANNAH (1958), *The Human Condition*, University of Chicago Press.

ARIÈS, PHILIPPE (1960), *L'Enfant et la vie familiale sous l'ancien régime*, Plon, Paris (trans. *Centuries of Childhood*, Cape, London, 1962).

ARIÈS, PHILIPPE (1975), *Essais sur l'histoire de la mort en Occident du Moyen Age à nos jours*, Seuil, Paris.

ARIÈS, PHILIPPE (1977), *L'Homme devant la mort*, Seuil, Paris (trans. *The Hour of our Death*, Knopf, New York, 1981).

ARMELAGOS, GEORGE J., a.o. (1981), 'Death and demography in prehistoric Sudanese Nubia', in Humphreys and King, eds, 1981, pp. 33-57.

ARRIGONI, GIAMPIERA (in press), 'Le Amazzoni a Roma', in Vegetti and Humphreys, eds, in press.

ARTHUR, MARYLIN (1982), 'Cultural strategies in Hesiod's *Theogony*: law, family, society', *Arethusa*, 15, pp. 63-82.

ARTHUR, MARYLIN (in press), 'Male and female in Hesiod's *Theogony*', Italian trans. in Vegetti and Humphreys, eds, in press.

ASGARI, N. and FIRATLI, N. (1978), 'Die Nekropole von Kalchedon', in *Studien zur Religion und Kultur Kleinasiens. Festschrift F. K. Dörner*, Brill, Leiden, pp. 1-92.

BACHOFEN, J. J. (1861), *Das Mutterrecht*, Krais & Hoffmann, Stuttgart.

BACHOFEN, J. J. (1870), *Die Sage von Tanaquil*, Mohr, Heidelberg.

BAKALAKIS, GEORGIOS (1971,) 'Die Lutrophoros Athen (ex Schliemann) -Berlin 3209', *Antike Kunst*, 14, pp. 74-83.

BARLEY, NIGEL (1981), 'The Dowayo Dance of Death', in Humphreys and King, eds, 1981, pp. 149-59.

BEAZLEY, J. D. (1956), *Attic Black-figure Vase Painters (ABV)*, Clarendon Press, Oxford.

BEAZLEY, J. D. (1963), *Attic Red-figure Vase Painters (ARV)*, 2nd edn, Clarendon Press, Oxford.

BEIDELMAN, T. O. (1974), *W. Robertson Smith and the Sociological Study of Religion*, University of Chicago Press.

BENARDETE, SETH (1969), *Herodotean Inquiries*, Nijhoff, The Hague.

BÉRARD, CLAUDE (1970), *Eretria. Fouilles et recherches III. L'Hérôon à la porte de l'ouest*, Francke, Berne.

BERGER, PETER, and KELLNER, HANSFRIED (1964), 'Marriage and the construction of reality', *Diogenes*, 46, pp. 1-24 (reprinted in Berger, *Facing up to Modernity*, Basic Books, New York, 1977; Penguin, Harmondsworth, 1979, pp. 27-47).

BERRY, R. J. (1981), 'The genetics of death – mortal, morbid and selfish genes', in Humphreys and King, eds, 1981, pp. 59-78.

BERTRAND, M., ed. (1973), *Marcelline Desbordes-Valmore: les oeuvres poétiques*, Presses Universitaires, Grenoble.

BEVAN, EDWYN (1923), 'Hellenistic popular philosophy', in J. B. Bury et al., *The Hellenistic Age*, Cambridge University Press, pp. 79-107.

BICKEL, ERNST (1915), *Diatribe in Senecae philosophi fragmenta. I. Fragmenta de matrimonio*, Teubner, Leipzig.

BICKERMAN, E. J. (1976), 'Love story in the Homeric Hymn to Aphrodite', *Athenaeum*, 54, pp. 229-254.

BINGEN, JEAN (1967), 'L'établissement géometrique et la nécropole ouest', *Thorikos 1965*, Comité des fouilles belges en Grèce, Brussels, pp. 31-56.

BINGEN, JEAN (1968), 'La nécropole ouest 4', *Thorikos 1963*, pp. 59-86.

BINGEN, JEAN (1969), 'L'établissement du IXe siècle et les nécropoles du secteur ouest', *Thorikos 1966/7*, pp. 25-46.

BLOCH, MAURICE (1971), *Placing the Dead: Tombs, Ancestral Villages and Kinship Organisation in Madagascar*, Seminar Press, London/New York.

BLOCH, MAURICE (1981), 'Tombs and states', in Humphreys and King, eds, 1981, pp. 137-47.

BLOCH, MAURICE (in press), 'Death, women and power', in J. Parry and M. Bloch, eds, *Death and the Regeneration of Life*, Cambridge University Press.

BOARDMAN, J. (1955), 'Painted funerary plaques and some remarks on prothesis', *Annual of the British School at Athens*, 50, pp. 51-66.

BOARDMAN, J. (1978), *Greek Sculpture: The Archaic Period*, Thames & Hudson, London.

BOEHLAU, J., and SCHEFOLD, K. (1940), *Larisa am Hermos* I, de Gruyter, Berlin.

BOTT, ELIZABETH (1957), *Family and Social Network*, Tavistock, London (2nd, rev. edn, 1971).

BOURDIEU, PIERRE (1977), *Outline of a Theory of Practice*, Cambridge University Press (original French edn, Droz, Geneva, 1972).

BOURRIOT, F. (1976), *Recherches sur la nature du génos*, H. Champion, Paris.

BRADEEN, D. W. (1969), 'The Athenian casualty lists', *Classical Quarterly*, 19, pp. 145-59.

BRADEEN, D. W. (1974), *The Athenian Agora XVII. Inscriptions. The Funerary Monuments*, American School of Classical Studies, Princeton.

BROWNE, THOMAS (1658), *Hydrotaphia, Urne Buriall*, Brome, London.

BRUCKNER, A., and PERNICE, E. (1893), 'Ein attischer Friedhof', *Athenische Mitteilungen*, 18, pp. 73-191.

BRUNT, P. (1965), ' "Amicitia" in the late Roman Republic', *Proceedings of the Cambridge Philological Society*, 191 (N. S. 11), pp. 1-20.

BUCK, C. D. (1955), *The Greek Dialects*, University of Chicago Press.

BURKERT, WALTER (1972), *Lore and Science in Early Pythagoreanism*, Harvard University Press, Cambridge, Mass. (revised version of *Weisheit und Wissenschaft*, Nürnberg, 1962).

BURNETT, ANNE PIPPIN (1971), *Catastrophe Survived. Euripides' plays of mixed reversal*, Oxford University Press, London.

BYRNES, ROBERT F. (1976), *Communal Families in the Balkans: the Zadruga*, University of Notre Dame Press, Notre Dame, Indiana.

CARBONELL, CH. -O. (1976), *Histoire et historiens, une mutation idéologique des historiens français, 1865-1885*, Privat, Toulouse.

CARLSON, D. S. (1974), 'Temporal variation in prehistoric Nubian crania', Ph. D. thesis, University of Massachusetts, Amherst.

CARLSON, D. S. (1976), 'Temporal variation in prehistoric Nubian crania', *American Journal of Physical Anthropology*, 45, pp. 467-84.

CARLSON, D. S., and VAN GERVEN, D. P. (1977), 'Masticatory function and post-Pleistocene evolution in Nubia', *American Journal of Physical Anthropology*, 46, pp. 495-506.

CASSIN, ELENA (1981), 'The Death of the Gods', in Humphreys and King, eds, 1981, pp. 317-25.

CHALMERS, A. F. (1976), *What is This Thing called Science?*, University of Queensland Press, St Lucia (Open University, Milton Keynes, 1978).

CHARITONIDES, S. I. (1961a), 'Anaskaphē klassikōn taphōn para tēn plateian Syntagmatos', *Archaiologikē Ephēmeris*, 1958, pp. 1-152.

CHARITONIDES, S. I. (1961b), 'The first half of a bouleutic list of the 4th century B.C.', *Hesperia*, 30, pp. 30-57.

CHATEAUBRIAND, F. R., Viscomte de (1802), *Le Génie du christianisme*, Migneret, Paris.

CHATEAUBRIAND, F. R., Viscomte de (1948), *Mémoires d'outre-tombe*, Flammarion, Paris (first published 1848-9).

CHRĒSTOS, CH. (1965), 'Spartiatikoi archaikoi taphoi', *Archaiologikon Deltion*, 19, A, 1964, pp. 123-63.

CLAIRMONT, CHRISTOPH (1970), *Gravestone and Epigram*, von Zabern, Mainz.

CLARYSSE, W. (1976), 'Note on the new temenos stele of King Antiochos I', *Zeitschrift für Papyrologie und Epigraphik*, 23, p. 264.

COLDSTREAM, NICHOLAS (1968), *Greek Geometric Pottery*, Methuen, London.

COLDSTREAM, NICHOLAS (1976), 'Hero-cults in the age of Homer', *Journal of Hellenic Studies*, 96, pp. 8-17.

COLDSTREAM, NICHOLAS (1977), *Geometric Greece*, Benn, London.

COLE, THOMAS W. (1967), *Democritus and the Sources of Greek Anthropology*, University of Michigan, Ann Arbor.

CONNOR, W. R. (1971), *The New Politicians of Fifth-century Athens*, Princeton University Press.

CONZE, A. (1893-1922), *Die attischen Grabreliefs*, Spemann & de Gruyter, Berlin.

COPPET, DANIEL DE (1981), 'The life-giving death: a Melanesian case', in Humphreys and King, eds, 1981, pp. 175-203.

COUCHOUD, P. -L. (1923), L'interprétation des stèles funéraires grecques', *Revue archéologigue*, 18, pp. 99-118, 233-260.

COURCELLE, PIERRE (1966), 'Le corps-tombeau (Platon, *Gorg.* 493a, *Cratyl.* 400c, *Phaedr*; 250c)', *Revue des études anciennes*, 68, pp. 101-22.

CROISSANT, F., and SALVIAT, F. (1966), 'Aphrodite gardienne des magistrats: gynéconomes de Thasos et polémarques de Thèbes', *Bulletin de correspondance hellénique*, 90, pp. 460-71.

CROOK, J. M. (1967), 'Patria Potestas', *Classical Quarterly*, 17, pp. 113-22.

CUNHA, MANUELA CARNEIRO DA (1973), 'Logique du mythe et de l'action Le mouvement messianique canela', *L'Homme*, 13(4), pp. 5-35.

CUNHA, MANUELA CARNEIRO DA (1981), 'Eschatology among the Krahó: reflection upon society, free field of fabulation', in Humphreys and King, eds, 1981, pp. 161-74.

CURTIUS, E. (1894), 'Personennamen', in Curtius, *Gesammelte Abhandlungen* I, Hertz, Berlin, pp. 516-528.

DARESTE, R., HAUSSOULLIER, B. and REINACH, TH. (1891-8), *Recueil des inscriptions juridiques*, Leroux, Paris.

DAUX, GEORGES (1975), 'Sur quelques stèles fúneraires grecques', *Archeologia classica*, 25/6, 1973/4, pp. 238-49.

DAVARAS, K. (1967), 'Anaskaphai Perisyllogēs kai tychaia heurémata. Attikē', *Archaiologikon Deltion*, 20, 1965, B, pp. 118-27.

DAVIES, J. K. (1971), *Athenian Propertied Families (APF)*, Clarendon Press, Oxford.

DETIENNE, M. (1967), *Les Maîtres de la vérité dans la Grèce ancienne*, Maspero, Paris.

DETIENNE, M. (1972), *Les Jardins d'Adonis*, Gallimard, Paris (Eng. trans., Harvester Press, Brighton, 1978).

DETIENNE, M. (1976), 'Potagerie de femmes ou comment engendrer seule', *Traverses*, 5/6, pp. 75-8.

DETIENNE, M. (1977), *Dionysos mis à mort*, Gallimard, Paris (Eng. trans., *Dionysos Slain*, Johns Hopkins University Press, Baltimore, 1979).

DETIENNE, M. (1979), 'Violentes "eugénies". En pleines Thesmophories: des femmes couvertes de sang', in Detienne and Vernant, eds, 1979, pp. 183-214.

DETIENNE, M. and VERNANT, J.-P., eds (1979), *La Cuisine du sacrifice*, Gallimard, Paris.

DIELS, HERMANN, and KRANZ, WALTHER, eds (1935), *Die Fragmente der Vorsokratiker*, vol. II, 5th edn, Weidmann, Berlin.

DIGGLE, J. (1970), *Euripides, Phaethon*, Cambridge University Press.

DODDS, E. R. (1973), 'The religion of the ordinary man in classical Greece', in Dodds, *The Ancient Concept of Progress and Other Essays on Greek Literature and Belief*, Clarendon Press, Oxford, pp. 140-55.

DONZELOT, JACQUES (1977), *La Police des familles*, Minuit, Paris (page-references to Eng. trans., *The Policing of Families. Welfare versus the State*, Hutchinson, London, 1980).

DOUGLAS, MARY (1966), *Purity and Danger*, Routledge & Kegan Paul, London.

DOVER, KENNETH J. (1964), 'Eros and Nomos', *Bulletin of the Institute of Classical Studies, London*, 11, pp. 31-42.

DOVER, KENNETH J. (1974), *Greek Popular Morality in the time of Plato and Aristotle*, Blackwell, Oxford.

DOVER, KENNETH J. (1978), *Greek Homosexuality*, Duckworth, London.

DUCAT, JEAN (1976), 'Fonctions de la statue dans la Grèce archaïque; *kouros* et *kolossos*', *Bulletin de correspondance hellénique*, 100, pp. 239-51.

DUMÉZIL, G. (1969), 'Les trois tribus primitives', in Dumézil, *Idées romaines*, Gallimard, Paris, pp. 209-23.

DUMONT, LOUIS (1967a), *Homo hierarchicus*, Gallimard, Paris (Eng. trans., Chicago University Press, 1970, rev. edn, 1980).

DUMONT, LOUIS (1967b), 'The individual as an impediment to sociological comparison and Indian history', in V. B. Singh and Baljit Singh, eds, *Social and Economic Change, Essays in Honour of D. P. Mukerji*, Allied Publishers, Bombay, pp. 226-48 (reprinted in Dumont, 1970, pp. 133-50).

DUMONT, LOUIS (1970), *Religion, Politics and History in India*, Mouton, Paris/ The Hague.

DUMONT, Louis (1975), 'On the comparative understanding of non-modern civilizations', *Daedalus*, 104 (2), pp. 153-72.

DUMONT, LOUIS (1977), *Homo aequalis. Genèse et épanouissement de l'idéologie économique*, Gallimard, Paris (English ed., *From Mandeville to Marx*, University of Chicago Press, 1977).

DUNANT, CHRISTIANE, and POUILLOUX, JEAN (1958), *Recherches sur l'histoire et les cultes de Thasos. II. De 196 avant J.-C. jusqu'à la fin de l'antiquité*, École française d'Athènes, Paris.

DUVAL, AMAURY (1801), *Des sépultures*, Panckoucke, Paris.

EHRENBERG, VICTOR (1954), *Sophocles and Pericles*, Blackwell, Oxford.

EICHLER, F. (1914), 'ΣHMA und MNHMA in älteren griechischen Grabinschriften', *Athenische Mitteilungen*, 39, pp. 138-43.

ERGON (1975 ff.), *To Ergon tēs en Athēnais archaiologikēs hetaireias*.

ETIENNE, ROLAND (1975), 'Collection Dolly Goulandris, II. Stèle funéraire attique', *Bulletin de correspondance hellénique*, 99, pp. 379-84.

FABRICIUS, JOHANNES ALBERTUS (1760), *Bibliographia Antiquaria*, 3rd ed, Bohn, Hamburg.

FANTHAM, ELAINE (1971), '*Heautontimoroumenos* and *Adelphoe*: a study of fatherhood in Terence and Menander', *Latomus*, 30, pp. 970-98.

FARNELL, L. R. (1904), 'Sociological hypotheses concerning the position of women in ancient religion', *Archiv für Religionswissenschaft*, 7, pp. 70-94.

FERRARIUS, O. (1699), *Dissertatio de veterum lucernis sepulcralibus*, in Graevius, 1694 ff. vol. XII.

FERRUA, A. (1962), 'Paralipomeni di Giona', *Rivista di archeologia cristiana*, 38, pp. 7-69.

FINLEY, MOSES (1965), 'The silent women of Rome' *Horizon* (New York) 7 (1), pp. 55-64 (reprinted in Finley, *Aspects of Antiquity*, Penguin, Harmondsworth, 1968, pp. 124-36).

FINLEY, MOSES (1970), 'Aristotle and economic analysis', *Past and Present*, 47, pp. 3-25.

FINLEY, MOSES (1977), 'The Ancient City: from Fustel de Coulanges to Max Weber and beyond', *Comparative Studies in Society and History*, 19, pp. 305-27.

FIRTH, RAYMOND (1936), *We, the Tikopia*, Allen & Unwin, London.

FOSTER, GEORGE M. (1965), 'The peasant society and the idea of limited good', *American Anthropologist*, 67, pp. 293-315.

FOUCAULT, MICHEL (1961), *Histoire de la folie à l'âge classique*, Plon, Paris (Eng. trans., *Madness and Civilisation*, Tavistock, London, 1971).

FOUCAULT, MICHEL (1969), *L'Archéologie du savoir*, Gallimard, Paris (Eng. trans., Tavistock, London, 1972).

FRANCIOSI, G. (1978), *Clan gentilizio e strutture monogamiche*, 2nd edn, Jovene, Naples.

FRASER, P. M. (1953), 'An inscription from Cos', *Bulletin de la société archéologique d'Alexandrie*, 40, pp. 35-62.

FRASER, P. M. (1977), *Rhodian Funerary Monuments*, Clarendon Press, Oxford.

FREEDMAN, MAURICE (1958), *Lineage Organisation in Southeastern China*, Athlone Press, London.

FREEDMAN, MAURICE (1966), *Chinese Lineage and Society: Fukien and Kwangtung*, Athlone Press, London.

FREEDMAN, MAURICE (1967), 'Ancestor worship: two facets of the Chinese case', in Freedman, ed, *Social Organisation. Essays Presented to Raymond Firth*, Cass, London, pp. 85-103.

FRENCH, S. (1974), 'The cemetery as cultural institution: the establishment of Mount Auburn and the "Rural Cemetery" movement', in D. Stannard, ed., *Death in America*, University of Pennsylvania Press, Philadelphia, pp. 69-91.

FREYTAG (Löringhoff), BETTINA VON (1976), 'Archaische und klassische Grabfunde auf dem Hang nördlich der "Eckterasse" im Kerameikos', *Athenische Mitteilungen*, 91, pp. 31-61.

FRIEDLÄNDER, PAUL (1948), *Epigrammata. Greek Inscriptions in Verse from the Beginnings to the Persian Wars*, University of California Press, Berkeley.

FRIEDRICH, PAUL (1979), *The Meaning of Aphrodite*, University of Chicago Press.

FUCHS, W. (1961), review of T. Dohrn, *Attische Plastik vom Tode des Phidias bis zum Wirken der grossen Meister des 4. Jh. v. Chr.*, Scherpe, Krefell, 1957, in *Gnomon*, 33, pp. 237-42.

FUSTEL DE COULANGES, NUMA DENIS (1856), *Mémoire sur l'île de Chio, Archives des missions scientifiques et littéraires*, 5, cahiers 10-12 (reprinted in Fustel de Coulanges, 1893, pp. 213-399).

FUSTEL DE COULANGES, NUMA DENIS (1858a), *Quid Vestae cultus in institutis veterum privatis publicisque valuerit*, Jeunet, Amiens.

FUSTEL DE COULANGES, NUMA DENIS (1858b), *Polybe ou la Grèce conquise par les Romains*, Jeunet, Amiens (reprinted in Fustel de Coulanges, 1893, pp. 119-211).

FUSTEL DE COULANGES, NUMA DENIS (1864), *La Cité antique*, Durand, Paris.

FUSTEL DE COULANGES, NUMA DENIS (1875-1892), *Histoire des institutions politiques de l'Ancienne France*, I-VI, Hachette, Paris.

FUSTEL DE COULANGES, NUMA DENIS (1893), *Questions historiques*, ed. C. Jullian, Hachette, Paris.

GARLAND, R. (1981), 'Greek attitudes and observances in regard to death', Ph.D. thesis, University of London.

GÉRIN, DOMINIQUE (1974), *L'Oikos dans la tragédie: Alceste et Médée:*

analyse comparée du fonctionnement de deux oikoi, Mémoire de maitrise, Ecole Pratique des Hautes Études, Paris.

GÉRIN, DOMINIQUE (in press), 'Alceste ou l'inversion des roles sexuels', Italian trans., in Vegetti and Humphreys, eds, in press.

GERNET, LOUIS (1920), 'La création du testament', *Revue des études grecques*, 33, pp. 123-68, 249-90 (rev. and abr. edn. in Gernet, *Droit et société dans la Grèce ancienne*, Sirev, Paris, 1955, pp. 121-49).

GERNET, LOUIS (1932), *La Génie grec dans la religion* (with A. Boulanger), La Renaissance du Livre (A. Michel), Paris.

GLOTZ, G. (1904), *La Solidarité de la famille dans la Grèce ancienne*, Fontemoing, Paris.

GLOTZ, G. (1928), *La Cité grecque*, La Renaissance du Livre, Paris (Eng. trans., Kegan Paul, Trench, Trubner, 1929).

GLUCKMAN, MAX (1962), 'Les rites de passage', in Gluckman, ed, *Essays on the Ritual of Social Relations*, Manchester University Press, pp. 1-52.

GOFFMAN, ERVING (1967), 'Where the Action is', in Goffman, *Interaction Ritual*, Doubleday, New York, pp. 149-270.

GOMME, A. W. (1945, 1956), *A Historical Commentary on Thucydides*, Clarendon Press, Oxford.

GOODY, JACK (1973), 'Strategies of heirship', *Comparative Studies in Society and History*, 15, pp. 3-20.

GORER, GEOFFREY (1965), *Death, Grief and Mourning in Contemporary Britain*, Cresset Press, London.

GOULD, J. P. (1978), 'Dramatic character and "human intelligibility" in Greek tragedy', *Proceedings of the Cambridge Philological Society*, 24, pp. 43-67.

GRACE, VIRGINIA (1969), 'Ancient cemetery and road at 28 Lenormant Street', *Archaiologikē Ephēmeris*, 1968, 'Chronika', pp. 44-8.

GRAEVEN, CHRISTIAN FRIEDRICH (1730), *De Coemeteriis ex urbibus tollendis*, Diss. (Canon law) Frankfurt (erroneously attributed to Christian Gottfried Hoffman, the presiding dean, by Fabricius).

GRAEVIUS, J. G. (1694 ff.), *Thesaurus Antiquitatum*, I-XII, Halma & van der Aa, Leiden/Utrecht.

GRANET, MARCEL (1922), 'Le langage de la douleur d'après le rituel funéraire de la Chine classique', *Journal de psychologie*, 19 (2), pp. 97-118 (reprinted in Granet, *Études sociologiques sur la Chine*, PUF, Paris, 1953, pp. 221-42).

GREENHILL, THOMAS (1705), *Nekrokedeia; or, the art of embalming, wherein is shewn the right of burial, the funeral ceremonies, and the several ways of preserving dead bodies in most nations of the world* . . ., the author, London.

GROSSI, P. (1977), *Un altro modo di possedere*, Giuffré, Milan.

GUARDUCCI, M. (1974), *Epigraffia greca* III, Instituto Poligrafico dello Stato, Rome.

GUERCI, L. (1979), *Libertà degli antichi e libertà dei moderni*, Guida, Naples.

GUIRAUD, P. (1896), *Fustel de Coulanges*, Hachette, Paris.

HABENSTEIN, R. W., and LAMERS, W. M. (1962), *The History of American Funeral Directing*, rev. edn. Bulfin Printers, Milwaukee (1st edn, 1955).

HAINSWORTH, J. B. (1972), *Tituli ad dialectos graecas illustrandas selecti. II. Tituli dorici et ionici* (Textus Minores, 44), Brill, Leiden.

HALLETT, JUDITH P. (n.d.), *Fathers and Daughters: Women in Roman Kinship and Society*, Princeton University Press.

HAMMOND, N. G. L. (1969), 'Strategia and hegemonia in 5th century Athens', *Classical Quarterly*, 19, pp. 111-44.

HAMMOND, N. G. L. (1977), *Migrations and Invasions in Greece and adjacent areas*, Noyes Press, Paul Ridge, N.J.

HAMP, ERIC P. (in press), 'Philos', *Bulletin de la Société de Linguistique de Paris*, 77.

HARRISON, A. R. W. (1968), *The Law of Athens. I. The Family and Property*, Clarendon Press, Oxford.

HARTOG, FRANÇOIS (1982), 'Les funérailles des rois scythes: la mort de l'autre', in Vernant and Gnoli, eds, 1982, pp. 143-54.

HARVEY, A. E. (1955), 'The classification of Greek lyric poetry', *Classical Quarterly*, 5, pp. 157-75.

HELBIG, W. (1900), 'Zu den homerischen Bestattungsgebräuchen,' *Sitzungsbericht der Akad. München*, Phil. -hist. Classe, pp. 199-279.

HERRICK, JANE (1954), *The Historical Thought of Fustel de Coulanges*, Catholic University of America, Washington, D. C.

HERTZ, ROBERT (1907), 'Contribution à une étude sur la représentation collective de la mort', *L'Année sociologique*, 10, pp. 48-137 (Eng. trans., *Death and The Right Hand*, Cohen & West, London, 1960).

HIRZEL, R. (1895), *Der Dialog*, I-II, S. Hirzel, Leipzig.

HODSON, F. R. and ORTON, C. R. (1981), 'Rank and class: interpreting the evidence from prehistoric cemeteries', in Humphreys and King, eds, 1981, pp. 103-15.

HONDIUS, J. J. E. (1921), 'A new inscription of the deme Halimous', *Annual of the British School at Athens*, 24, pp. 151-60.

HOPKINS, KEITH (1965), 'Contraception in the Roman empire', *Comparative Studies in Society and History*, 8, pp. 124-51.

HORKHEIMER, MAX, ed. (1936), *Studien über Autorität und Familie; Forschungsbericht aus dem Institut für Sozialforschung*, Alcan, Paris.

HORNSTEIN, ÉDOUARD (1868), *Les Sépultures*, Albanel, Paris.

HORTON, R. (1967), 'African traditional thought and Western science', *Africa*, 37, pp. 50-71, 155-87.

HUMPHREYS, S. C. (1974), 'The *nothoi* of Kynosarges', *Journal of Hellenic Studies*, 94, pp. 88-95.

HUMPHREYS, S. C. (1978), *Anthropology and the Greeks*, Routledge & Kegan Paul, London.

HUMPHREYS, S. C., and KING, HELEN, eds (1981), *Mortality and Immortality:*

the Anthropology and Archaeology of Death, Academic Press, London.

HUMPHREYS, S. C. (1982), 'Fustel de Coulanges and the Greek *genos*', *Sociologia del Diritto* (in press).

HUMPHREYS, S. C. (1983), 'The date of Hagnias' death', *Classical Philology* (in press).

HUNTINGTON, RICHARD, and METCALF, PETER (1979), *Celebrations of Death. The Anthropology of Mortuary Ritual*, Cambridge University Press.

JACOBSEN, T. W., and CULLEN, TRACEY (1981), 'A consideration of mortuary practices in neolithic Greece: burials from Franchthi Cave', in Humphreys and King, eds, 1981, pp. 79-101.

JACOBY, FELIX (1923-1958), *Die Fragmente der griechischen Historiker* (*FGH*), Weidmann, Berlin, and Brill, Leiden.

JACOBY, FELIX (1944a), 'Genesia. A forgotten festival of the dead', *Classical Quarterly*, 38, pp. 65-75 (in Jacoby, 1956, pp. 243-59).

JACOBY, FELIX (1944b), 'Patrios nomos: state burial in Athens and the public cemetery in the Kerameikos', *Journal of Hellenic Studies*, 64, pp. 37-66 (in Jacoby, 1956, pp. 260-315).

JACOBY, FELIX (1956), *Abhandlungen zur griechischen Geschichtsschreibung*, Brill, Leiden.

JEFFERY, L. H. (1961), *The Local Scripts of Archaic Greece*, Clarendon, Oxford.

JEFFERY, L. H. (1962), 'The inscribed gravestones of archaic Attica', *Annual of the British School at Athens*, 57, pp. 115-53.

JONES, A. H. M. (1952), *The Athens of Demosthenes*, Cambridge University Press (reprinted in Jones, *Athenian Democracy*, Blackwell, Oxford, 1957, pp. 23-38).

JONES, JOHN (1962), *On Aristotle and Greek Tragedy*, Chatto & Windus, London.

JUST, ROGER (1975), 'Conceptions of women in Classical Athens', *Journal of the Anthropological Society of Oxford*, 6 (1), pp. 153-70 (Italian trans. in Vegetti and Humphreys, eds, in press).

KAHN, LAURENCE (1978), *Hermès passe ou les ambiguités de la communication*, Maspero, Paris.

KAHRSTEDT, U. (1936), *Untersuchungen zur Magistratur in Athen*, Kohlhammer, Stuttgart/Berlin.

KALLIPOLITIS, V. G. (1964), 'Anaskaphai taphōn Anagyrountos', *Archaiologikon Deltion*, 18, 1963, A, pp. 115-32.

KALLIPOLITIS, V. G. (1967), 'Archaiotētes kai mnēmeia Attikēs kai nēsōn', *Archaiologikon Deltion*, 20, 1965, B, pp. 110-17.

KALLIPOLITIS, V. G., and PETRAKOS, V. Ch. (1965), 'Attikē kai Aigina', *Archaiologikon Deltion*, 18, 1963, B, pp. 43-52.

KAMPS, W. (1937), 'Les origines de la fondation cultuelle dans la Grèce ancienne', *Archives d'histoire du droit oriental*, 1, pp. 145-79.

KARO, G. (1936), 'Archäologische Funde vom Sommer 1935 bis Sommer 1936', *Archäologischer Anzeiger*, cols 94-181.

KAROUZOU, S. (1947/8), 'Un cimetière de l'époque classique à Athènes', *Bulletin de correspondance hellénique*, 71/2, pp. 385-91.

KAROUZOU, S. (1957), 'Epitymbia stēlē titthēs sto Ethniko Mouseio', *Hellenika*, 15, pp. 311-23.

KAROUZOU, S. (1963), *Angeia tou Anagyrountos*, Archaiologikē Hetaireia, Athens.

KASTRIOTIS, P., and PHILADELPHEUS, A. (1912), 'Anaskaphai Anavysou: perigraphē anaskaphēs taphōn', *Praktika tēs en Athēnais archaiologikēs hetaireias*, 1911, pp. 110-31.

KERN, Otto (1900), *Die Inschriften von Magnesia am Maeander*, Spemann, Berlin.

KEULS, EVA (1974), *The Water-carriers in Hades. A study of catharsis through toil in classical antiquity*, Hakkert, Amsterdam.

KLEIN, ANITA (1932), *Child Life in Greek Art*, Columbia University Press, New York.

KNIGGE, URSULA (1972), 'Untersuchungen bei den Gesandtenstelen im Kerameikos', *Archäologischer Anzeiger*, pp. 584-629.

KNIGGE, URSULA (1976), *Der Sudhügel* (*Kerameikos. Ergebnisse der Ausgrabungen*, IX), de Gruyter, Berlin.

KNOX, B. M. W. (1964), *The Heroic Temper*, University of California, Berkeley; Cambridge University Press.

KOTZIAS, N. CH. (1948), 'Epigraphai Attikēs', *Polemon*, 3, pp. 145-51.

KÜBLER, KARL (1954), *Die Nekropole des 10. bis 8. Jahrhunderts* (*Kerameikos* V), de Gruyter, Berlin.

KÜBLER, KARL (1959), *Die Nekropole des späten 8. bis frühen 6. Jahrhunderts* (*Kerameikos* VI. 1), de Gruyter, Berlin.

KÜBLER, KARL (1976), *Die Nekropole der Mitte des 6. bis Ende des 5. Jahrhunderts* (*Kerameikos* VII. I.), de Gruyter, Berlin.

KUHN, THOMAS S. (1963), *The Structure of Scientific Revolutions*, University of Chicago Press (2nd rev. edn, 1970).

KURTZ, DONNA C. (1975), *Athenian White Lekythoi*, Clarendon Press, Oxford.

KURTZ, DONNA C., and BOARDMAN, JOHN (1971), *Greek Burial Customs*, Thames & Hudson, London.

KYPARISSES, N. (1925), 'Hai anaskaphai tōn Vasilikōn Stavlōn', *Parartēma tou Archaiologikou Deltiou 1922-1925*, pp. 68-72.

LANZA, DIEGO (1980), 'La morte esclusa', *Quaderni di Storia*, 11, pp. 157-72.

LATTIMORE, RICHMOND (1942), *Themes in Greek and Roman Epitaphs*, University of Illinois Press, Urbana.

LAUM, B. (1914), *Stiftungen in der griechischen und römischen Antike*, Teubner, Leipzig.

LEACH, E. R. (1955), 'Polyandry, inheritance and the definition of marriage: with particular reference to Sinhalese customary law', *Man*, 55, pp. 182-6, (reprinted in Leach, *Rethinking Anthropology*, Athlone Press, London, 1961, pp. 105-13).

LEACH, E. R. (1977), 'A view from the bridge', in M. Spriggs, ed., *Archaeology and Anthropology: Areas of Mutual Interest*, British Archaeological Reports Supplementary Series, 19, pp. 161-76.

LEBRUN, FRANCQIS (1971), *Les Hommes et la mort en Anjou aux XVIIe et XVIIIe siècles. Essai de démographie et de psychologie historiques*, Mouton, Paris/Hague.

LEFKOWITZ, MARY (1981), 'Women's Heroism', in Lefkowitz, *Heroines and Hysterics*, Duckworth, London, pp. 1-11.

LEMERLE, PAUL (1937), 'Chronique des fouilles 1937', *Bulletin de correspondance hellénique*, 61, pp. 441-76.

LE PLAY, FREDERIC (1855), *Les Ouvriers européens*, Imprimerie Nationale, Paris.

LE PLAY, FREDERIC (1864), *La Réforme sociale en France*, Plon, Paris.

LEWIS, D. M. (1979), 'Notes on Athenian casualty lists', *Zeitschrift für Papyrologie und Epigraphik*, 34, pp. 240-6.

LEWIS, I. M. (1965), 'Problems in the comparative study of unilineal descent', in M. Banton, ed., *The Relevance of Models for Social Anthropology*, Tavistock, London, pp. 87-112.

LIAKOURAS, A. G. (1976), 'B' Ephoreia klassikōn archaiotētōn', *Archaiologikon Deltion*, 27, 1972, B, I, pp. 147-82.

LINDERS, T. (1972), *Studies in the Treasure Records of Artemis Brauronia found in Athens*, Astrom, Lund.

LLOYD, G. E. R. (in press), 'The treatment of women in the Hippocratic corpus', in G. E. R. Lloyd, *Science, Folklore and Ideology*, Cambridge University Press. (Italian trans. to appear in Vegetti and Humphreys, eds, in press).

LORAUX, NICOLE (1978), 'Sur la race des femmes et quelques-unes de ses tribus', *Arethusa*, 11, pp. 43-87 (Italian trans. to appear in Vegetti and Humphreys, eds, in press).

LORAUX, NICOLE (1982), 'Mourir devant Troie, tomber pour Athènes: de la gloire du héros à l'idée de la cité', in Vernant and Gnoli, eds, 1982, pp. 27-43.

LUKÁCS, GEORG (1955), *Der historische Roman*, Aufbau-Verlag, Berlin (written 1936/7; Eng. trans., *The Historical Novel*, Merlin Press, London, 1962).

MACFARLANE, ALAN (1981), 'Death and the demographic transition: a note on English evidence on death 1500-1750', in Humphreys and King, eds, 1981, pp. 249-59.

McLENNAN, J. F. (1865), *Primitive Marriage*, A. & C. Black, Edinburgh.

McNAMARA, JO ANN (1979), 'Wives and widows in early Christian thought', *International Journal of Women's Studies*, 2, pp. 575-92.

MAINE, H. S. (1861), *Ancient Law*, John Murray, London.

MAINE, H. S. (1883), *Dissertations on Early Law and Custom*, John Murray, London.

MALINOWSKI, BRONISLAW (1913), *The Family among the Australian Aborigines*, University of London Press.

MALINOWSKI, BRONISLAW (1927), *The Father in Primitive Psychology*,

Basic English Publishing Co., London.

MALINOWSKI, BRONISLAW (1929), 'Kinship', *Encyclopedia Britannica*, 14th ed., pp. 403-9.

MALINOWSKI, BRONISLAW (1930), 'Kinship', *Man*, 30, pp. 19-29.

MARRIS, PETER (1974), *Loss and Change*, Routledge & Kegan Paul, London.

MASTROKOSTAS, E. I. (1966), 'Epistēmata ek Myrrhinountos', *Charistērion eis Anastasion K. Orlandon*, III, Archaiologikē Hetaireia, Athens, pp. 281-99.

MASTROKOSTAS, E. I. (1972), 'Hē korē Phrasikleia Aristiōnos tou Pariou kai kouros marmarinos anekalyphthēsan en Myrrhinounti', *Athens Annals of Archaeology*, 5, pp. 298-324.

MAUSS, MARCEL (1938), 'Une catégorie de l'esprit humain: la notion de personne, celle de "moi", un plan de travail', *Journal of the Royal Anthropological Institute*, 68, pp. 263-81 (reprinted in Mauss, *Sociologie et anthropologie*, PUF, Paris, 4th edn, 1968, pp. 331-62).

MAYER, ADRIAN (1966), 'The significance of quasi-groups in the study of complex societies', in M. Banton, ed., *The Social Anthropology of Complex Societies*, Tavistock, London, pp. 97-122.

MEAD, MARGARET (1928), *Coming of Age in Samoa: a psychological study of primitive youth for Western civilization*, W. Morrow, New York.

MEAD, MARGARET (1935), *Sex and Temperament in Three Societies*, W. Morrow, New York.

MEIGGS, RUSSELL, and LEWIS, D. M. (1969), *A Selection of Greek Historical Inscriptions to the end of the 5th century B. C.*, Clarendon Press, Oxford.

MELIADES, I. (1955), 'Anaskaphai notiōs tēs Akropoleōs', *Praktika tēs en Athēnais archaiologikēs hetaireias*, pp. 36-52.

METZGER, H. (1951), *Les Représentations dans la céramique attique du IVe siècle*, de Boccard, Paris.

MEYERSON, IGNACE (1948), *Les Fonctions psychologiques et les oeuvres*, Vrin, Paris.

MILES, D. (1965), 'Socio-economic aspects of secondary burial', *Oceania*, 35, pp. 161-74.

MÖBIUS, HANS (1966), 'Eigenartige attische Grabreliefs', *Athenische Mitteilungen*, 81, pp. 136-60.

MOLLESON, THEYA (1981), 'The archaeology and anthropology of death: what the bones tell us', in Humphreys and King, eds, 1981, pp. 15-32.

MOMIGLIANO, A. D. (1970), 'La città antica di Fustel de Coulanges', *Rivista storica italiana*, 87, pp. 81-98 (Eng. trans. in Momigliano, 1977, pp. 325-43).

MOMIGLIANO, A. D. (1975), *Alien Wisdom*, Cambridge University Press.

MOMIGLIANO, A. D. (1977), *Essays in Ancient and Modern Historiography*, Blackwell, Oxford.

MOMIGLIANO, A. D., and HUMPHREYS, S. C. (1974), 'The social structure of the ancient city', *Annali della Scuola Normale, Pisa*, ser. 3, 4, pp. 329-67 (reprinted in Humphreys, 1978, pp. 177-208).

MOMMSEN, A. (1898), *Feste der Stadt Athen im Altertum*, Teubner, Leipzig.

MOORE, SALLY FALK (1981), 'Chagga customary law and the property of the dead', in Humphreys and King, eds, 1981, pp. 225-48.

MORENZ, SIEGFRIED (1973), *Egyptian Religion*, Methuen, London (German edn, 1960).

MORETTI, L. (1979), *Inscriptiones Graecae Urbis Romae* III, Istituto Italiano per la Storia Antica, Rome.

MORGAN, EDMUND S. (1944), *The Puritan Family*, Public Library, Boston (expanded edition, Harper & Row, New York, 1966).

MORGAN, L. H. (1877), *Ancient Society*, Holt, New York.

MÜLLER, C. W. (1981), 'Der griechische Roman', in E. Vogt, ed., *Griechische Literatur* (Neues Handbuch der Literaturwissenschaft), Athenaion, Wiesbaden, pp. 377-412.

MYLONAS, G. (1975), *To dytikon nekrotapheion tés Elefsinos*, Archaiologikē Hetaireia, Athens.

NAUCK, A. (1889), *Tragicorum Graecorum Fragmenta*, 2nd edn, Teubner, Leipzig.

NEEDHAM, RODNEY (1971), 'Remarks on the analysis of kinship and marriage', in Needham, ed, *Rethinking Kinship and Marriage*, Tavistock, London, pp. 1-34.

NILSSON, MARTIN (1911), 'Der Ursprung der Tragödie', *Neue Jahrbücher für das klassische Altertum*, 27 (14), pp. 609-42, 673-96.

NORTH, HELEN (1966), *Sophrosyne. Self-Knowledge and Self-Restraint in Greek Literature*, Cornell University Press, Ithaca.

OGLE, M. B. (1933), 'The Sleep of Death', *Memoirs of the American Academy in Rome*, 11, pp. 81-117.

OLTRAMARE, ANDRE (1926), *Les Origines de la diatribe romaine*, Payot, Paris.

PANOFSKY, ERWIN (1964), *Tomb Sculpture*, Thames & Hudson, London.

PANTOS, A. (1974), 'Epitymbion epigramma ex Athēnōn', *Athens Annals of Archaeology*, 7, pp. 406-15.

PEEK, WERNER (1942), 'Attische Inschriften', *Athenische Mitteilungen*, 57, pp. 1-217.

PEEK, WERNER (1955), *Griechische Vers-Inschriften I. Grab-Epigramme*, Akademie-Verlag, Berlin.

PEEK, WERNER (1957), *Attische Grabschriften II*, *Abhandlungen der deutschen Akademie der Wissenschaft zu Berlin*, Kl. für Sprache, Lit. u. Kunst, 1956. 3.

PEMBROKE, S. G. (1967), 'Women in charge: the function of alternatives in early Greek tradition and the ancient idea of matriarchy', *Journal of the Warburg and Courtauld Institutes*, 30, pp. 1-35.

PEMBROKE, S. G. (1971), 'Oikeiōsis', in A. A. Long, ed., *Problems in Stoicism*, Athlone Press, London, pp. 114-49.

PEMBROKE, S. G. (1978), 'The early human family: some views 1770-1870', in R. R. Bolgar, ed., *Classical Influences on Western Thought A. D. 1650-1870*,

Cambridge University Press, pp. 275-91 (Italian trans. to appear in Humphreys and Vegetti, eds, in press).

PERDRIZET, PAUL (1934), 'Le mort qui sentait bon', *Mélanges Bidez (Annuaire de l'Institut de Philologie et d'histoire)* II, pp. 719-27.

PERRY, BEN EDWIN (1967), *The Ancient Romances*, University of California Press, Berkeley.

PETRAKOS, V. CH. (1977), 'Anaskaphē Rhamnountos', *Praktika tēs en Athēnais archaiologikeēs hetaireias tou etous 1975*, pp. 5-35.

PETRAKOS, V. CH. (1978), 'Anaskaphē Rhamnountos', *Praktika tēs en Athēnais archaiologikēs hetaireias tou etous 1976*, pp. 5-60.

PETRAKOS, V. CH. (1980), 'Anaskaphē Rhamnountos', *Praktika tēs en Athēnais archaiologikēs hetaireias tou etous 1977*, pp. 3-22.

PFOHL, G. (1967), *Greek Poems on Stones, I. Epitaphs from the 7th to the 5th centuries B. C.*, Brill, Leiden.

PICKARD-CAMBRIDGE, ARTHUR (1968), *The Dramatic Festivals of Athens*, (2nd edn, ed. John Gould and D. M. Lewis), Clarendon Press, Oxford.

PIRCHER, JOSEF (1979), *Das Lob der Frau im vorchristlichen Grabepigramm der Griechen*, Wagner, Innsbruck.

PITT-RIVERS, J. (1977), *The Fate of Shechem or the Politics of Sex*, Cambridge University Press.

PLEKET, H. W. (1969), *Epigraphica II. Texts on the Social History of the Greek World*, Brill, Leiden.

POSTER, MARK (1978), *Critical Theory of the Family*, Seabury Press, New York; Pluto Press, London.

POTTER, JOHN (1699), *Archaeologiae Graecae, or the Antiquities of Greece*, II, Child, London.

POUILLOUX, JEAN (1954), *La Forteresse de Rhamnonte*, de Boccard, Paris.

PRÉAUX, CLAIRE (1959), 'Le statut de la femme à l'époque hellénistique, principalement en Égypte', *Recueils de la Société Jean Bodin*, 11, pp. 127-75.

PRICE, THEODORA HADZISTELIOU (1973), 'Hero-cult and Homer', *Historia*, 22, pp. 129-44.

RADCLIFFE-BROWN, A. R. (1952), 'Social anthropology past and present', *Man*, 52, pp. 13-14.

RADCLIFFE-BROWN, A. R. (1957), *A Natural Science of Society*, Free Press, Chicago.

RADITSA, LEO FERRERO (1980), 'Augustus' legislation concerning marriage, procreation, love affairs and adultery', *Aufstieg und Niedergang der römischen Welt*, H. Temporini, ed., II. 13, de Gruyter, Berlin, pp. 278-339.

RAHTZ, PHILIP (1981), 'Archaeological sources for death after A. D. 1200 – from grave-goods to memorials', in Humphreys and King, eds, 1981, pp. 117-36.

REDFIELD, JAMES (1975), *Nature and Culture in the Iliad. The Tragedy of Hector*, University of Chicago Press.

REDFIELD, JAMES (1978), 'The women of Sparta', *Classical Journal*, 73, pp. 146-61.

192	*Bibliography*

RICHARD, J.-C. (1978), *Les Origines de la plèbe romaine*, École Française, Rome.

RICHARDSON, NICHOLAS (1974), *The Homeric Hymn to Demeter*, Clarendon Press, Oxford.

RICHTER, GISELA M. A. (1961), *The Archaic Gravestones of Attica*, Phaidon Press, London.

RIEMANN, HANS (1937), 'Archäologische Funde vom Sommer 1936 bis Sommer 1937. Griechenland' *Archäologischer Anzeiger*, cols 86-184.

RIEZLER, W. (1914), *Weissgrundige attische Lekythen*, Bruckmann, Munich.

RIVERS, W. H. R. (1926), 'The primitive conception of death', in Rivers, *Psychology and Ethnology*, Kegan Paul, London, pp. 36-50.

ROBINSON, D. M., and GRAHAM, J. WALTER (1938), *Olynthus VIII. The Hellenic House*, Johns Hopkins University Press, Baltimore.

ROMILLY, J. de (1956), *Histoire et raison chez Thucydide*, Les Belles Lettres, Paris.

ROSSELLINI, MICHELE, and SAID, SUZANNE (1978), 'Usages de femmes et autres nomoi chez les "sauvages" d'Hérodote: essai de leçon structurale', *Annali della Scuola Normale, Pisa*, ser. 3, 8, pp. 949-1005.

ROUSSELLE, ALINE (1980), 'En Grèce: observation féminine et idéologie masculine', *Annales E.S.C.*, 35, pp. 1089-115.

ROUX, GEORGES (1967), 'Les grimaces de Cleisthenes', *Revue des études grecques*, 80, pp. 165-75.

SASSI, MARIA MICHELA (1981), 'Riflessione filosofica e ideologia funeraria: la stele di Aristocle', *Dialoghi di Archeologia*, N.S.3, pp. 33-40.

SAURMANN, JOHANNES FRIEDRICH (1737), *Tractatus historico-juridicus de Jure circa sepulchra et hominum demortuorum cadavera*, Saurmann, Bremen.

SCHAPS, D. M. (1979), *Economic Rights of Women in Ancient Greece*, Edinburgh University Press.

SCHILARDIS, DEMETRIOS-UMBERTOS (1969a), 'Anaskaphai para tas "Ērias Pylas" kai topographica problēmata tēs periochēs', *Archaiologikē Ephēmeris*, 1968, *Chronika*, pp. 8-52.

SCHILARDIS, DEMETRIOS-UMBERTOS (1969b), 'Tymbos klassikou taphou ex Athēnōn', *Athens Annals of Archaeology*, 2, pp. 334-8.

SCHILARDIS, DEMETRIOS-UMBERTOS (1976), 'Anaskaphē para ta Makra Teichē kai hē oinochoē tou Taurou', *Archaiologikē Ephēmeris*, 1975, pp. 66-149.

SCHLORB-VIERNEISEL, BARBARA (1966), 'Eridanos-Nekropole', *Athenische Mitteilungen*, 81, pp. 1-111.

SCHMITT-PANTEL, PAULINE (1982), 'Évergétisme et mémoire du mort: à propos des fondations de banquets publics dans les cités grecques à l'époque hellénistique et romaine', in Vernant and Gnoli, eds, 1982, pp. 177-188.

SCHNEIDER, D. M. (1972), 'What is kinship all about?', in Priscilla Reining, ed., *Kinship Studies in the Morgan Centennial Year*, Anthropological Society, Washington, pp. 32-63.

SENNETT, RICHARD (1970), *Families against the City*, Harvard University Press, Cambridge, Mass.

SENNETT, RICHARD (1977), *The Fall of Public Man*, Knopf, New York.

S.G.D.I. - *Sammlung der grieschischen Dialekt-Inschriften*, ed. H. Collitz, F. Bechtel, Vandenhoeck & Ruprecht, Göttingen, 1884-1915.

- SHAW, MICHAEL (1975), 'The female intruder: women in fifth-century drama', *Classical Philology*, 70, pp. 255-66.

SLATER, PHILIP (1968), *The Glory of Hera*, Beacon Press, Boston.

SMITH, W. ROBERTSON (1885), *Kinship and Marriage in Early Arabia*, Cambridge University Press.

SMITH, W. ROBERTSON (1889), *Lectures on the Religion of the Semites*, A. &. C. Black, Edinburgh.

SMITHSON, EVELYN LORD (1961), 'The Protogeometric cemetery at Nea Ionia, 1949', *Hesperia*, 30, pp. 147-78.

SMITHSON, EVELYN LORD (1974), 'A Geometric cemetery on the Areopagus: 1897, 1932, 1947', *Hesperia*, 43, pp. 325-90.

SNODGRASS, A. M. (1982), 'Les origines du culte des héros dans la Grèce antique', in Vernant and Gnoli, eds, 1982, pp. 107-19.

SOKOLOWSKI, F. (1955), *Lois sacrées de l'Asie Mineure*, de Boccard, Paris.

SOKOLOWSKI, F. (1969), *Lois sacrées des cités grecques*, de Boccard, Paris.

SONTHEIMER, G.-D. (1977), *The Joint Hindu Family: its Evolution as a legal institution*, Munshiram Manoharlal, New Delhi.

SOTERIADES, G. (1940), 'Anaskaphē Marathōnos', *Praktika tēs en Athēnais archaiologikēs hetaireias tou etous 1939*, pp. 27-39.

STÄDELE, A. (1980), *Die Briefe des Pythagoras und der Pythagoreer*, Hain, Meisenheim am Glan.

STÄHLIN, G. (1974), 'Das Bild der Witwe. Ein Beitrag zur Bildersprache der Bibel und zum Phänomen der Personifikation in der Antike', *Jahrbuch für Antike und Christentum*, 17, pp. 5-20.

STAIS, V. (1890a), 'Ho tymbos en Vourvai', *Athenische Mitteilungen*, 15, pp. 318-29.

STAIS, V. (1890b), 'Anaskaphai tymbōn en Attikē', *Archaiologikon Deltion*, 6, pp. 16-28, 49, 100, 105-13.

STAIS, V. (1891), 'Peri tōn en Vari anaskaphōn', *Archaiologikon Deltion*, 7, pp. 28-32.

STAVROPOULOS, PHOIBOS D. (1967), 'Athenai-Attikē: B'. Anaskaphikai ereunai kai tychaia heurēmata', *Archaiologikon Deltion*, 20, 1965, B, pp. 44-109.

- STONE, LAWRENCE (1977), *The Family, Sex and Marriage in England 1500-1800*, Weidenfeld & Nicolson, London.

- STONE, LAWRENCE (1981), 'Family History in the 1980s. Past achievements and future trends', *Journal of Interdisciplinary History*, 12, pp. 51-87.

STRATHERN, ANDREW (1981), 'Death as exchange: two Melanesian cases', in Humphreys and King, eds, 1981, pp. 205-23.

STUIBER, A. (1957), *Refrigerium interim*, Hanstein, Bonn.

STUPPERICH, REINHARD (1977), *Staatsbegrabnis und Privatgrabmal im klassischen Athen*, Diss, Münster.

SUDNOW, DAVID (1967), *Passing On: The Social Organization of Dying*, Prentice-Hall, Englewood Cliffs, N. J.

SVENBRO, JESPER (1976), *La Parole et le marbre. Aux origines de la poétique grecque*, Studentlitteratur, Lund.

SYKUTRIS, J. (1931), 'Epistolographie', Pauly-Wissowa, *Realencyclopädie*, Supplementband V, coll. 185-220.

TECHNAU, WERNER (1936), *Exekias*, Keller, Leipzig.

THAPAR, ROMILA (1981), 'Death and the hero', in Humphreys and King, eds, 1981, pp. 293-315.

THIMME, JÜRGEN (1964), 'Die Stele des Hegeso als Zeugnis des attischen Grabkultes', *Antike Kunst*, 7, pp. 16-29.

THÖNGES-STRINGARIS, RHEA N. (1965), 'Das griechische Totenmahl', *Athenische Mitteilungen*, 80, pp. 1-99.

THOMPSON, WESLEY E. (1967), 'The marriage of first cousins in Athenian society', *Phoenix*, 21, pp. 273-82.

THOMPSON, WESLEY E. (1970), 'Some Attic kinship terms', *Glotta*, 48, pp. 75-81.

THOMPSON, WESLEY E. (1976), *De Hagniae Hereditate*, Brill, Leiden.

TOD, MARCUS N. (1948), *A Selection of Greek Historical Inscriptions. II. From 403 to 323 B. C.*, Clarendon Press, Oxford.

TOLSON, ANDREW (1977), *The Limits of Masculinity*, Tavistock, London.

TUPLIN, C. J. (1980), 'Some emendations to the family-tree of Isocrates', *Classical Quarterly*, 30, pp. 299-305.

TYLOR, E. B. (1871), *Primitive Culture*, J. Murray, London.

UCKO, P. J. (1969), 'Ethnography and the archaeological interpretation of funerary remains', *World Archaeology*, 1, pp. 262-77.

URBAIN, JEAN-DIDIER (1979), *La Société de conservation*, Payot, Paris.

VAN BREMEN, H. C. (1983), 'Women and wealth', in A. Cameron, ed., *Images of Women in Antiquity*, Croom Helm, London.

VANSTIPHOUT, H. L. J. (1980), 'The death of an era: the Great Mortality in the Sumerian City Laments', in B. Alster, ed., *Death in Mesopotamia*, Akademisk Forlag, Copenhagen, pp. 83-9.

VAN TIEGHEM, PAUL (1921), 'La poésie de la nuit et des tombeaux en Europe au 18e siècle', *Mémoires de l'Académie Royale de Belgique*, Cl. des lettres et des sciences morales et politiques, ser. 2, 16.

VATIN, CLAUDE (1970), *Recherches sur le mariage et la condition de la femme mariée à l'époque hellénistique*, de Boccard, Paris.

VEGETTI, MARIO and HUMPHREYS, S. C., eds (in press), *La Donna antica*, Boringhieri, Milan.

VERMEULE, EMILY (1970), 'Five vases from the grave precinct of Dexileos', *Jahrbuch des deutschen archäologischen Instituts*, 85, pp. 94-111.

VERMEULE, EMILY (1979), *Aspects of Death in Early Greek Art and Poetry*, University of California Press, Berkeley.

VERNANT, J.-P. (1956), 'Le pur et l'impur', *L'Année sociologique*, 1953/4, pp. 331-52 (reprinted in Vernant, 1974, pp. 121-40).

VERNANT, J.-P. (1959), 'Aspects mythiques de la mémoire', *Journal de psychologie*, 56, pp. 1-29 (reprinted in Vernant, 1965, pp. 51-78).

VERNANT, J.-P. (1960), 'Le fleuve "Amélès" et la "Mélété Thanatou"', *Revue philosophique*, 85, pp. 163-79 (reprinted in Vernant, 1965, pp. 79-94).

VERNANT, J.-P. (1962), 'Figuration de l'invisible et catégorie psychologique du double: le colossos', contribution to *Le Signe et les systèmes de signes*, colloque of the Centre de recherches de psychologie comparative, Royaumont 1962 (in Vernant, 1965, pp. 251-64).

VERNANT, J.-P. (1965), *Mythe et pensée chez les Grecs*, Maspero, Paris (Eng. trans. as *Myth and Thought among the Greeks*, Routledge & Kegan Paul, London, 1982).

VERNANT, J.-P. (1966), 'La société des dieux', in *La Naissance des dieux*, Éditions Rationalistes, Paris, pp. 55-78 (reprinted in Vernant, 1974, pp. 103-20).

VERNANT, J.-P. (1967), 'Oedipe sans complexe', *Raison présente*, 4, pp. 3-20 (reprinted in Vernant and Vidal-Naquet, 1972, pp. 77-98; 1981, pp. 63-86).

VERNANT, J.-P. (1969), 'Tensions and ambiguities in Greek tragedy', in C. Singleton, ed., *Interpretation. Theory and Practice*, Johns Hopkins University Press, Baltimore, pp. 105-21 (reprinted in Vernant and Vidal-Naquet, 1972, pp. 19-40; 1981, pp. 6-27).

VERNANT, J.-P. (1974), *Mythe et société en Grèce ancienne*, Maspero, Paris.

VERNANT, J.-P. (1976), 'Étude comparée des religions antiques', *Annuaire du Collège de France*, 76, pp. 367-76.

VERNANT, J.-P. (1977), 'Étude comparée des religions antiques', *Annuaire du Collège de France*, 77, pp. 423-43.

VERNANT, J.-P. (1978), 'Étude comparée des religions antiques', *Annuaire du Collège de France*, 78, pp. 451-66.

VERNANT, J.-P. (1981), 'Death with two faces', in Humphreys and King, eds, 1981, pp. 285-91.

VERNANT, J.-P. (1982), 'La belle mort et le cadavre outragé', in Vernant and Gnoli, eds, 1982, pp. 45-76.

VERNANT, J.-P., and DETIENNE, MARCEL (1974), *Les Ruses de l'intelligence. La Métis des Grecs*, 2nd edn, Flammarion, Paris (Eng. trans., *Cunning Intelligence in Greek Culture and Society*, Harvester Press, Brighton, 1977).

VERNANT, J.-P., and GNOLI, G. eds (1982), *La Mort, les morts dans les sociétés anciennes*, Cambridge University Press.

VERNANT, J.-P., and VIDAL-NAQUET, PIERRE (1972), *Mythe et tragédie en Grèce ancienne*, Maspero, Paris (Eng. trans., *Tragedy and Myth in Ancient Greece*, Harvester Press, Brighton, 1981).

VEYNE, PAUL (1978), 'La famille et l'amour sous le haut empire romain', *Annales E.S.C.*, 33, pp. 35-63.

VIDAL-NAQUET, PIERRE (1968), 'Le chasseur noir et l'origine de l'ephébie athénienne', *Annales E.S.C.*, 23, pp. 947-64 (reprinted in Vidal-Naquet, 1981, pp. 151-75; Eng. version in *Proceedings of the Cambridge Philological Society*, 194, pp. 49-64).

VIDAL-NAQUET, PIERRE (1970), 'Esclavage et gynécocratie dans la tradition, le mythe, l'utopie', in C. Nicolet, ed., *Recherches sur les structures sociales dans l'antiquité classique*, CNRS., Paris, pp. 63-80 (revised edn in Vidal-Naquet, 1981, pp. 267-88).

VIDAL-NAQUET, PIERRE (1971), 'Le Philoctète de Sophocle et l'ephébie', *Annales E.S.C.*, 26, pp. 623-38 (reprinted in Vernant and Vidal-Naquet, 1972, pp. 159-84; 1981, pp. 175-99).

VIDAL-NAQUET, PIERRE (1974), 'Le cru, l'enfant grec et le cuit', in J. Le Goff and P. Nora, eds, *Faire de l'histoire* III, Gallimard, Paris, pp. 137-68 (reprinted in Vidal-Naquet, 1981, pp. 177-207).

VIDAL-NAQUET, PIERRE (1981), *Le Chasseur noir. Formes de pensée et formes de société dans le monde grec*, Maspero, Paris.

VIERNEISEL, K. (1964), 'Die Grabung in der Nekropole 1962', *Archäologischer Anzeiger*, cols 420-67.

WAGNER, J. and PETZL, G. (1976), 'Ein neue Temenos-stele des Königs Antiochos I von Commagene', *Zeitschrift für Papyrologie und Epigraphik*, 20, pp. 201-23.

WALDMANN, HELMUT (1973), *Die kommagenischen Kultreformen unter König Mithradates I Kallinikos und seinem Sohne Antiochos I*, Brill, Leiden.

WALLACE, M. B. (1970), 'Notes on early Greek grave epigrams', *Phoenix*, 24, pp. 95-105.

WALTER, OTTO (1940), 'Archäologische Funde in Griechenland von Frühjahr 1939 bis Frühjahr 1940', *Archäologischer Anzeiger*, cols. 121-308.

WATSON, ALAN (1975), *Rome of the XII Tables*, Princeton University Press.

WEBER, MAX (1904), 'Die "Objektivität" sozialwissenschaftlicher und sozial-politischer Erkenntnis', *Archiv für Sozialwissenschaft und Sozialpolitik*, 19, pp. 22-87 (reprinted in Weber, *Gesammelte Aufsätze zur Wissenschaftslehre*, Mohr, Tübingen, 1922, pp. 146-214; Eng. trans., Weber, *Essays on the Methodology of the Social Sciences*, Free Press, Chicago, 1949, pp. 49-112).

WEHRLI, F., ed. (1949), *Die Schule des Aristoteles, IV. Demetrius von Phaleron*, Schwabe, Basel.

WEHRLI, F. (1962), 'Les gynéconomes', *Museum Helveticum*, 19, pp. 33-8.

WEST, M. L. (1971/2), *Iambi et Elegi Graeci*, I-II, Clarendon Press, Oxford.

WILAMOWITZ, U. VON (1930), 'Lesefrüchte CCLXXVI', *Hermes*, 65, pp. 253-4.

WILHELM, A. (1978), 'Bemerkungen zu den attischen Grabinschriften *I.G.* II^2, *Zeitschrift für Papyrologie und Epigraphik*, 29, pp. 57-90.

WIRSZUBSKI, CHAIM (1950), *Libertas as a Political Idea at Rome during the Late Republic and the Early Principate*, Cambridge University Press.

WISEMAN, JAMES and SHAW, JOSEPH W. (1970), 'An archaic inscription from Attica', *Hesperia*, 39, pp. 139-44.

WOLFF, CHRISTIAN (n.d.), 'Public and private in Euripides'.

XANTHAKIS-KARAMANOS, G. (1980), *Studies in Fourth-century Tragedy*, Academy, Athens.

YOUNG, RODNEY S. (1939), *Late Geometric Graves and a 7th Century Well in the Agora, Hesperia*, Supplement II.

YOUNG, RODNEY, S. (1951), 'Sepulturae intra urbem', *Hesperia*, 20, pp. 67-134.

ZAPHEIROPOULOS, N. S. (1958), 'Marmarinē lēkythos met'epitymbiou parastaseōs', *Archaiologikē Ephēmeris*, 1953/4, II, pp. 237-46.

ZEITLIN, FROMA (1978), 'The Dynamics of Misogyny: myth and myth-making in the *Oresteia*', *Arethusa*, 11, pp. 149-84.

ZEITLIN, FROMA (in press), 'Male-female polarities in the *Oresteia* of Aeschylus', (Italian trans. to appear in Vegetti and Humphreys, eds, in press).

ZSCHIETZSCHMANN, W. (1928), 'Die Darstellung der Prothesis in der griechischen Kunst', *Athenische Mitteilungen*, 53, pp. 17-47.

Index of inscriptions

Index

Routledge Social Science Series

Routledge & Kegan Paul   London, Henley and Boston

39 Store Street,
London WC1E 7DD
Broadway House,
Newtown Road,
Henley-on-Thames,
Oxon RG9 1EN
9 Park Street,
Boston, Mass. 02108

Contents

*Authors wishing to submit manuscripts for any series
in this catalogue should send them to the Social Science Editor,
Routledge & Kegan Paul Ltd, 39 Store Street,
London WC1E 7DD.*
● *Books so marked are available in paperback.*
○ *Books so marked are available in paperback only.*
*All books are in metric Demy 8vo format (216 × 138mm approx.)
unless otherwise stated.*

International Library of Sociology
General Editor   John Rex

GENERAL SOCIOLOGY

Barnsley, J. H. The Social Reality of Ethics. *464 pp.*
Brown, Robert. Explanation in Social Science. *208 pp.*
●   Rules and Laws in Sociology. *192 pp.*
Bruford, W. H. Chekhov and His Russia. *A Sociological Study. 244 pp.*
Burton, F. and **Carlen, P.** Official Discourse. *On Discourse Analysis, Government Publications, Ideology. About 140 pp.*
Cain, Maureen E. Society and the Policeman's Role. *326 pp.*
● **Fletcher, Colin.** Beneath the Surface. *An Account of Three Styles of Sociological Research. 221 pp.*
Gibson, Quentin. The Logic of Social Enquiry. *240 pp.*
Glassner, B. Essential Interactionism. *208 pp.*
Glucksmann, M. Structuralist Analysis in Contemporary Social Thought. *212 pp.*
Gurvitch, Georges. Sociology of Law. *Foreword by Roscoe Pound. 264 pp.*
Hinkle, R. Founding Theory of American Sociology 1881–1913. *About 350 pp.*
Homans, George C. Sentiments and Activities. *336 pp.*
Johnson, Harry M. Sociology: *A Systematic Introduction. Foreword by Robert K. Merton. 710 pp.*
● **Keat, Russell** and **Urry, John.** Social Theory as Science. *278 pp.*
Mannheim, Karl. Essays on Sociology and Social Psychology. *Edited by Paul Keckskemeti. With Editorial Note by Adolph Lowe. 344 pp.*
Martindale, Don. The Nature and Types of Sociological Theory. *292 pp.*
● **Maus, Heinz.** A Short History of Sociology. *234 pp.*
Myrdal, Gunnar. Value in Social Theory: *A Collection of Essays on Methodology. Edited by Paul Streeten. 332 pp.*
Ogburn, William F. and **Nimkoff, Meyer F.** A Handbook of Sociology. *Preface by Karl Mannheim. 656 pp. 46 figures. 35 tables.*
Parsons, Talcott and **Smelser, Neil J.** Economy and Society: *A Study in the Integration of Economic and Social Theory. 362 pp.*
Payne, G., Dingwall, R., Payne, J. and **Carter, M.** Sociology and Social Research. *About 250 pp.*
Podgórecki, A. Practical Social Sciences. *About 200 pp.*
Podgórecki, A. and **Łos, M.** Multidimensional Sociology. *268 pp.*
Raffel, S. Matters of Fact. *A Sociological Inquiry. 152 pp.*
● **Rex, John.** Key Problems of Sociological Theory. *220 pp.*
   Sociology and the Demystification of the Modern World. *282 pp.*
● **Rex, John.** (Ed.) Approaches to Sociology. *Contributions by Peter Abell, Frank Bechhofer, Basil Bernstein, Ronald Fletcher, David Frisby, Miriam Glucksmann, Peter Lassman, Herminio Martins, John Rex, Roland Robertson, John Westergaard and Jock Young. 302 pp.*
Rigby, A. Alternative Realities. *352 pp.*
Roche, M. Phenomenology, Language and the Social Sciences. *374 pp.*
Sahay, A. Sociological Analysis. *220 pp.*
Strasser, Hermann. The Normative Structure of Sociology. *Conservative and Emancipatory Themes in Social Thought. About 340 pp.*
Strong, P. Ceremonial Order of the Clinic. *267 pp.*
Urry, John. Reference Groups and the Theory of Revolution. *244 pp.*
Weinberg, E. Development of Sociology in the Soviet Union. *173 pp.*

FOREIGN CLASSICS OF SOCIOLOGY

● **Gerth, H. H.** and **Mills, C. Wright.** From Max Weber: *Essays in Sociology. 502 pp.*

● **Tönnies, Ferdinand.** Community and Association *(Gemeinschaft und Gesellschaft).|Translated and Supplemented by Charles P. Loomis. Foreword by Pitirim A. Sorokin. 334 pp.*

SOCIAL STRUCTURE

Andreski, Stanislav. Military Organization and Society. *Foreword by Professor A. R. Radcliffe-Brown. 226 pp. 1 folder.*

Broom, L., Lancaster Jones, F., McDonnell, P. and **Williams, T.** The Inheritance of Inequality. *About 180 pp.*

Carlton, Eric. Ideology and Social Order. *Foreword by Professor Philip Abrahams. About 320 pp.*

Clegg, S. and **Dunkerley, D.** Organization, Class and Control. *614 pp.*

Coontz, Sydney H. Population Theories and the Economic Interpretation. *202 pp.*

Coser, Lewis. The Functions of Social Conflict. *204 pp.*

Crook, I. and **D.** The First Years of the Yangyi Commune. *304 pp., illustrated.*

Dickie-Clark, H. F. Marginal Situation: *A Sociological Study of a Coloured Group. 240 pp. 11 tables.*

Giner, S. and **Archer, M. S.** (Eds) Contemporary Europe: *Social Structures and Cultural Patterns, 336 pp.*

● **Glaser, Barney** and **Strauss, Anselm L.** Status Passage: *A Formal Theory. 212 pp.*

Glass, D. V. (Ed.) Social Mobility in Britain. *Contributions by J. Berent, T. Bottomore, R. C. Chambers, J. Floud, D. V. Glass, J. R. Hall, H. T. Himmelweit, R. K. Kelsall, F. M. Martin, C. A. Moser, R. Mukherjee and W. Ziegel. 420 pp.*

Kelsall, R. K. Higher Civil Servants in Britain: *From 1870 to the Present Day. 268 pp. 31 tables.*

● **Lawton, Denis.** Social Class, Language and Education. *192 pp.*

McLeish, John. The Theory of Social Change: *Four Views Considered. 128 pp.*

● **Marsh, David C.** The Changing Social Structure of England and Wales, 1871–1961. *Revised edition. 288 pp.*

Menzies, Ken. Talcott Parsons and the Social Image of Man. *About 208 pp.*

● **Mouzelis, Nicos.** Organization and Bureaucracy. *An Analysis of Modern Theories. 240 pp.*

● **Ossowski, Stanislaw.** Class Structure in the Social Consciousness. *210 pp.*

● **Podgórecki, Adam.** Law and Society. *302 pp.*

Renner, Karl. Institutions of Private Law and Their Social Functions. *Edited, with an Introduction and Notes, by O. Kahn-Freud. Translated by Agnes Schwarzschild. 316 pp.*

Rex, J. and **Tomlinson, S.** Colonial Immigrants in a British City. *A Class Analysis. 368 pp.*

Smooha, S. Israel: Pluralism and Conflict. *472 pp.*

Wesolowski, W. Class, Strata and Power. *Trans. and with Introduction by G. Kolankiewicz. 160 pp.*

Zureik, E. Palestinians in Israel. *A Study in Internal Colonialism. 264 pp.*

SOCIOLOGY AND POLITICS

Acton, T. A. Gypsy Politics and Social Change. *316 pp.*

Burton, F. Politics of Legitimacy. *Struggles in a Belfast Community. 250 pp.*

Crook, I. and **D.** Revolution in a Chinese Village. *Ten Mile Inn. 216 pp., illustrated.*

Etzioni-Halevy, E. Political Manipulation and Administrative Power. *A Comparative Study. About 200 pp.*

Fielding, N. The National Front. *About 250 pp.*

● **Hechter, Michael.** Internal Colonialism. *The Celtic Fringe in British National Development, 1536–1966. 380 pp.*

Kornhauser, William. The Politics of Mass Society. *272 pp. 20 tables.*

Korpi, W. The Working Class in Welfare Capitalism. *Work, Unions and Politics in Sweden. 472 pp.*

Kroes, R. Soldiers and Students. *A Study of Right- and Left-wing Students. 174 pp.*

Martin, Roderick. Sociology of Power. *About 272 pp.*

Merquior, J. G. Rousseau and Weber. *A Study in the Theory of Legitimacy. About 288 pp.*

Myrdal, Gunnar. The Political Element in the Development of Economic Theory. *Translated from the German by Paul Streeten. 282 pp.*

Varma, B. N. The Sociology and Politics of Development. *A Theoretical Study. 236 pp.*

Wong, S.-L. Sociology and Socialism in Contemporary China. *160 pp.*

Wootton, Graham. Workers, Unions and the State. *188 pp.*

CRIMINOLOGY

Ancel, Marc. Social Defence: *A Modern Approach to Criminal Problems. Foreword by Leon Radzinowicz. 240 pp.*

Athens, L. Violent Criminal Acts and Actors. *104 pp.*

Cain, Maureen E. Society and the Policeman's Role. *326 pp.*

Cloward, Richard A. and **Ohlin, Lloyd E.** Delinquency and Opportunity: *A Theory of Delinquent Gangs. 248 pp.*

Downes, David M. The Delinquent Solution. *A Study in Subcultural Theory. 296 pp.*

Friedlander, Kate. The Psycho-Analytical Approach to Juvenile Delinquency: *Theory, Case Studies, Treatment. 320 pp.*

Gleuck, Sheldon and **Eleanor.** Family Environment and Delinquency. *With the statistical assistance of Rose W. Kneznek. 340 pp.*

Lopez-Rey, Manuel. Crime. *An Analytical Appraisal. 288 pp.*

Mannheim, Hermann. Comparative Criminology: *A Text Book. Two volumes. 442 pp. and 380 pp.*

Morris, Terence. The Criminal Area: *A Study in Social Ecology. Foreword by Hermann Mannheim. 232 pp. 25 tables. 4 maps.*

Rock, Paul. Making People Pay. *338 pp.*

● **Taylor, Ian, Walton, Paul** and **Young, Jock.** The New Criminology. *For a Social Theory of Deviance. 325 pp.*

● **Taylor, Ian, Walton, Paul** and **Young, Jock.** (Eds) Critical Criminology. *268 pp.*

SOCIAL PSYCHOLOGY

Bagley, Christopher. The Social Psychology of the Epileptic Child. *320 pp.*

Brittan, Arthur. Meanings and Situations. *224 pp.*

Carroll, J. Break-Out from the Crystal Palace. *200 pp.*

● **Fleming, C. M.** Adolescence: Its Social Psychology. *With an Introduction to recent findings from the fields of Anthropology, Physiology, Medicine, Psychometrics and Sociometry. 288 pp.*

● The Social Psychology of Education: *An Introduction and Guide to Its Study. 136 pp.*

Linton, Ralph. The Cultural Background of Personality. *132 pp.*

● **Mayo, Elton.** The Social Problems of an Industrial Civilization. *With an Appendix on the Political Problem. 180 pp.*

Ottaway, A. K. C. Learning Through Group Experience. *176 pp.*

Plummer, Ken. Sexual Stigma. *An Interactionist Account. 254 pp.*

● **Rose, Arnold M.** (Ed.) Human Behaviour and Social Processes: *an Interactionist Approach. Contributions by Arnold M. Rose, Ralph H. Turner, Anselm Strauss, Everett C. Hughes, E. Franklin Frazier, Howard S. Becker et al. 696 pp.*

Smelser, Neil J. Theory of Collective Behaviour. *448 pp.*

Stephenson, Geoffrey M. The Development of Conscience. *128 pp.*

Young, Kimball. Handbook of Social Psychology. *658 pp. 16 figures. 10 tables.*

SOCIOLOGY OF THE FAMILY

Bell, Colin R. Middle Class Families: *Social and Geographical Mobility. 224 pp.*
Burton, Lindy. Vulnerable Children. *272 pp.*
Gavron, Hannah. The Captive Wife: *Conflicts of Household Mothers. 190 pp.*
George, Victor and **Wilding, Paul.** Motherless Families. *248 pp.*
Klein, Josephine. Samples from English Cultures.
    1. Three Preliminary Studies and Aspects of Adult Life in England. *447 pp.*
    2. Child-Rearing Practices and Index. *247 pp.*
Klein, Viola. The Feminine Character. *History of an Ideology. 244 pp.*
McWhinnie, Alexina M. Adopted Children. *How They Grow Up. 304 pp.*
● **Morgan, D. H. J.** Social Theory and the Family. *About 320 pp.*
● **Myrdal, Alva** and **Klein, Viola.** Women's Two Roles: *Home and Work. 238 pp.*
    27 tables.
Parsons, Talcott and **Bales, Robert F.** Family: Socialization and Interaction Process.
    In collaboration with James Olds, Morris Zelditch and Philip E. Slater. 456 pp.
    50 figures and tables.

SOCIAL SERVICES

Bastide, Roger. The Sociology of Mental Disorder. *Translated from the French by*
    Jean McNeil. 260 pp.
Carlebach, Julius. Caring For Children in Trouble. *266 pp.*
George, Victor. Foster Care. *Theory and Practice. 234 pp.*
    Social Security: *Beveridge and After. 258 pp.*
George, V. and **Wilding, P.** Motherless Families. *248 pp.*
● **Goetschius, George W.** Working with Community Groups. *256 pp.*
Goetschius, George W. and **Tash, Joan.** Working with Unattached Youth. *416 pp.*
Heywood, Jean S. Children in Care. *The Development of the Service for the Deprived*
    Child. Third revised edition. 284 pp.
King, Roy D., Ranes, Norma V. and **Tizard, Jack.** Patterns of Residential Care.
    356 pp.
Leigh, John. Young People and Leisure. *256 pp.*
● **Mays, John.** (Ed.) Penelope Hall's Social Services of England and Wales.
    368 pp.
Morris, Mary. Voluntary Work and the Welfare State. *300 pp.*
Nokes, P. L. The Professional Task in Welfare Practice. *152 pp.*
Timms, Noel. Psychiatric Social Work in Great Britain (1939–1962). *280 pp.*
●   Social Casework: *Principles and Practice. 256 pp.*

SOCIOLOGY OF EDUCATION

Banks, Olive. Parity and Prestige in English Secondary Education: a Study in
    Educational Sociology. *272 pp.*
● **Blyth, W. A. L.** English Primary Education. *A Sociological Description.*
    2. Background. *168 pp.*
Collier, K. G. The Social Purposes of Education: *Personal and Social Values in*
    Education. 268 pp.
Evans, K. M. Sociometry and Education. *158 pp.*
● **Ford, Julienne.** Social Class and the Comprehensive School. *192 pp.*
Foster, P. J. Education and Social Change in Ghana. *336 pp. 3 maps.*
Fraser, W. R. Education and Society in Modern France. *150 pp.*
Grace, Gerald R. Role Conflict and the Teacher. *150 pp.*
Hans, Nicholas. New Trends in Education in the Eighteenth Century. *278 pp.*
    19 tables.
●   Comparative Education: *A Study of Educational Factors and Traditions. 360 pp.*
● **Hargreaves, David.** Interpersonal Relations and Education. *432 pp.*
●   Social Relations in a Secondary School. *240 pp.*
    School Organization and Pupil Involvement. *A Study of Secondary Schools.*

● **Mannheim, Karl** and **Stewart, W. A. C.** An Introduction to the Sociology of
Education. *206 pp.*
● **Musgrove, F.** Youth and the Social Order. *176 pp.*
● **Ottaway, A. K. C.** Education and Society: An Introduction to the Sociology of
Education. *With an Introduction by W. O. Lester Smith. 212 pp.*
  Peers, Robert. Adult Education: *A Comparative Study. Revised edition. 398 pp.*
  Stratta, Erica. The Education of Borstal Boys. *A Study of their Educational
Experiences prior to, and during, Borstal Training. 256 pp.*
● **Taylor, P. H., Reid, W. A.** and **Holley, B. J.** The English Sixth Form. *A Case Study in
Curriculum Research. 198 pp.*

SOCIOLOGY OF CULTURE

  Eppel, E. M. and **M.** Adolescents and Morality: *A Study of some Moral Values and
Dilemmas of Working Adolescents in the Context of a changing Climate of
Opinion. Foreword by W. J. H. Sprott. 268 pp. 39 tables.*
● **Fromm, Erich.** The Fear of Freedom. *286 pp.*
●   The Sane Society. *400 pp.*
  Johnson, L. The Cultural Critics. *From Matthew Arnold to Raymond Williams.
233 pp.*
  Mannheim, Karl. Essays on the Sociology of Culture. *Edited by Ernst Mannheim in
co-operation with Paul Kecskemeti. Editorial Note by Adolph Lowe. 280 pp.*
  Merquior, J. G. The Veil and the Mask. *Essays on Culture and Ideology. Foreword
by Ernest Gellner. 140 pp.*
  Zijderfeld, A. C. On Clichés. *The Supersedure of Meaning by Function in Modernity.
150 pp.*

SOCIOLOGY OF RELIGION

  Argyle, Michael and **Beit-Hallahmi, Benjamin.** The Social Psychology of Religion.
256 pp.
  Glasner, Peter E. The Sociology of Secularisation. *A Critique of a Concept.
146 pp.*
  Hall, J. R. The Ways Out. *Utopian Communal Groups in an Age of Babylon. 280 pp.*
  Ranson, S., Hinings, B. and **Bryman, A.** Clergy, Ministers and Priests. *216 pp.*
  Stark, Werner. The Sociology of Religion. *A Study of Christendom.*
    Volume II. *Sectarian Religion. 368 pp.*
    Volume III. *The Universal Church. 464 pp.*
    Volume IV. *Types of Religious Man. 352 pp.*
    Volume V. *Types of Religious Culture. 464 pp.*
  Turner, B. S. Weber and Islam. *216 pp.*
  Watt, W. Montgomery. Islam and the Integration of Society. *320 pp.*

SOCIOLOGY OF ART AND LITERATURE

  Jarvie, Ian C. Towards a Sociology of the Cinema. *A Comparative Essay on the
Structure and Functioning of a Major Entertainment Industry. 405 pp.*
  Rust, Frances S. Dance in Society. *An Analysis of the Relationships between the Social
Dance and Society in England from the Middle Ages to the Present Day. 256 pp.
8 pp. of plates.*
  Schücking, L. L. The Sociology of Literary Taste. *112 pp.*
  Wolff, Janet. Hermeneutic Philosophy and the Sociology of Art. *150 pp.*

SOCIOLOGY OF KNOWLEDGE

  Diesing, P. Patterns of Discovery in the Social Sciences. *262 pp.*

● **Douglas, J. D.** (Ed.) Understanding Everyday Life. *370 pp.*
● **Hamilton, P.** Knowledge and Social Structure. *174 pp.*
Jarvie, I. C. Concepts and Society. *232 pp.*
Mannheim, Karl. Essays on the Sociology of Knowledge. *Edited by Paul Kecskemeti. Editorial Note by Adolph Lowe. 353 pp.*
Remmling, Gunter W. The Sociology of Karl Mannheim. *With a Bibliographical Guide to the Sociology of Knowledge, Ideological Analysis, and Social Planning. 255 pp.*
Remmling, Gunter W. (Ed.) Towards the Sociology of Knowledge. *Origin and Development of a Sociological Thought Style. 463 pp.*
Scheler, M. Problems of a Sociology of Knowledge. *Trans. by M. S. Frings. Edited and with an Introduction by K. Stikkers. 232 pp.*

URBAN SOCIOLOGY

Aldridge, M. The British New Towns. *A Programme Without a Policy. 232 pp.*
Ashworth, William. The Genesis of Modern British Town Planning: *A Study in Economic and Social History of the Nineteenth and Twentieth Centuries. 288 pp.*
Brittan, A. The Privatised World. *196 pp.*
Cullingworth, J. B. Housing Needs and Planning Policy: *A Restatement of the Problems of Housing Need and 'Overspill' in England and Wales. 232 pp. 44 tables. 8 maps.*
Dickinson, Robert E. City and Region: *A Geographical Interpretation. 608 pp. 125 figures.*
The West European City: *A Geographical Interpretation. 600 pp. 129 maps. 29 plates.*
Humphreys, Alexander J. New Dubliners: *Urbanization and the Irish Family. Foreword by George C. Homans. 304 pp.*
Jackson, Brian. Working Class Community: *Some General Notions raised by a Series of Studies in Northern England. 192 pp.*
● **Mann, P. H.** An Approach to Urban Sociology. *240 pp.*
Mellor, J. R. Urban Sociology in an Urbanized Society. *326 pp.*
Morris, R. N. and **Mogey, J.** The Sociology of Housing. *Studies at Berinsfield. 232 pp. 4 pp. plates.*
Mullan, R. Stevenage Ltd. *About 250 pp.*
Rex, J. and **Tomlinson, S.** Colonial Immigrants in a British City. *A Class Analysis. 368 pp.*
Rosser, C. and **Harris, C.** The Family and Social Change. *A Study of Family and Kinship in a South Wales Town. 352 pp. 8 maps.*
● **Stacey, Margaret, Batsone, Eric, Bell, Colin** and **Thurcott, Anne.** Power, Persistence and Change. *A Second Study of Banbury. 196 pp.*

RURAL SOCIOLOGY

Mayer, Adrian C. Peasants in the Pacific. *A Study of Fiji Indian Rural Society. 248 pp. 20 plates.*
Williams, W. M. The Sociology of an English Village: *Gosforth. 272 pp. 12 figures. 13 tables.*

SOCIOLOGY OF INDUSTRY AND DISTRIBUTION

Dunkerley, David. The Foreman. *Aspects of Task and Structure. 192 pp.*
Eldridge, J. E. T. Industrial Disputes. *Essays in the Sociology of Industrial Relations. 288 pp.*
Hollowell, Peter G. The Lorry Driver. *272 pp.*
● **Oxaal, I., Barnett, T.** and **Booth, D.** (Eds) Beyond the Sociology of Development.

Economy and Society in Latin America and Africa. 295 pp.

Smelser, Neil J. Social Change in the Industrial Revolution: *An Application of Theory to the Lancashire Cotton Industry, 1770–1840. 468 pp. 12 figures. 14 tables.*

Watson, T. J. The Personnel Managers. *A Study in the Sociology of Work and Employment, 262 pp.*

ANTHROPOLOGY

Brandel-Syrier, Mia. Reeftown Elite. *A Study of Social Mobility in a Modern African Community on the Reef. 376 pp.*

Dickie-Clark, H. F. The Marginal Situation. *A Sociological Study of a Coloured Group. 236 pp.*

Dube, S. C. Indian Village. *Foreword by Morris Edward Opler. 276 pp. 4 plates.* India's Changing Villages: *Human Factors in Community Development. 260 pp. 8 plates. 1 map.*

Fei, H.-T. Peasant Life in China. *A Field Study of Country Life in the Yangtze Valley. With a foreword by Bronislaw Malinowski. 328 pp. 16 pp. plates.*

Firth, Raymond. Malay Fishermen. *Their Peasant Economy. 420 pp. 17 pp. plates.*

Gulliver, P. H. Social Control in an African Society: a Study of the Arusha, Agricultural Masai of Northern Tanganyika. *320 pp. 8 plates. 10 figures.* Family Herds. *288 pp.*

Jarvie, Ian C. The Revolution in Anthropology. *268 pp.*

Little, Kenneth L. Mende of Sierra Leone. *308 pp. and folder.* Negroes in Britain. *With a New Introduction and Contemporary Study by Leonard Bloom. 320 pp.*

Tambs-Lyche, H. London Patidars. *About 180 pp.*

Madan, G. R. Western Sociologists on Indian Society. *Marx, Spencer, Weber, Durkheim, Pareto. 384 pp.*

Mayer, A. C. Peasants in the Pacific. *A Study of Fiji Indian Rural Society. 248 pp.*

Meer, Fatima. Race and Suicide in South Africa. *325 pp.*

Smith, Raymond T. The Negro Family in British Guiana: *Family Structure and Social Status in the Villages. With a Foreword by Meyer Fortes. 314 pp. 8 plates. 1 figure. 4 maps.*

SOCIOLOGY AND PHILOSOPHY

Adriaansens, H. Talcott Parsons and the Conceptual Dilemma. *About 224 pp.*

Barnsley, John H. The Social Reality of Ethics. *A Comparative Analysis of Moral Codes. 448 pp.*

Diesing, Paul. Patterns of Discovery in the Social Sciences. *362 pp.*

● **Douglas, Jack D.** (Ed.) Understanding Everyday Life. *Toward the Reconstruction of Sociological Knowledge. Contributions by Alan F. Blum, Aaron W. Cicourel, Norman K. Denzin, Jack D. Douglas, John Heeren, Peter McHugh, Peter K. Manning, Melvin Power, Matthew Speier, Roy Turner, D. Lawrence Wieder, Thomas P. Wilson and Don H. Zimmerman. 370 pp.*

Gorman, Robert A. The Dual Vision. *Alfred Schutz and the Myth of Phenomenological Social Science. 240 pp.*

Jarvie, Ian C. Concepts and Society. *216 pp.*

Kilminster, R. Praxis and Method. *A Sociological Dialogue with Lukács, Gramsci and the Early Frankfurt School. 334 pp.*

● **Pelz, Werner.** The Scope of Understanding in Sociology. *Towards a More Radical Reorientation in the Social Humanistic Sciences. 283 pp.*

Roche, Maurice. Phenomenology, Language and the Social Sciences. *371 pp.*

Sahay, Arun. Sociological Analysis. *212 pp.*

● **Slater, P.** Origin and Significance of the Frankfurt School. *A Marxist Perspective. 185 pp.*

Spurling, L. Phenomenology and the Social World. *The Philosophy of Merleau-Ponty and its Relation to the Social Sciences. 222 pp.*

Wilson, H. T. The American Ideology. *Science, Technology and Organization as Modes of Rationality. 368 pp.*

International Library of Anthropology
General Editor Adam Kuper

⬤ Ahmed, A. S. Millennium and Charisma Among Pathans. *A Critical Essay in Social Anthropology. 192 pp.*
  Pukhtun Economy and Society. *Traditional Structure and Economic Development. About 360 pp.*

Barth, F. Selected Essays. *Volume I. About 250 pp.* Selected Essays. *Volume II. About 250 pp.*

Brown, Paula. The Chimbu. *A Study of Change in the New Guinea Highlands. 151 pp.*

Foner, N. Jamaica Farewell. *200 pp.*

Gudeman, Stephen. Relationships, Residence and the Individual. *A Rural Panamanian Community. 288 pp. 11 plates, 5 figures, 2 maps, 10 tables.*
  The Demise of a Rural Economy. *From Subsistence to Capitalism in a Latin American Village. 160 pp.*

Hamnett, Ian. Chieftainship and Legitimacy. *An Anthropological Study of Executive Law in Lesotho. 163 pp.*

Hanson, F. Allan. Meaning in Culture. *127 pp.*

Hazan, H. The Limbo People. *A Study of the Constitution of the Time Universe Among the Aged. About 192 pp.*

Humphreys, S. C. Anthropology and the Greeks. *288 pp.*

Karp, I. Fields of Change Among the Iteso of Kenya. *140 pp.*

Lloyd, P. C. Power and Independence. *Urban Africans' Perception of Social Inequality. 264 pp.*

Parry, J. P. Caste and Kinship in Kangra. *352 pp. Illustrated.*

Pettigrew, Joyce. Robber Noblemen. *A Study of the Political System of the Sikh Jats. 284 pp.*

Street, Brian V. The Savage in Literature. *Representations of 'Primitive' Society in English Fiction, 1858–1920. 207 pp.*

Van Den Berghe, Pierre L. Power and Privilege at an African University. *278 pp.*

International Library of Phenomenology and Moral Sciences
General Editor John O'Neill

Apel, K.-O. Towards a Transformation of Philosophy. *308 pp.*

Bologh, R. W. Dialectical Phenomenology. *Marx's Method. 287 pp.*

Fekete, J. The Critical Twilight. *Explorations in the Ideology of Anglo-American Literary Theory from Eliot to McLuhan. 300 pp.*

Medina, A. Reflection, Time and the Novel. *Towards a Communicative Theory of Literature. 143 pp.*

International Library of Social Policy
General Editor Kathleen Jones

Bayley, M. Mental Handicap and Community Care. *426 pp.*

Bottoms, A. E. and McClean, J. D. Defendants in the Criminal Process. *284 pp.*

Bradshaw, J. The Family Fund. *An Initiative in Social Policy. About 224 pp.*

Butler, J. R. Family Doctors and Public Policy. *208 pp.*

Davies, Martin. Prisoners of Society. *Attitudes and Aftercare. 204 pp.*

Gittus, Elizabeth. Flats, Families and the Under-Fives. *285 pp.*

Holman, Robert. Trading in Children. *A Study of Private Fostering. 355 pp.*

Jeffs, A. Young People and the Youth Service. *160 pp.*

Jones, Howard and Cornes, Paul. Open Prisons. *288 pp.*

Jones, Kathleen. History of the Mental Health Service. *428 pp.*

Jones, Kathleen with **Brown, John, Cunningham, W. J., Roberts, Julian** and **Williams, Peter.** Opening the Door. *A Study of New Policies for the Mentally Handicapped. 278 pp.*

Karn, Valerie. Retiring to the Seaside. *400 pp. 2 maps. Numerous tables.*

King, R. D. and **Elliot, K. W.** Albany: Birth of a Prison—End of an Era. *394 pp.*

Thomas, J. E. The English Prison Officer since 1850: *A Study in Conflict. 258 pp.*

Walton, R. G. Women in Social Work. *303 pp.*

● **Woodward, J.** To Do the Sick No Harm. *A Study of the British Voluntary Hospital System to 1875. 234 pp.*

International Library of Welfare and Philosophy
General Editors Noel Timms and David Watson

● **McDermott, F. E.** (Ed.) Self-Determination in Social Work. *A Collection of Essays on Self-determination and Related Concepts by Philosophers and Social Work Theorists. Contributors: F. P. Biestek, S. Bernstein, A. Keith-Lucas, D. Sayer, H. H. Perelman, C. Whittington, R. F. Stalley, F. E. McDermott, I. Berlin, H. J. McCloskey, H. L. A. Hart, J. Wilson, A. I. Melden, S. I. Benn. 254 pp.*

● **Plant, Raymond.** Community and Ideology. *104 pp.*

Ragg, Nicholas M. People Not Cases. *A Philosophical Approach to Social Work. 168 pp.*

● **Timms, Noel** and **Watson, David.** (Eds) Talking About Welfare. *Readings in Philosophy and Social Policy. Contributors: T. H. Marshall, R. B. Brandt, G. H. von Wright, K. Nielsen, M. Cranston, R. M. Titmuss, R. S. Downie, E. Telfer, D. Donnison, J. Benson, P. Leonard, A. Keith-Lucas, D. Walsh, I. T. Ramsey. 320 pp.*

● Philosophy in Social Work. *250 pp.*

● **Weale, A.** Equality and Social Policy. *164 pp.*

Library of Social Work
General Editor Noel Timms

● **Baldock, Peter.** Community Work and Social Work. *140 pp.*

○ **Beedell, Christopher.** Residential Life with Children. *210 pp. Crown 8vo.*

● **Berry, Juliet.** Daily Experience in Residential Life. *A Study of Children and their Care-givers. 202 pp.*

○ Social Work with Children. *190 pp. Crown 8vo.*

● **Brearley, C. Paul.** Residential Work with the Elderly. *116 pp.*

● Social Work, Ageing and Society. *126 pp.*

● **Cheetham, Juliet.** Social Work with Immigrants. *240 pp. Crown 8vo.*

● **Cross, Crispin P.** (Ed.) Interviewing and Communication in Social Work. *Contributions by C. P. Cross, D. Laurenson, B. Strutt, S. Raven. 192 pp. Crown 8vo.*

- **Curnock, Kathleen** and **Hardiker, Pauline.** Towards Practice Theory. *Skills and Methods in Social Assessments. 208 pp.*
- **Davies, Bernard.** The Use of Groups in Social Work Practice. *158 pp.*
- **Davies, Martin.** Support Systems in Social Work. *144 pp.*
  Ellis, June. (Ed.) West African Families in Britain. *A Meeting of Two Cultures. Contributions by Pat Stapleton, Vivien Biggs. 150 pp. 1 Map.*
- **Hart, John.** Social Work and Sexual Conduct. *230 pp.*
- **Hutten, Joan M.** Short-Term Contracts in Social Work. *Contributions by Stella M. Hall, Elsie Osborne, Mannie Sher, Eva Sternberg, Elizabeth Tuters. 134 pp.*
  Jackson, Michael P. and **Valencia, B. Michael.** Financial Aid Through Social Work. *140 pp.*
- **Jones, Howard.** The Residential Community. *A Setting for Social Work. 150 pp.*
- (Ed.) Towards a New Social Work. *Contributions by Howard Jones, D. A. Fowler, J. R. Cypher, R. G. Walton, Geoffrey Mungham, Philip Priestley, Ian Shaw, M. Bartley, R. Deacon, Irwin Epstein, Geoffrey Pearson. 184 pp.*
  Jones, Ray and **Pritchard, Colin.** (Eds) Social Work With Adolescents. *Contributions by Ray Jones, Colin Pritchard, Jack Dunham, Florence Rossetti, Andrew Kerslake, John Burns, William Gregory, Graham Templeman, Kenneth E. Reid, Audrey Taylor. About 170 pp.*
- **Jordon, William.** The Social Worker in Family Situations. *160 pp. Crown 8vo.*
- **Laycock, A. L.** Adolescents and Social Work. *128 pp. Crown 8vo.*
- **Lees, Ray.** Politics and Social Work. *128 pp. Crown 8vo.*
- Research Strategies for Social Welfare. *112 pp. Tables.*
- **McCullough, M. K.** and **Ely, Peter J.** Social Work with Groups. *127 pp. Crown 8vo.*
- **Moffett, Jonathan.** Concepts in Casework Treatment. *128 pp. Crown 8vo.*
  Parsloe, Phyllida. Juvenile Justice in Britain and the United States. *The Balance of Needs and Rights. 336 pp.*
- **Plant, Raymond.** Social and Moral Theory in Casework. *112 pp. Crown 8vo.*
  Priestley, Philip, Fears, Denise and **Fuller, Roger.** Justice for Juveniles. *The 1969 Children and Young Persons Act: A Case for Reform? 128 pp.*
- **Pritchard, Colin** and **Taylor, Richard.** Social Work: Reform or Revolution? *170 pp.*
- **Pugh, Elisabeth.** Social Work in Child Care. *128 pp. Crown 8vo.*
- **Robinson, Margaret.** Schools and Social Work. *282 pp.*
- **Ruddock, Ralph.** Roles and Relationships. *128 pp. Crown 8vo.*
- **Sainsbury, Eric.** Social Diagnosis in Casework. *118 pp. Crown 8vo.*
- Social Work with Families. *Perceptions of Social Casework among Clients of a Family Service. 188 pp.*
  Seed, Philip. The Expansion of Social Work in Britain. *128 pp. Crown 8vo.*
- **Shaw, John.** The Self in Social Work. *124 pp.*
  Smale, Gerald G. Prophecy, Behaviour and Change. *An Examination of Self-fulfilling Prophecies in Helping Relationships. 116 pp. Crown 8vo.*
  Smith, Gilbert. Social Need. *Policy, Practice and Research. 155 pp.*
- Social Work and the Sociology of Organisations. *124 pp. Revised edition.*
- **Sutton, Carole.** Psychology for Social Workers and Counsellors. *An Introduction. 248 pp.*
- **Timms, Noel.** Language of Social Casework. *122 pp. Crown 8vo.*
- Recording in Social Work. *124 pp. Crown 8vo.*
- **Todd, F. Joan.** Social Work with the Mentally Subnormal. *96 pp. Crown 8vo.*
- **Walrond-Skinner, Sue.** Family Therapy. *The Treatment of Natural Systems. 172 pp.*
- **Warham, Joyce.** An Introduction to Administration for Social Workers. *Revised edition. 112 pp.*
- An Open Case. *The Organisational Context of Social Work. 172 pp.*
- **Wittenberg, Isca Salzberger.** Psycho-Analytic Insight and Relationships. *A Kleinian Approach. 196 pp. Crown 8vo.*

12

Primary Socialization, Language and Education
General Editor   Basil Bernstein

Adlam, Diana S., *with the assistance of Geoffrey Turner and Lesley Lineker.* Code in Context. *272 pp.*
Bernstein, Basil. Class, Codes and Control. *3 volumes.*
● 1. *Theoretical Studies Towards a Sociology of Language. 254 pp.*
  2. *Applied Studies Towards a Sociology of Language. 377 pp.*
● 3. *Towards a Theory of Educational Transmission. 167 pp.*
Brandis, W. and **Bernstein, B.** Selection and Control. *176 pp.*
Brandis, Walter and **Henderson, Dorothy.** Social Class, Language and Communication. *288 pp.*
Cook-Gumperz, Jenny. Social Control and Socialization. *A Study of Class Differences in the Language of Maternal Control. 290 pp.*
● **Gahagan, D. M.** and **G. A.** Talk Reform. *Exploration in Language for Infant School Children. 160 pp.*
Hawkins, P. R. Social Class, the Nominal Group and Verbal Strategies. *About 220 pp.*
Robinson, W. P. and **Rackstraw, Susan D. A.** A Question of Answers. *2 volumes. 192 pp. and 180 pp.*
Turner, Geoffrey J. and **Mohan, Bernard A.** A Linguistic Description and Computer Programme for Children's Speech. *208 pp.*

Reports of the Institute of Community Studies

Baker, J. The Neighbourhood Advice Centre. *A Community Project in Camden. 320 pp.*
● **Cartwright, Ann.** Patients and their Doctors. *A Study of General Practice. 304 pp.*
Dench, Geoff. Maltese in London. *A Case-study in the Erosion of Ethnic Consciousness. 302 pp.*
Jackson, Brian and **Marsden, Dennis.** Education and the Working Class: *Some General Themes Raised by a Study of 88 Working-class Children in a Northern Industrial City. 268 pp. 2 folders.*
Marris, Peter. The Experience of Higher Education. *232 pp. 27 tables.*
●   Loss and Change. *192 pp.*
Marris, Peter and **Rein, Martin.** Dilemmas of Social Reform. *Poverty and Community Action in the United States. 256 pp.*
Marris, Peter and **Somerset, Anthony.** African Businessmen. *A Study of Entrepreneurship and Development in Kenya. 256 pp.*
Mills, Richard. Young Outsiders: *a Study in Alternative Communities. 216 pp.*
Runciman, W. G. Relative Deprivation and Social Justice. *A Study of Attitudes to Social Inequality in Twentieth-Century England. 352 pp.*
Willmott, Peter. Adolescent Boys in East London. *230 pp.*
Willmott, Peter and **Young, Michael.** Family and Class in a London Suburb. *202 pp. 47 tables.*
Young, Michael and **McGeeney, Patrick.** Learning Begins at Home. *A Study of a Junior School and its Parents. 128 pp.*
Young, Michael and **Willmott, Peter.** Family and Kinship in East London. *Foreword by Richard M. Titmuss. 252 pp. 39 tables.*
  The Symmetrical Family. *410 pp.*

Reports of the Institute for Social Studies in Medical Care

Cartwright, Ann, Hockey, Lisbeth and **Anderson, John J.** Life Before Death. *310 pp.*
Dunnell, Karen and **Cartwright, Ann.** Medicine Takers, Prescribers and Hoarders. *190 pp.*
Farrell, C. My Mother Said. . . *A Study of the Way Young People Learned About Sex and Birth Control. 288 pp.*

Medicine, Illness and Society
General Editor   W. M. Williams

Hall, David J. Social Relations & Innovation. *Changing the State of Play in Hospitals. 232 pp.*
Hall, David J. and **Stacey, M.** (Eds) Beyond Separation. *234 pp.*
Robinson, David. The Process of Becoming Ill. *142 pp.*
Stacey, Margaret *et al.* Hospitals, Children and Their Families. *The Report of a Pilot Study. 202 pp.*
Stimson, G. V. and **Webb, B.** Going to See the Doctor. *The Consultation Process in General Practice. 155 pp.*

Monographs in Social Theory
General Editor   Arthur Brittan

● **Barnes, B.** Scientific Knowledge and Sociological Theory. *192 pp.*
Bauman, Zygmunt. Culture as Praxis. *204 pp.*
● **Dixon, Keith.** Sociological Theory. *Pretence and Possibility. 142 pp.*
   The Sociology of Belief. *Fallacy and Foundation. About 160 pp.*
Goff, T. W. Marx and Mead. *Contributions to a Sociology of Knowledge. 176 pp.*
Meltzer, B. N., Petras, J. W. and **Reynolds, L. T.** Symbolic Interactionism. *Genesis, Varieties and Criticisms. 144 pp.*
● **Smith, Anthony D.** The Concept of Social Change. *A Critique of the Functionalist Theory of Social Change. 208 pp.*

Routledge Social Science Journals

The British Journal of Sociology. *Editor – Angus Stewart; Associate Editor – Leslie Sklair. Vol. 1, No. 1 – March 1950 and Quarterly. Roy. 8vo. All back issues available. An international journal publishing original papers in the field of sociology and related areas.*
Community Work. *Edited by David Jones and Marjorie Mayo. 1973. Published annually.*
Economy and Society. *Vol. 1, No. 1. February 1972 and Quarterly. Metric Roy. 8vo. A journal for all social scientists covering sociology, philosophy, anthropology, economics and history. All back numbers available.*

Ethnic and Racial Studies. *Editor – John Stone. Vol. 1 – 1978. Published quarterly.*

Religion. Journal of Religion and Religions. *Chairman of Editorial Board, Ninian Smart. Vol. 1, No. 1, Spring 1971. A journal with an inter-disciplinary approach to the study of the phenomena of religion. All back numbers available.*

Sociology of Health and Illness. *A Journal of Medical Sociology. Editor – Alan Davies; Associate Editor – Ray Jobling. Vol. 1, Spring 1979. Published 3 times per annum.*

Year Book of Social Policy in Britain. *Edited by Kathleen Jones. 1971. Published annually.*

Social and Psychological Aspects of Medical Practice
Editor   Trevor Silverstone

Lader, Malcolm. Psychophysiology of Mental Illness. *280 pp.*

● **Silverstone, Trevor** and **Turner, Paul.** Drug Treatment in Psychiatry. *Revised edition. 256 pp.*

Whiteley, J. S. and **Gordon, J.** Group Approaches in Psychiatry. *240 pp.*